WORKFARE:

WHY GOOD SOCIAL POLICY IDEAS GO BAD

One of the most debated social policy ideas of the 1980s and 1990s in
North America was workfare. In *Workfare: Why Good Social Policy Ideas
Go Bad*, Maeve Quaid delves into the definition and history of workfare,
and then continues with a critical and comparative analysis of workfare programs in six jurisdictions: three American (California, Wisconsin, New York) and three Canadian (Alberta, Ontario, New Brunswick).
Drawing from these case studies, Quaid develops an analytic model
that illustrates how workfare falls prey to a series of hazards whereby
good social policy ideas fail. Their demise, argues Quaid, begins with
politicians with a zest for big ideas but little interest in implementation,
continues with short-sighted policy-makers, resistant bureaucrats,
cynical recipients, and flawed evaluations, and culminates in fleeting
and fickle public attention and support. Quaid's identification and
analysis of these hazards is especially valuable because they can also
be applied to innovation in other areas of social policy, such as health
care, education, pension plans, child care, and unemployment insurance.

MAEVE QUAID is an Associate Professor in the Administrative Studies
Program at Trent University.

MAEVE QUAID

WORKFARE

Why Good Social Policy Ideas Go Bad

UNIVERSITY OF TORONTO PRESS
Toronto Buffalo London

© University of Toronto Press Incorporated 2002
Toronto Buffalo London
Printed in Canada

ISBN 0-8020-4261-9 (cloth)
ISBN 0-8020-8101-0 (paper)

Printed on acid-free paper

National Library of Canada Cataloguing in Publication Data

Quaid, Maeve
    Workfare : why good social policy ideas go bad

    Includes bibliographical references and index.
    ISBN 0-8020-4261-9 (bound).   ISBN 0-8020-8101-0 (pbk.)

    1. Welfare recipients – Employment – Canada – Evaluation.
    2. Welfare recipients – Employment – United States – Evaluation.
    3. Public welfare administration – Canada – Evaluation.   4. Public
    welfare administration – United States – Evaluation.   I. Title.

    HV105.Q35 2002   362.5'8'0971   C2002-901027-6

University of Toronto Press acknowledges the financial assistance to
its publishing program of the Canada Council for the Arts and the
Ontario Arts Council.

University of Toronto Press acknowledges the financial support for
its publishing activities of the Government of Canada through the
Book Publishing Industry Development Program (BPIDP).

This book is dedicated to my son Berke.

Contents

Acknowledgments

I thank the Donner Canadian Foundation for providing me with the funding required to undertake the research for this book. I am also grateful to the many people in the states of California, New York, and Wisconsin and the provinces of New Brunswick, Alberta, and Ontario who answered my questions and shared their workfare experiences with me.

WORKFARE:

WHY GOOD SOCIAL POLICY IDEAS GO BAD

1.

Introduction

The Nature of a Good Idea – Policy Fads and Fashions

We have all had our share of good ideas – sometimes even great ideas. We have all worked for organizations that have introduced 'transforming ideas' and 'groundbreaking innovations,' but which have ultimately effected little change. In some cases, the 'good idea' never finds its way out of policy reports, the document standing as the only vestige of an honourable intention. In other cases, the good idea goes ahead, full steam, spreading across jurisdictions far and wide – and then, slowly but surely, it turns from good to bad, not quite delivering what it promised, or collapsing into confusion as expectations turn to dust. As one good idea meets its death, another waits in the wings, ready to take its turn in the spotlight. The organizational world is a graveyard of good ideas.

The policy field is littered with good ideas. But the good idea always seems to be linked to its own demise. What is it about good ideas that defeats them before they achieve their promise? In this book, I look at why good ideas go bad, focusing on workfare, one of the most popular social policy good ideas to surface in the 1980s and 1990s. In this period of cost-cutting, deficit reduction, and social program reform, few policies have enjoyed such skyrocketing notoriety and widespread dissemination as workfare. Workfare – a policy that obliges the welfare recipient to engage in training or public work in order to receive benefits – has been trumpeted as the instant solution to one of the most intractable of all social-policy problems. It is positioned as the perfect policy idea. Workfare is claimed to reduce welfare rolls, save money, and miraculously transform welfare recipients into productive citizens.

There are plenty of good ideas around. Indeed, the single, occasional act of innovating has become an everyday occurrence. The so-called good idea is now a fixture of the policy landscape. The world of organizational consulting is itself based on the creation, development, and dissemination of the good idea. The instant, non-problematic solution has been institutionalized as the implicit basis of the client-consultant contract. Good ideas are now practically routine. We are forging a culture in which innovation is an expectation, and policy is the vehicle for meeting this expectation. The 'good idea' also attains visible abundance within the political sphere. Politicians promise, constituents believe, and with every election everywhere hundreds of good ideas appear and disappear. Politics is about conjuring up the perfect 'good idea,' and policy-making is about developing the perfect 'good idea.'

What is a 'good idea'? First, a good idea is generally a concept that is believed to be new. By 'new,' I mean something that is believed to represent a significant departure from the status quo. A good idea is one that is better than that which is prevalent at the time the idea first appears. By 'better,' I don't mean that it has to be better, e.g., more technically efficient, it has only to be *believed* to be better, an improvement over the old. Sometimes, however, upon closer inspection, there are such inherent problems associated with the good idea that some might suggest that it should not even qualify as such at all. I do not agree. I argue here that the practical value of a good idea is basically irrelevant to the essence of a good idea – that one of the inherent characteristics of a good idea is that it need not, in practical terms, actually *be* a good idea. A good idea may, in fact, be seriously flawed. Take, for example, the Quality of Working Life (QWL) craze of the 1970s and 1980s. Under the influence of QWL, thousands of organizations scrambled to transform the quality of working life. Conferences and case studies validated the innovative management practice. Eventually, however, it all unravelled. QWL reduced organizational complexity by defining a problem in relatively simple terms. It also provided a useful rhetoric that appeared to produce order out of disorder. But at a basic level, little changed. Assumptions and expectations about the 'good idea' can often be illogical and ridiculous, but this circumstance in no way detracts from its importance or appeal.

Second, a good idea generally offers an all-encompassing solution to otherwise complex problems. Good ideas take on the most difficult problems. They tend not to limit themselves to one small part of a problem, but bravely tackle it whole. Never content with small victories, good ideas want massive successes; never content with just a battle, they want the war. Because they take on too much, good ideas often sidestep the problem at hand. This sidestepping of deeply rooted or complex organizational problems has been noted in research on management fads. Byrne, for example, claims that executives will latch on to any management idea that looks like a quick fix: 'There's nothing inherently wrong with any of these ideas (corporate culture, intrapreneurship, quality circles, wellness, etc.). What's wrong is that too many companies use them as gimmicks to evade the basic challenges they face ... They quickly become meaningless buzzwords, hollow symbols, mere fads ... Business fads are something of a necessary evil and have always been with us. What's different – and alarming – today is the sudden rise and fall of so many conflicting fads and how they influence the modern manager' (1990, 11).

Thus, good ideas can be negative in that they provide a way of hiding from problems rather than confronting them. The preferred action is to invent a 'solution,' a program or policy that will deal with the problem once and for all. While most corporations appear to survive this constant rash of trends, some good ideas have clearly proved to be a step backward, not a step forward. For example, Byrne (1990) refers us to the mounting piles of paper and the tangled web of bureaucracy that accompanied such innovations as management by objectives, PERT (program evaluation and review technique), and operations research. Most of us, whether in our professional or personal lives, have abandoned a good idea owing to its cumbersome administration.

Third, the good idea fits the moral truth that commands broad support within society at that time. Foucault claims that reality, or rather our concept of reality, changes according to prevailing ideologies, to what is 'in the truth' at the time. A good idea is something that is 'in the truth' at the time that the idea appears. And fourth, the good idea provides a rhetoric of efficiency that appears to resolve the irresolvable. A good idea, in this sense, is like magic – we are willing to suspend our disbelief for a good trick. The good idea emerges within this analogy as sleight of hand. The key characteristics of a good idea are summarized in Figure 1.1.

Rhetoric seems central to the good idea – both in terms of the selling of the idea and the elaboration of the idea itself in a compelling and appropriate jargon. Research on management fads and fashions suggests that the production of the collective belief that certain management techniques are both innovative and an improvement, relative to

Figure 1.1 Key Characteristics of a Good Idea

THE GOOD IDEA:
- Believed to be new
- Provides an all-encompassing solution
- Fits the 'truth' of the time
- Couched in the rhetoric of efficiency

the status quo, involves the elaboration of a 'convincing rhetoric.' Abramson explains how rhetoric is used to convince fashion followers that a management technique is both (a) rational and (b) at the forefront of management progress:

> It [rhetoric] must create the belief that the technique allows managers to pursue an important managerial goal in the most efficient fashion. It must, therefore, articulate (a) why it is imperative for managers to pursue this goal and (b) why this technique provides the most efficient means to attain these goals ...
>
> Certain rhetorics clearly indicate how a management technique consti- tutes an innovation ... other management rhetorics provide no careful evidence that techniques constitute improvements. Moreover, they present old and forgotten management goals as if they had just been invented. (Abramson 1996, 268)

In terms of a 'good idea' we can call this a rhetoric of justification. Rhetoric provides the reason and rationale for the good idea, and it also shapes the content and substance of the bigger and better new thing. Rhetoric acts as a 'promoting logic,' a kind of institutional public rela- tions that serves to stimulate interest in, and action on, the new idea. Sometimes rhetoric will also explain the way in which the good idea is actually new, or it might merely serve to promote the idea as new. (All managerial innovators declare the previous way of doing things to be old and outdated.) Rhetoric also invents or manufactures a crisis or need, bringing it to the forefront, and the good idea is sold to us as the only way out. And finally, on closer inspection, many new ideas are really old ideas, repackaged and relabelled for the sake of innovation ('old wine in new bottles'). Today, the profusion of management fads poses considerable distraction for both the business manager and the policy-maker. Business fads such as formal job evaluation, QWL (quality of working life), and zero-base budgeting have been adopted by both private and public organizations, often with dubious results.

Politicians and policy-makers are particularly susceptible to the pursuit of the 'new.' Innovation in the private sector differs, of course, from innovation in the public sector. Each sector faces its own set of pressures. The private sector must show that an innovation is profitable. Government, on the other hand, must show that an innovation is bound to advance the public good. Abramson also claims that managers who do not innovate are at risk of losing their followers: 'fashion setters who tend to lag in the dissemination of progressive management rhetorics also will tend to be perceived as lagging behind management progress and, consequently, as undeserving of their stakeholder support' (1996, 270).

This can be seen as the 'careerist' dimension of the good idea, where political or organizational career success is a 'good idea language game' in which those who are more skilled in the use of fanciful organizational rhetoric, at the packaging of good ideas, attain desired career success. Of course, this career interpretation has largely been ignored in the popular literature of career success with the exception of those writing from a symbolic perspective.

Thus there are deep incentives to develop or align oneself with fad and fashion – perhaps the most powerful relating to the idea of personal and departmental career incentives. To date, institutional theory (Berger and Luckmann 1967; Meyer and Rowan 1977; Zucker 1987; Powell and DiMaggio 1991), has provided one useful explanation for the popular diffusion of innovation in organizational settings, explicitly focusing on the ways in which organizations conform to the strategies used by other organizations' structures and processes. Meyer and Rowan (1977), for example, suggest that modern societies contain many complexes of institutionalized rules and patterns – products of professional groups, the state, and public opinion. This constellation of institutional social patterns is seen to provide a basis for the creation, elaboration, and legitimation of formal organization. The process by which actions are repeated and given similar meanings is referred to as 'institutionalization.'

Another aspect of institutional theory that helps us to understand the concept of 'fads and fashions' is the idea of 'institutional isomorphism,' or one organization's copycatting of another's institutional structures, strategies, systems, processes, etc. Meyer and Rowan argue that organizations are driven to incorporate the practices and procedures 'defined by prevailing rationalized concepts of organizational work and institutionalized in society' (1977, 340). They suggest that organizations incorporate institutional structures and rules partly to garner social legitimacy; appearing to be like other organizations sends a comforting message to clients, customers and other stakeholders. They go so far as to suggest that this organizational mimicry is 'independent of the immediate efficacy of the acquired practice and procedure' (Meyer and Rowan 1977, 340). Adopting what is widely considered to be a successful program elsewhere, for example, can make an organization look up-to-date and progressive, regardless of whether or not that program proves to be efficacious. With respect to our concept of the 'good idea,' institutional theory shows how organizations might be more interested in external legitimation than in efficiency. Good ideas become one key tool for managing organizational legitimacy. Institutional theory also provides us with a glimpse of how the imitation of supposedly rational structures and systems can prove to be useful when faced with an intractable problem. Good ideas are imported to resolve the irresolvable.

Management or policy fads constitute a good idea at the point at which the idea appears. Such good ideas are typically considered to be a significant departure from the status quo and an improvement over the old way of doing things. They are also disseminated effectively through their own particular rhetoric.

What is a 'good idea'? A good idea is a transforming idea, one that promises new solutions to problems. A good idea is true because it is believed. Each good idea has its followers who share a system of collective beliefs, however transitory those beliefs may be. In fact, it can be argued that an essential aspect of the nature of a good idea is that there is a limited time in which it is believed. In a recent discussion of organizational change, a set of organizational theorists commented on how the literature grows and consulting firms become created around the idea of 'massive programs of comprehensive change, namely transformation': 'Just about every writer and consulting firm has his or her or its own formula for success. There is no consensus at all as to what works best, although there are certain periodic fads – galore. But all this seems to reveal mainly what doesn't work – namely last year's fad' (Mintzberg, Ahlstrand, and Lampel 1998, 330).

Workfare: The Perfect Good Idea

If ever there was a good idea drummed up by politicians and policy-makers alike, workfare is it. Workfare has been embraced as a policy panacea by governments and the public alike. It has burst on the scene as the latest and best good idea. It has been trumpeted as something new and highly innovative. It is believed to be better than what was there before, and it also conveniently fits the ascendant conservative agenda of cost-cutting and efficiencies, of tax cuts and deficit reductions. Workfare also provides a compelling rhetoric, both in terms of justification for the problem and as a defined formula for success.

Workfare arrived on the scene full of promise and hope. Everyone would win with workfare. Welfare recipients would get real job skills and experience, welfare rolls would be reduced, and money would be saved. Workfare would also appeal to those voters who had become less tolerant of government hand-outs. What's more, moral arguments for the policy abound. Four familiar moral arguments are incessantly advanced in its favour: (1) a work requirement distinguishes the deserving from the undeserving; (2) workfare maintains the self-respect of the welfare recipient; (3) the right to income support imposes reciprocal work obligations on recipients; and (4) workfare safeguards welfare recipients' status as citizens able to participate fully in a democratic society (Jacobs 1995). While many of the debates on workfare have focused on moral concerns about the nature of social justice, this book is more concerned with the implementation of policy. Workfare, at least on the surface, meets the criteria of both a good social policy idea and a 'perfect' good idea. It is 'new' and 'better,' it fits the predominant moral tone, and it has all the larger-than-life, mythical qualities of resolving the seemingly irresolvable welfare problem.

Of course, as we will see, good ideas tend to possess glaring limitations. In fact, at the end of the day, I will come to define good ideas in terms of their limitations and problems. Because the good idea is made up of diverse and competing energy currents, it is often laden with contradictory elements and technical flaws. Because it seeks broad and sweeping change, it often attempts too much, leaving one small policy battling a complex and intractable program. Although the basic notion of requiring people to train or perform community work in exchange for benefits can be construed as 'good,' the reality of the situation is not so simple as the idea would lead us to believe. But this too is central to the 'good idea': behind the veneer of the 'good' is a train of problems and internal contradictions.

Theoretical Framework: Why It Is Hard to Study a Good Idea

As an academic in the area of organizational behaviour and human resource management I have a keen interest in employment policies in general. In 1996 I took a leave of absence from Trent University to work at Ontario's Social Assistance Review Board, which is a board of appeals, so to speak, for welfare applicants who feel that they have unjustly been denied welfare in the first place, or for existing welfare recipients who have been cut off welfare, or had the amount of their welfare payment reduced. During my time as an adjudicator on this Progressive Conservative board, the Conservative government of Ontario announced that workfare (then an American concept, a campaign promise of the Progressive Conservative Party in the recent successful political election) would soon apply to Ontario welfare recipients. In Ontario, this initiative had received mass public support during the previous election campaign, and in the government it was heavily endorsed as a policy that would magically solve a welfare problem that had gone out of control. The Ontario government's workfare policy initiative coincided with my interest in organizational panaceas, so I returned to academia to study how the 'good idea' of workfare would play out in Ontario, and also to find out what had happened when workfare had been introduced elsewhere. Another concern that prompted this study was the question of why we were going to force people to participate in even more training, when it has been proven, over and over again, that government training programs so rarely improve the earnings or job prospects of their clients ('Training and Jobs,' 1996).

With governments around the world spending large amounts of public money on introducing and maintaining social policy programs, what do we really know about what we are getting in exchange for that money? We actually know very little, if anything, about what happens once a program has been announced. For example, what happens between the time that politicians sell workfare to the public and the time that formal evaluators descend upon the program to evaluate results? What are the key constraints that destabilize a social policy program? To what extent does the public play a role, and how long do we wait until we want the next good idea to come along?

This book should be seen as an exploratory search for an answer to the question that frames this research: 'Why do good ideas go bad?' Using the example of workfare, I take a close look at certain key forces that have prevented the workfare 'good idea' from meeting its stated objectives of 'moving people into real jobs.' Workfare has certain characteristics that make it particularly suitable for the study of policy implementation. As Nathan points out, welfare employment strategies are good case material for the study of policy implementation owing, first, to their 'breadth' and, second, to their 'vertical or federalism dimension.' In terms of breadth, 'They involve a wide array of organizations – welfare agencies, child care providers, employment services, training programs, schools and community colleges, as well as health and transportation agencies. This can be thought of as the horizontal/coordination challenge of welfare employment strategies.' And in terms of the vertical or federalism dimension, 'They involve the national government, state governments, county governments, other local governments (for example school districts), and thousands of community organizations that administer services for welfare families' (Nathan 1993, 6).

Not only is workfare a policy with which most people are familiar, but it is current and controversial and reveals a great deal about the workings of government. So, why did workfare – so highly publicized, so carefully planned and organized – so often fail? Given such a major commitment of workforce and financial resources, what happened? What went wrong? Could anything have been done differently? To understand why such a good idea as workfare has achieved, at best, only limited results, I have studied the workfare efforts of three American jurisdictions (California, Wisconsin, and New York) and three Canadian jurisdictions (New Brunswick, Alberta, and Ontario), focusing on the way in which the good idea eroded over time. The three American states were selected because of the celebrated status of their workfare programs compared with other American states. California, for example, claims to have America's longest running workfare program (Greater Avenues for Independence established in [GAIN], 1982). GAIN was apparently used by Washington as a model in the design of the 1988 national Job Opportunities and Basic Skills (JOBS) program. Wisconsin has attracted broad attention because it reduced its welfare rolls by a greater percentage than any other state. As Carl Horowitz notes in the article 'Welfare Reform: Passing Phase? Congress Is Already Opening Workfare Loopholes': 'In all, Wisconsin's welfare rolls have dropped by some 60% since Thompson became governor in 1987, the largest drop of all the states' (by 1999 welfare rolls had subsequently dropped by 90 per cent since Thompson became governor) (*Los Angeles Investor's Business Daily*, 16 July 1997). And New York was chosen because its policies and programs exhibit both features that are unique and others that are common to a number of other states. Rather than covering the whole state, this chapter focuses on the New York City's workfare program, which is interesting because of the massive movement of welfare recipients into public service placements.

New Brunswick, Alberta, and Ontario were selected because, out of Canada's ten provinces, these three have had the highest profile in workfare-related activities. New Brunswick's 'learnfare' program attracted national attention, and other provinces were advised by Ottawa to emulate it (despite a price tag of fifty-nine thousand dollars per participant and a drop-out rate of more than two-thirds). Alberta was selected because of the drastic drop in the welfare rolls after the Progressive Conservative government of Ralph Klein came to power. During his campaign Klein pledged to crack down on welfare recipients if he won the election. In 1993, the province experienced a huge drop in the welfare rolls, only one year after he had become premier. Ontario was selected because it provides the most typical example of American-style workfare in a Canadian context. Sold in the campaign promises of 1995, designed in 1996, and introduced in 1997, Ontario's workfare program is relatively new, but it still presents some interesting findings, especially in relation to cross-border policy adoption.

There is an old Canadian political maxim: In the West politics is a religion, in Ontario it's a business, and in the Maritimes it's a disease. The Canadian workfare case stories provide samples from all three geographic areas. The main reason why I did not include Quebec's 1988 welfare reforms is because there were so many employment experiments that applied to such a wide range of constituents that the system, as a whole, proved almost impossible to study. This problem is confirmed by Canada's National Council of Welfare, which has declared: 'One point is clear: the new Quebec system is complex, perhaps the most complex of any provincial or territorial welfare system' (1992, 15). Quebec's Ministère de la Sécurité de Revenu (1994, 14) claims that almost fifty thousand adult welfare recipients are available and waiting to participate in welfare employability programs. There is widespread agreement that none of the workfare-related programs was successful in gaining long-term employment for participants. It is not because of its failure, however, that Quebec was not selected, but rather because of its overwhelmingly complex two-tiered structure.

The choice of three U.S. and three Canadian jurisdictions not only allows for some useful insights into what happens in different places to a social policy that is considered to be a 'good idea,' but it also provides a unique and timely opportunity to conduct a U.S.-Canada cross-border analysis with a view, in particular, to uncover the lessons that

Canadian government organizations might have learned from the American workfare experience. The Canada/U.S. juxtaposition allows for the possibility of some interesting cross-cultural references emerging, for example, in terms of how and why certain governments follow others. In other words, it is to be hoped that we might gain more knowledge about how Canadians adapt American policies to fit their needs. As well as providing a useful guide to implementation, the questions asked in this book – e.g., What is the background of the reform initiative? How was the program designed? What were the administrative challenges? Did welfare recipients participate? What do the evaluators say? Did the public play a role? And, finally, whatever happened to the good idea? – are also designed to stimulate policy-makers to consider whether or not they would like to pursue workfare as a social policy in the first place.

The method that I have used to conduct this research is the narrative, or the case story. This book is a collection of six stories. While the narrative might lack the scientific weight and general applicability of conventional research methods, it is sometimes the only possible research strategy. It is my opinion that conventional research methods are not altogether relevant to studying the processes of decision-making and implementation in organizations. Moreover, when there is more than one story, I believe that these narratives might serve as a basis of fruitful theoretical development and provide guidelines for future practice. The realm of the narrative, by contrast with the case study, has more to do with the telling of a story, the relaying of an account to an audience. I chose this research method because it can accommodate and explicate multiple, conflicting, and often unaggregatable realities. Moreover, since human behaviour is rarely as rational as policy or management textbooks would have us believe, the case story was a particularly appropriate mode of enquiry. Its strengths are precisely those I needed in order to act in sympathy with the careerist, emotional, and affiliative motivations of the key actors. The case story, as a narrative, describes interpretations that people attach to their own experiences, making it an ideal way to depict key actors and their own individual realities. Sen (1980) defends description in contrast to prediction and prescription in a seminal work entitled *Description as Choice*, part of the Oxford Economic Papers. In this study, Sen (1980, 353) points out that, in making descriptions, one has to make choices, and these choices are guided by our paradigm, our access, and our preunderstanding. One's own analysis and interpretation are thus inevitable.

Each story begins more or less the same way, pointing out the stated objectives of the work-for-welfare program, and ends with a conclusion as to whether or not these objectives were perceived to be met. The data for the research come from extensive data collection and analysis, specifically, a survey of the relevant academic literature; an analysis of data available in relevant employment offices; the collection and analysis of documents and records as well as new data at the six jurisdictions; the collection and analysis of newspaper and journal articles on welfare reform and workfare; the collection and analysis of information on training programs and courses offered to welfare recipients; and interviews (personal or telephone) with key individuals connected to the selling, design, delivery, and evaluation of workfare, as well as those groups and individuals most affected by the policy.

My greatest research challenge lay in gathering useful evaluation data (basically, administrators did not measure their programs). Workfare is an extremely complex and detailed subject. Each jurisdiction operates a number of different types of welfare-to-work programs, all with different eligibility criteria, exemptions, sanctions, rewards, and, in certain cases, time limits. At the same time, all jurisdictions have their own special variety of carrots or sticks to encourage able-bodied welfare recipients to find jobs. Sometimes people on welfare are in full- or part-time jobs but still receive welfare to meet the budgetary requirements of their family. In some jurisdictions welfare recipients are classified according to who they are, for example, as 'sole-support parent' or 'disabled' while in other jurisdictions they are classified according to the amount of effort it will take for them to attain employment. Some jurisdictions have moved children, older people, students, and persons with disabilities from the welfare category to other government programs. Others have not.

This book represents a comprehensive account of six high-profile welfare-to-work policies in one volume. Based on the experiences of these government organizations, I have identified six forces, or 'hazards,' that can destabilize a social policy such as workfare, and I have developed a model, which stems from the findings of the six case stories, to explain why good ideas go bad. Although this study was not intended to develop a model from the data, certain 'hazard' patterns emerged throughout the six jurisdictions that are most clearly illustrated in the form of a model. Essentially, the model I have developed is a force-field analytic model that identifies the behavioural hazards associated with the roles of six sets of major actors involved in social policy innovation (politicians, policy-makers, administrators, target group/welfare recipients, evaluators, and the general public, including activists and the media). From the model, it is not possible to make a generalization about how common these interaction patterns are, but the model does help us to understand the destabilizing process and its driving forces or hazards.

Organization of the Book

The thesis of this book is that workfare falls prey to a process whereby good policy ideas go bad. In Chapter 2, before starting in on the six workfare stories, I discuss the challenge of trying to define workfare. The term 'workfare' is commonly used to define any one of a range of programs, from a simple voluntary employment enhancement program aimed at a small part of a jurisdiction's total welfare population, to the overall requirement for mandatory participation in a work/school/training program in exchange for social assistance. I have tried to simplify my analysis of workfare by developing three categories into which various definitions may fit: (1) workfare is 'something' (i.e., real change with supports such as child care and transportation); (2) workfare is 'nothing' (i.e., relabelling of the same old job preparation and training programs; (3) workfare is 'anything and everything' (e.g., substance abuse counselling, university attendance). What is included under the workfare umbrella? What does workfare mean? (Workfare has come to mean many things). How do different jurisdictions use the word workfare? How can claims be made to the public about the role that workfare plays in bringing down the welfare caseload when workfare may in fact be anything? I conclude the chapter by suggesting that it is precisely the open-ended nature of workfare that makes it so attractive to those who want to appear to be resolving the irresolvable.

In Chapter 3, I discuss why workfare has been the centrepiece of so many attempts at social welfare reform. In this chapter I provide a brief history of workfare set against the backdrop of the efficiency and accountability mania that swept so many Western countries in the 1980s. The United States is considered to be the birthplace of workfare, which emerged in a mature form during the Reagan administration. U.S.-style workfare-related programs came to Canada only in the 1990s, and, since welfare in Canada is a provincial, not a federal, responsibility, each of the ten provinces has implemented its own style of welfare reforms. Some include workfare-related activities and others do not.

In Chapters 4, 5, and 6 I tell the story of the mandatory workfare experience in three American states: California, Wisconsin, and New

York. In Chapters 7, 8, and 9 I move north of the border to Canada, to describe a voluntary learnfare program in New Brunswick, supposedly voluntary work experience 'opportunities' for welfare recipients in Alberta, and American-style mandatory workfare in Ontario.

In each of the six cases, the welfare-to-work program is placed in the context of the particular jurisdiction, in terms of the politicians' stated objectives in introducing the program and how the policy-makers designed the program. An explanation is also provided as to how each plan works, followed by how the plan is administered, how the welfare recipients have reacted, what the evaluators have reported in terms of results, and how high the level of public interest has been (e.g., amongst general public, activists, and the media). Each case story concludes with a discussion of what happened to the good idea. My use of the word 'success' in relation to workfare is always in quotation marks, precisely because of the types of issues surrounding the 'evaluator hazard.' My interests lie not in individuals or in personalities, but in the forces that threaten each selected jurisdiction from reaching its originally stated goal.

In Chapter 10 I present a force-field analytic model that is drawn from the phases of implementation of a social policy initiative such as workfare. Each of the hazards is a type of behaviour associated with one of the key groups of actors in the social policy process. The key actors are identified as the politicians, the policy-makers, the administrators, the target group (welfare recipients), the evaluators, and the general public (including activists and the media). The model is basically a codifying process in which, interactively, I name the key workfare actors and frame the context in which each of them, by a particular behaviour, may cause the demise of the good idea. The pie-shaped model moves from the outside circle towards the inside circle, depicting the journey from good to bad. The model does not preclude any or all of the six key actor groups engaging in a form of collusion to keep the good idea good for an extended period of time. The hazards are identified as follows:

1. *Political Hazard:* Politicians are very interested in selling a catchy idea, but they are less concerned with actually implementing it.

2. *Policy-maker Hazard:* Policy-makers, who are cut from the bureaucratic mould, tend to design the 'good idea' in a one-size-fits-all fashion, without due attention to the messy, but important, details that inevitably emerge.

3. *Administrator Hazard:* Bureaucratic administrators are not only resistant to change, as may be expected, but they are also adept at making it look as though change has taken place when it has not (e.g., the complicity of otherwise upright bureaucrats who may not be in support of the innovation).

4. *Target-Group Hazard:* The clients whom the good idea is designed to help are also often resistant to change and sceptical of new ideas, having seen so many come and go. They are also adept at interpreting the new as the old and subverting the new until it resembles the old (or literally does become old). Or sometimes the target group might engage in a superficial, theatrical enactment of the institutional demands of the new – in other words, 'just putting in time.'

5. *Evaluator Hazard:* It is difficult for independent evaluators of the good idea to be critical, since to do so would reflect badly on the very people who retained them in the first place. What can take place is a form of 'goal displacement' where the measurement of subsidiary, but more 'successful,' goals (e.g., running training sessions on time) replaces the evaluation of the original 'meta' goal (e.g., moving welfare recipients into the workplace).

6. *Public Hazard:* The general public, lobby groups, and the media are all swept up by the good idea. But our attention is fleeting and fickle, and we do not generally sustain enough interest over a sufficiently long time for the good idea to work.

The model depicted in Chapter 10 attempts to illustrate more *generalized* hazards but recognizes that other, less dominant forces are, of course, always potential hazards. In each one of the six stories, some forces are particularly relevant and others are downplayed. I do believe that, by identifying relevant hazards, this book makes an important contribution to social policy analysis. Also, by watching out for these hazards, various organizations such as the government and the research community might stand a greater chance of protecting the welfare state. The book concludes with some thoughts on how this study can inform research on other social policy innovations, for example, in such areas as education, pension plans, child care, unemployment insurance, and medical care.

2.

What Is Workfare? Something, Nothing, or Anything and Everything?

Some Definitional Problems

As is so often the case with anything that at first glance seems to be dramatically innovative, that which claims to be 'new' is rarely original. Workfare is no exception. Workfare has existed for many years and has appeared in many different guises. Yet to say that workfare offers nothing new is to underestimate it. While workfare has certainly been 'out there' for a while, it is now here to be noticed. Part of its new appeal lies in the clever and simple name of 'workfare.' It condenses, in one word, all of the hopes and dreams of politicians and policy-makers. 'Work' now leads the rallying cry. It is no wonder that many great ideas have been pitched in a catch-all of one word or phrase – e.g., 're-engineering,' 'quality circles,' 'quality of work life,' etc. These short catch-alls simplify and condense a complex problem into an easily imagined solution.

Workfare has come to mean many things. For this reason, the precise form and character of workfare are difficult to sketch out, mostly because, as workfare has moved up the social policy agenda, it has constantly been redefined. There are probably as many forms of workfare as there are jurisdictions operating such a program; as a result, the various definitions of workfare do not always coincide. Any attempt at definition will be an admitted simplification, as all definitions tend to blur together at the edges. Part of the study of a good idea such as workfare lies in examining the different meanings associated with the term. This raises several questions: Does the term have a core definition, both from a formal, conceptual point of view and from a practical, applied point of view? And can the term survive our disagreement over how to define it, measure it, study it, and apply it? In some ways, the term 'workfare' promotes a singular view of reality, suggesting closure and denying complexity.

Like many good ideas, workfare defies any precise definition. In one way it is a rallying cry for reform. It provides for a socially acceptable way of attacking 'welfare bums' and 'cheats.' It provides a quasi-technical jargon that can be used to uphold or condemn particular positions. As to the question 'What is workfare?' I have come to realize that, depending on one's point of view, workfare can be seen either as 'something' (a defined, tangible program that people fight over), 'nothing' (just more training), or 'anything and everything' (from transportation, child care, and drug and alcohol counselling to university attendance, etc.). It is this third 'definition' that is allied most closely with our construct of the 'good idea.' It is the nature of good ideas that they may be everything or they may be nothing. Because they tend to be solve-alls (with the power to solve complex problems in one fell swoop) they need to be multidimensional and multifaceted. In the face of criticism, advocates of a good idea can always point to any one dimension or facet of the good idea and are not limited by a precise or narrowly specified policy or platform. Moreover, new dimensions or facets of the policy may be invented or created as the good idea is introduced. This malleable nature of the good idea, changing and growing as it is introduced and implemented (often in response to criticism), virtually ensures that it will evolve into a large, amorphous, and vague policy initiative.

In both the United States and Canada conceptual distinctions also exist between the terms 'workfare,' 'work-for-welfare,' 'welfare-to-work,' 'work experience,' 'subsidized job placements,' and 'community service.' I believe that, generally, these differences are largely semantic and reflect more the preference of the politicians for how the words might sound to the voter's or taxpayer's ear than any actual, tangible distinctions between types of programs. Basically, workfare signifies a form of welfare for which recipients undertake some labour-market-related activities (e.g., training, job searching, apprenticeships, volunteer work, subsidized work, paid work) in return for government payments. In other words, workfare merely codifies the efforts that are supposed to be made anyway, in any welfare office, to help welfare recipients prepare for and find work.

Workfare as Something

In this first scenario of 'workfare as something,' workfare may cover a great variety of situations, but, within each group of individuals, there is some common understanding about what workfare means. Activists who protest against workfare, for instance, have a shared view of the policy, which they often describe with terms such as 'exploitation,' 'slavery,' 'chain-gangs,' etc. Those who support workfare also have a shared view – one in which welfare recipients engage in a work-related activity in exchange for their benefits: 'a hand up, not a hand out,' 'an opportunity for the client to update résumé and references,' 'dignity,' 'pride,' 'work habits,' etc. To both these camps, workfare is a real something, a specific policy. A number of policy-makers, case workers, welfare recipients, evaluators, and members of the general public also see workfare as 'something.'

While there is a certain amount of debate over what actually constitutes workfare, probably the most common dimension quoted, or complained about, is its mandatory nature. Even so, there is controversy over the issue of whether a 'real' workfare program needs to be mandatory. Many of the people for whom workfare is 'something' appear to agree that its mandatory nature is probably an essential defining aspect of the term. The importance of the mandatory nature of workfare has been discussed by Patricia Evans, who, for example, sees the requirement to work as a critical aspect of modern workfare: 'The key word is *requirement*. Programs of apprenticeship, training, and further education for those receiving social assistance have been available for many years. The change is linking benefits or the levels of benefits to participation in programs' (1995, 18).

Workfare as Nothing

It can be argued that workfare is really nothing more than a relabelling of the same old employment support training programs that governments have been offering to welfare recipients over the years. The fact that such training programs might now include an element of job shadowing or co-op/community work placement does not make them new or revolutionary. In fact, the case stories in this book show that most caseworkers and welfare recipients within the system do not consider workfare to be anything new. Caseworkers know that it's up to them to make a revolutionary change such as mandatory 'community service' happen. Such a change, however, usually requires a serious turnaround in the administrative culture of social service agencies. It is just so much easier for these agencies to send welfare recipients to the same old training programs to which they have been sending them for years than to a new work placement that first has to be *found* and then *monitored*. And welfare recipients know that, despite the promises of politicians, very little really ever changes. It is a truism that if you stay around an organization long enough, you will see the same old proposed solutions presented as the new and better way of doing things. Even a cursory examination of the history of workfare turns up the same old programs, sometimes under different or new names, but, for the most part, there is little innovation. The first aspect of workfare as 'nothing' relates to its repackaging and relabelling as 'new'. Workfare is 'nothing' because it is not new – it has always been around in one form of training or another, and it is far from revolutionary. It is not the purpose of this study to debate the value of 'education first' versus 'job first' welfare-to-work strategies. Whether entry-level, usually lower-paid, jobs lead to further and better jobs, over the long run, than does a period of education and/or training is not central to the measure of workfare's success *per se*, since evaluation itself is so often a reflection of who is doing the hiring. My sense is that any significant discussion of placement versus training is already well covered by large and substantial debate in the field (Dunk, McBride, and Nelson 1996). Ushering welfare recipients directly into the workplace is a central feature of Wisconsin's (Wisconsin capped all training/job readiness programs at a maximum time frame of twelve weeks) and, to a lesser extent, Alberta's strategies, and therefore is discussed, but only in relation to the stated objectives of the program.

The theme of workfare as 'nothing' can also be found in the more rational or technical critiques of workfare, critiques which undermine the program and show workfare to be so laden with problems that the concept dissolves before one's eyes. Sometimes a good idea might have so many challenges or obstacles attached to it that it is never likely to become anything more than an idea. Torjman (1996) provides a perfect example of this in her attack on Ontario workfare, pointing out a long list of problems and limitations. Taken individually or together, such attacks question the content and substance of workfare. Torjman points to the prolonged duration of unemployment and its high rates (hovering at the 10 per cent mark at the time) as affecting the success of workfare. As Torjman explains, 'In short, the root of the welfare problem lies in the fact that there is not enough work' (1996, 6). She also alludes to the cost of monitoring and enforcing a mandatory approach, problems related to the health and safety of the jobs, problems associated with making social workers into welfare police, the question of a fair and equitable appeal system, the burden that workfare places on volunteer organizations, and the evidence from a New York project (MCSS, 1995, 5) which supports the argument that workfare displaces workers who are already employed, so that it actually contributes to a loss of jobs, not a gain. Torjman concludes, in fact, that there is no evidence that workfare programs succeed in getting people into real jobs: 'While the programs may save money in the short run by cutting people off welfare, they do not improve the long-term employability of the participants' (1996, 7). Citing a study by Richards and Vining (1995, 20), Torjman states: 'The people cut off eventually return to welfare or turn to some other program for assistance, thereby merely shifting the responsibility and associated costs to another level of government' (1996, 7).

Torjman's list of the practical problems associated with workfare makes one wonder if the idea is not so inherently flawed as to make it unfeasible in the first place. In other words, such a long list of problems associated with workfare could easily make it appear a non-starter. Apart from this, workfare as something 'real' is somewhat diminished by the added realization that, to date, it has not been proved that work leads to employment.

Other practical problems that make the good idea not so good relate to the fact that training programs (the bulk of what workfare is about) are rarely successful. Study after study has shown that there is very little, if any, benefit to be had from dollars spent on training, not just in North America but in all industrialized countries. An article in the *Economist* entitled 'Training and Jobs – What Works' shows that training has very little effect, with both North American and international studies showing 'gloomy' results:

A growing body of research shows most government training schemes fail to improve either the earnings or the employment prospects of their clients. After surveying the results of various broadly based training programs for unemployed adults, even the training friendly OECD concluded in 1994 that there is 'remarkably little support for the hypothesis that such programs are effective.'

In the United States, the Department of Labour runs $5-billion worth of elaborate training schemes directed at the disadvantaged. How much do they help their clientele? 'Zero is not a bad number' concludes James Heckman of the University of Chicago, who directed a government financed study of the Job Training Partnership Act, America's largest such program. (1996, 19)

The expenses related to workfare (such as child care) are also very high. And governments hardly ever direct enough resources at workfare for it to meet its objectives (for example, child care for all those workfare participants who require it). There is also little financial incentive for the welfare recipient to get off welfare. For example, the low wages that welfare recipients are likely to earn and the requirement that they pay for their own medications provide little formal incentive for recipients to move off welfare, especially in Canada, where time limits on welfare have not been introduced. In other words, sometimes the 'good idea' is actually not a good idea at all. It might sound great, for political purposes, but, when someone unravels it, it might actually be nothing.

Workfare as Anything and Everything

Workfare, of course, can also be seen as anything and everything. In fact, the history of workfare finds expression in the ever-widening definition of the term. The expanding definition of what constitutes acceptable work-related activities under workfare can be seen as a result of a shift from old-style workfare (punitive, 1970s) to new-style workfare (combination of liberal and conservative elements, 1980s). Nathan (1993, 15) draws this distinction between old-style and new-style workfare. In the 1970s, workfare was seen to signify a restrictive and punitive approach to welfare reform, one in which welfare payments would be made available only as compensation for work. In the 1980s, however, workfare took on connotations that were broader and less harsh. New-style workfare, whose operative concept is that of mutual obligation, is considered to embody a political bargain between liberals and conservatives. Workfare now refers to a wide range of strategies that help able-bodied welfare recipients make the transition from reliance on welfare to economic independence.

Evidence of Nathan's new-style, catch-all definition of workfare can be seen in the December 1996 *Time* magazine article entitled 'Workfare Means Daycare' (Collins 1996), followed by a description of Wisconsin's progressive efforts in the area of workfare. Workfare can now mean a lot of things. In fact, workfare may be understood to mean almost anything and everything. This also holds true in Canada. Workfare can be mandatory or voluntary, work oriented or training oriented, have penalties and sanctions or merely guidelines, and cover anything from job preparation to job searching to job placement.

Further evidence of the 'workfare as anything and everything' concept can be seen in the legal expansion of the definition of 'work-related activity' required of workfare participants in the United States. Since 1981, a certain percentage of welfare recipients has been required to participate in work-related activity (these targets were not met under WIN, nor under the 1988 JOBS program). Currently, states that don't meet their workfare participation rates suffer financial penalties. So, for a variety of reasons (the most important of which being political expediency), the definition of 'work-related activity' has been expanded to include almost anything.

Washington's preoccupation with the workfare participation rate of each state (as opposed to actual job placement) probably has a lot to do with how the definition of workfare has evolved and is still evolving. According to Clinton's 1996 welfare reform bill, by October 1997, each state had to place at least 25 per cent of welfare caseloads in work-related activities (a figure set to rise to 50 per cent by 2002). States have reacted to this pressure by changing the definition of 'work-related activity' to allow them to label more people as workfare participants, thereby meeting their participation targets. Evidence of this can be found in a 16 July 1997 *Los Angeles Investor's Business Daily* article by Carl Horowitz entitled 'Welfare Reform: Passing Phase? Congress Is Already Opening Workfare Loopholes.' Here, Horowitz claims that Congress was joining forces with those Democrats who were leading the fight to weaken the landmark 1996 federal welfare law (according to the 1996 act, adults must be involved in some work-related activity after two years on welfare). For example, Congress, in an attempt to assist states in reaching their workfare participation requirements, proposed a Senate bill that expands the definition of 'work' to include going to school or enrolling in a job-training program unrelated to a job currently held. Horowitz points out that these modifications 'would also give states resisting reform, such as New York and California, an easy way to meet the welfare-to-work targets ... To some extent, the '96 law, like previous welfare laws, has loopholes to get around work mandates. The latest measures would widen them much further.' The Senate bill to broaden the definition of work-related activity was passed in 1997.

Other attempts to get state participation numbers up by changing the definition of workfare requirements have been recorded by the U.S. General Accounting Office (U.S. GAO/HEHS-97-80:13), which reported that a total of thirteen states had expanded the definition of work-related activity to include activities that would not have met the 'participation' requirement under the previous JOBS program, such as family counselling or drug- and alcohol-abuse counselling. Twelve of the thirteen states added parenting- or family-skills training as an option. In addition, nineteen states waived the JOBS program limits on job-search activities, extending the amount of time that a job search could reasonably be counted as a work activity. In other words, workfare is constantly redefined to fit political objectives, most recently to meet the welfare recipient 'work participation' targets set out in President Clinton's 1996 welfare reform act. Moreover, the U.S General Accounting Office has claimed that the states are working to achieve greater levels of participation by changing their policies over who must participate, eliminating certain exemptions categories – e.g., lowering the age of the youngest child – that had existed under JOBS (U.S. GAO/HEHS-97-80).

In Canada, the meaning of workfare has also been defined by political pressures, although these have not necessarily had anything to do with the U.S. obsession with requiring that certain percentages of welfare recipients achieve workfare participation targets by certain set dates (although Ontario did require the municipalities to set workfare participation targets of 15 per cent of the total welfare population and moved this target to 30 per cent in 2000). The challenge for Canadian politicians is to appear to be tough enough to resolve a serious welfare problem while not appearing to be mean-spririted. When it comes to welfare in Canada, what you see is not always what you get. Sometimes, a program that the public has been told is one of voluntary workfare may in fact be quite coercive, while a so-called mandatory program may in fact offer the client a very wide range of choice. During Ontario's 1995 election campaign, for example, Progressive Conservative Party leader Mike Harris portrayed his workfare proposal as a tough, mandatory program in which welfare recipients would be required to work for their benefits. During a time of high unemployment and serious voter disenchantment with the New Democratic Party, Harris was elected premier of the province in a resounding victory. The following year, puzzled Ontario journalists expressed disappointment that there would actually be some choice, or options

Figure 2.1. Entitlement to Social Assistance – A Continuum of
Work-Related Qualifications

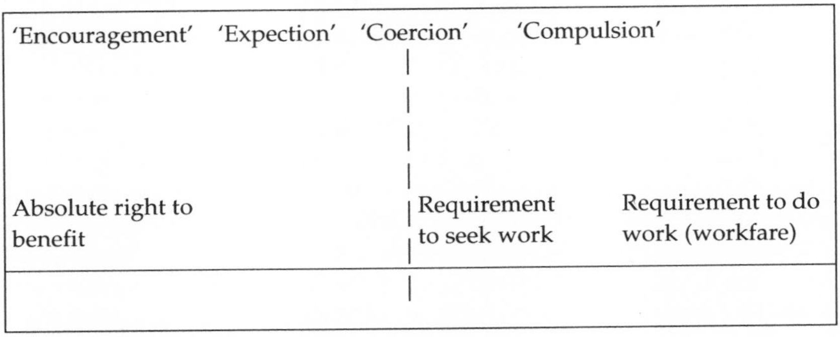

'Encouragement' 'Expection' 'Coercion' 'Compulsion'		
Absolute right to benefit	Requirement to seek work	Requirement to do work (workfare)

Source: Lightman, 1991, 123

(such as job training or job searching), other than forced community
service.

The academic community appears to have settled on a very broad
definition of workfare, which, in the context of this dicussion, can be
seen as 'anything and everything.' Ernie Lightman (1991), an economist
and professor of social policy at the University of Toronto's Faculty of
Social Work, refers to a technical continuum from voluntary to compulsory participation in programs as well as an ideological continuum
from the 'right to benefit' (or entitlement) to that of responsibilities and
obligations on the part of program participants. Figure 2.1 depicts
Lightman's two dimensions of workfare.

Joan McFarland and Robert Mullaly (1996) have tried to capture all
the nuances of the concept of workfare and divided these into three key
dimensions (the third of which draws from Ernie Lightman's ideas): (1)
the mandatory versus the voluntary nature of the programs; (2) the
welfare recipient's inherent right to a benefit, versus the participant's
responsibilities and obligations; and (3) the active (work/train) versus
the passive (stay home) nature of the program. Regarding the first
dimension of workfare, McFarland and Mullaly claim that the term
'workfare' can be applied to both mandatory and voluntary programs,
depending on the conditions. Regarding the second dimension (the
extent to which welfare recipients have an inherent right to a benefit
compared to a requirement to fulfil responsibilities and obligations),
they assert that the true definition of workfare demands the concept of

Figure 2.2. Employability and Workfare Programs

Source: McFarland and Mullaly 1996, 205

reciprocal obligations. Regarding the third dimension of workfare, active (employment/training participation) versus passive (stay home) programs, McFarland and Mullally (1996) have expanded upon Ernie Lightman's (1991) ideas. Here they try to clarify some of the issues surrounding the definition of workfare. Their model (see Figure 2.2) further focuses on employability, claiming that it is employability that best represents the reality of the changes that are taking place in welfare programs. They look at three continuums rather than two and explain their model as follows: 'In addition to the voluntary/compulsory and right/obligations aspects, we add the passive/active aspect of such programs. In addition, we include the role of such measures as earnings exemptions, tax-back rates, service and financial strategies and guaranteed annual income schemes. We also try to incorporate such issues as the role of full employment policies, the cost of the programs and the creation of a low wage labour force for employers' (McFarland and Mullaly 1996, 205–6).

There are four quadrants to their model, and mandatory workfare appears in quadrant IV. Mandatory workfare is 'compulsory, active, and involves obligations and responsibilities on the part of participants.' However, workfare is just one of several types of programs that have been categorized in quadrant IV. Also included are mandatory learnfare, the financial strategy (the manipulation of financial rewards, such as the raising or lowering of benefits that make it impossible for recipients to live without joining a program), and a Guaranteed Annual Income that sets basic rates too low for survival without labour-force participation. McFarland and Mullaly also include the effect of 'stigma' in quadrant IV, because 'the stigma attached to "not working or learning," especially if there is a lot of public rhetoric around this idea, can itself add a compulsory aspect to participation in a program' (1996, 206).

McFarland and Mullaly's model is interesting in that it attempts to capture the consequences of a program rather than its publicly stated objective. This is a particularly relevant model for understanding Canada, which, to date, has had more experience with voluntary training and employment programs than with more obviously mandatory programs. McFarland and Mullaly, both academics at St. Thomas University in New Brunswick, demonstrate how Canada's first, high-profile 'learnfare' program, New Brunswick Works (NB Works), fits into their model: 'We would place programs like NB Works, in quadrant III, at the top right. The program is officially voluntary. It involves work and training and is therefore active along the passive/active continuum. It is based on the concept of "opportunity" as contrasted to that of either a "right" or "obligation" of participants. Such programs have been referred to by some as "welfare to work" (Evans 1993: 56); "programs of attitudinal and psychological support, T-groups, education, and training activity" (Rein 1983 cited in Lightman 1991); or employability enhancement programs, characterized by Evans (1993: 62) as "carrots" as opposed to "sticks"' (1996, 206).

McFarland's and Mullaly's model can be used to better understand the true nature of voluntary workfare programs in other jurisdictions too. For example, with their model we are likely to relabel Quebec's so-called voluntary workfare as, in fact, coercive, since Quebec's restructuring of social assistance to pay lower benefits (e.g., a penalty or reduction of one hundred dollars per month for employable recipients who do not make themselves available for voluntary workfare makes it very difficult for recipients to make ends meet.

It is no coincidence that it is the continuum which has been employed to define the nature of workfare. The continuum is a catch-all that provides any number of definitions of workfare. The continuum and the multi-cell model are trotted out simply because workfare has evolved into so many different things. Workfare thus appears to carry a hundred different possible meanings as we move along the continuum or move around quadrants in a multi-cell model.

It does seem, at times, that the term 'workfare' is employed so broadly that it can apply to anything and everything. Although there may be a general consensus amongst policy-makers and academics that workfare involves the notion of linking welfare benefits to participation in work-related activity, agreement about a rigorous definition of workfare breaks down along a number of semantic dividing lines, such as those described above. An infinite combination of alternatives allows different and varying ways to put together the elements that constitute workfare. Workfare's lack of a specific definition is attractive to the desperate politician and the disillusioned taxpayer alike. Its absence of unity is both a strength and a weakness. Part of its magic lies in its open-endedness. The six case stories contained in this volume further illustrate the different meanings that have come to be attached to the term 'workfare.'

3.

Policy Chic: Putting the Poor to Work

The Nature and Development of Workfare

It is the nature of a good idea that it emerges from whatever wider set of social beliefs happen to be in vogue at the time. In the case of workfare, it was the 1980s rhetoric of efficiency and accountability that proved to be a congenial ideological environment for the development of workfare policies. Thus, workfare did not develop in isolation of a social context, but it was consistent with values that commanded broad support within society. Indeed, workfare was itself borne of another good idea – that of 'public accountability.'

Sometimes the same, or a very similar, good idea materializes in different places, often far apart, at the same time. During the past two decades, the term 'workfare' has been used in countries on both sides of the Atlantic, and workfare policies have been adopted in a number of jurisdictions. The present chapter takes a closer look at the development of this far-reaching 'good idea.'

The history of workfare is very much the history of adaptation. During the 1980s, welfare reform became a central policy issue in a number of countries. However, welfare reform was only one part of a wider social policy review that was occurring in most Western countries at around that time. During the 1980s, governments far and wide, large and small, federal, state, provincial, and local began to re-evaluate their long-standing economic and social principles. Although public sector reform has had a long history in most developed countries (usually linked to government life cycles), the government reforms of the 1980s appear to have been more significant and more comprehensive than previous efforts. Those reforms stand out because they were aimed at effecting an ideological shift in government from a public service, whose purpose was to promote public welfare, to an enterprise culture based on the rhetoric of efficiency and economy.

Mascarenhas (1993, 319–20) suggests that the high interest in public sector reform during the 1980s was due to the following three factors: (1) the significant growth of public bureaucracies – a product of the post-Keynesian welfare state, which had become increasingly complex and unable to deliver the goods, leading to public disenchantment; (2) funding expenditure on public services through taxation was seen as diverting resources to less productive purposes and crowding out the private sector; (3) the emergence of conservative regimes in Britain and the United States with the elections of Margaret Thatcher (1979) and Ronald Reagan (1980) led to what is now regarded as the neoliberalism or conservatism of the 1980s.

According to Mascarenhas, governments in the 1980s began introducing a range of public sector reforms that were largely based on economic theories of organization, the most significant of which was public choice. Managers were to be given responsibility and were to be held accountable for results. The rhetoric of public sector accountability was itself pitched as a good idea. If public sector organizations were to be transformed, it would be through accountability: let the bureaucracy be accountable for results. In the United States as well as Canada a number of aggressive public reforms were attempted, emphasizing so-called good ideas of the private sector – instant solve-alls such as: rationalization, downsizing, zero-based budgeting, job evaluation, re-engineering – their stated objective being to bring about efficiency.

It was during this period when the rhetoric of wider efficiency and accountability predominated that the great welfare debate emerged. According to the politicians, the postwar welfare system had apparently crumbled somewhere along the way and was no longer any good. Things were out of control. Reforms then began to the way in which the social assistance plan was delivered; these reforms are still evolving. To date, some reforms have included cutting welfare rates and tightening eligibility requirements. In many cases, the old assumption that the state owed unfettered payments to those in need began to be replaced by a new operative concept: that of 'mutual obligation.' The idea of a reciprocal agreement between the welfare recipient and the state seemed to make sense, workfare began to be heralded as the means of getting welfare recipients off the welfare rolls and into permanent employment.

The wave of welfare reform that swept many countries was part of a larger attempt at rationalizing public services. Britain, Australia, New Zealand, Canada, and the United States all undertook reforms, yet the variety and complexity of these reforms make it difficult to explain why mandatory workfare proved to be a good idea in some jurisdictions and not others. Ultimately, each country's response to the problem of long-term unemployment among welfare recipients is a reflection of the individual country's unique history and the ideology dominating social and economic thought. This book is confined to workfare in the United States, where the policy originated, and Canada, where U.S.-style welfare programs have been gaining popularity. The following section explores how workfare came to be hailed as such a good idea, first in the United States and later, in Canada. The specifics of how workfare has actually worked in three U.S. states and in three Canadian provinces will be explored in later chapters describing the welfare-to-work experience of each jurisdiction.

Before tracing the roots of workfare in the United States and Canada, I would like to draw the reader's attention to two important differences between welfare in the United States and welfare in Canada. First, welfare in the United States is federally controlled, with a system of capped block grants distributed to the states. Each state administers its welfare system on a county-by-county basis, according to general standards established in Washington. In Canada, while contributions to welfare are made by the federal government to the provinces in the form of transfer payments, Ottawa is not involved. The management of welfare in Canada is strictly a provincial matter. While there are similarities between welfare management in all the provinces, there were also differences in such areas as eligibility criteria, payout rates, rules, and sanctions. Moreover, each province is free to embrace workfare or ignore it.

Second, the term 'welfare' doesn't really cover the same client base in the United States as it does in Canada. When we hear about American welfare in the news media, the references are usually to single mothers on welfare. For many years the U.S. welfare system was called Aid to Families with Dependent Children (AFDC; replaced with Temporary Aid to Needy Families [TANF] after Clinton's 1996 reforms). In fact, the U.S. welfare system applies only to single parents, the overwhelming majority of whom are single mothers. Americans who are single, able-bodied, employable, and with no dependants are not included in the cash-payment welfare system. Such individuals do not qualify for welfare, but they may receive food stamps, hostel allocation, and possibly emergency cash under the General Assistance Program, a program funded and delivered solely by state governments and targeted at people who are excluded from AFDC/TANF. Most states do not have service programs for the single employable (New York and Illinois are two exceptions).

Canada, on the other hand, has a far more generous attitude toward the single employable person without dependants. This group is fully entitled to welfare benefits in the form of regular monthly welfare payments, and it makes up almost half of the welfare caseload of the country. In fact, the single employable man or woman in Canada who qualifies for welfare (and fulfils job search requirements) is entitled to receive regular welfare cheques until he or she moves to old age security payments. David Brown has made the following comparison between American and Canadian welfare benefits: 'Although a single employable individual may be able to get help in the form of food stamps and state-provided GA, these programs alone will not provide a level of income that meets a basic-needs budget. In the United States, if you are not a single parent and you do not have other sources of income, surviving without earned income is a much more difficult matter than it is in Canada' (1995, 52).

While welfare in the United States applies only to single mothers, welfare in Canada covers both employables (made up of single or married able-bodied persons without dependent children) and unemployables (single parents with children under a certain age, the aged, and persons with disabilities). The unemployables generally receive considerably higher welfare benefits than do the employables. In 1993, employable welfare recipients in Canada made up 45 per cent of the total, single parents another 28 per cent, persons with disabilities 20 per cent; all others were 7 per cent (Canada 1994a, 12).

The different client base between the two countries is one of the significant distinctions between welfare in Canada and welfare in the United States. The reader should bear in mind that the entire U.S. welfare system (and any subsequent workfare program) is built around the concept of the single mother, with only minor, state-financed programs available to single employables. Total General Assistance recipients (single employables) in the United States in 1991 were 1.3 million – much smaller than the 11 million recipients of AFDC (Brown 1995, 52) – whereas in Canada, single employables make up approximately 45 per cent of the total cash-payment welfare rolls (Canada 1994a, 12).

A third major difference between the Canadian and American welfare systems is that American states have had permission since 1987 to experiment with welfare benefit 'termination' after a set time limit. So, even before the ink was dry on Clinton's momentous August 1996 welfare reform law (mandating work as a condition for aid and a lifetime maximum welfare entitlement of five years), forty-six states had already obtained approval for waiver provisions experimenting with their welfare-to-work programs and thirty-three states had already implemented benefit termination provisions (welfare time limits) similar to those eventually outlined in Clinton's new federal law (U.S. GAO/HEHS-97-74). Clinton's new law will be discussed in some detail in this chapter, but it is important for the reader to bear this important difference in mind. The idea of time-limited welfare is completely abhorrent to Canadians, and the concept has shown not the slightest sign of life in Canada.

Workfare in the United States

The receipt of welfare has never been completely unconditional for able-bodied recipients, who have usually had to demonstrate that they were available for, and willing to, work. Over the years, different jurisdictions have varied in the extent to which they bother to require recipients to search for a job. Workfare, like most good ideas, has taken many different shapes and forms over time, appearing and reappearing in different periods and under different guises. In the United States, there is, in fact, a long history of developing education and training programs to move people out of welfare and into gainful employment. During the 1930s, Franklin D. Roosevelt helped the unemployed by marshalling federal funds to pay for a massive public service jobs strategy. Later, Kennedy, Johnson, and Nixon all experimented with substituting work for welfare. Reagan made workfare a policy fad of the 1980s, and Clinton 're-invented' workfare in the 1990s. Contemporary workfare, as seen by the 1980s style, represented a possible solution to a social problem that was out of control. The convenient catch-all label served to simplify an otherwise complex problem – which seemed irresolvable and intractable. It also reflected the growing consensus among politicians and the public that existing welfare practices should encompass the concept of reciprocity. The attempts at welfare reform in 1981, 1988, and 1996 all represented good ideas. Each piece of legislation seemed to introduce something new and seemed to represent an improvement over the old. Finally, each good idea had its believers, at least until the next good idea came along. What is most interesting about the United States is that the same good idea came along three times, and each time it was found by many to be convincing.

The formal U.S welfare system began with a program entitled Aid to Families with Dependent Children (AFDC). AFDC was a federally prescribed welfare program developed in the 1930s to help single mothers who had been widowed or abandoned by their husbands. It was originally designed as a permanent entitlement so that mothers could stay at home with their children, rather than be forced out to work. There were no work expectations for these women, and it was believed that, once they remarried, their need for welfare would end. The AFDC remained the core of the welfare system, the overwhelming majority of recipients being single female parents. Other important components of the welfare system such as Medicare, Medicaid, and the Food Stamp Program were introduced in the 1960s, during President Lyndon Johnson's administration, but AFDC remained the principal welfare program in America.

Along with many other social changes taking place in North America during the 1960s and 1970s, the traditional labour market was also changing. Technology was rapidly changing the workplace, and social movements such as women's liberation stressed the career potential of women and the liberating effect of having financial independence. People's perceptions began to change about who should go to work. The idea that mothers should stay at home with their children instead of pursuing careers was increasingly challenged. Even though society's expectations and conditions were evolving, the objectives of the AFDC program remained unchanged throughout these years. But pressure slowly began to build to change AFDC from a permanent measure to a temporary one, with the idea of gradually integrating recipients into the workforce. In 1981, President Ronald Reagan developed the idea of replacing the 1971 general regulation that required social assistance recipients to 'register' for employment and training with a more specific obligation for recipients to 'engage in' activities to increase their employment potential (except mothers with children under six years of age). The legislation, known as the Omnibus and Budget Reconciliation Act, 1981 (OBRA), was modified several times as the initial requirements were found to be too strict and too many welfare recipients lost their benefits (Evans 1993).

The Omnibus and Budget Reconciliation Act, 1981, may be considered to be America's first real step towards workfare due to its requirement that recipients participate in, and not just register for, work-related activity. Unlike Nixon, Reagan focused on the state level. The Community Work Experience Program (CWEP) was a central feature of the act and was mandated for all states: 'Each state shall be required to establish and maintain a community work experience program approved by the Secretary of Health and Human Services for those individuals required to work (exceptions would be the disabled, persons under 18 or over 65, those with very young children) as a condition of receiving AFDC. Community jobs would be provided if private sector jobs were unavailable' (Nathan 1993, 22). According to Nathan (1993, 23), the act's 'all state' requirement was too much for Congress to swallow. Congress would only agree to provide authority for the states to 'experiment' with CWEP, along with other approaches (including job search and training) aimed at enabling welfare recipients to get a job. Another important change made by Congress was the authority to shift the 1967 Work Incentive Program (WIN) directly to a single-state welfare agency and away from joint state employment service/welfare agency management.

Although the 1981 act was roundly criticized after its inception, it did encourage individual states to develop their own programs and alternatives to WIN, resulting in a proliferation of programs with a wide assortment of acronyms: GAIN (Greater Avenues for Independence) in California, JEDI (Jobs for Employable Dependent Individuals) in Maryland, MOST (Michigan Opportunities for Skills and Training) in Michigan, ET (Employment and Training) Choices in Massachusetts, PEACH (Promoting Economic Achievement) in Georgia, and many others. These programs included all or some of the following: 'education and training components, support services such as child care and transportation allowances, job search, and, often Community Work Experience Programs (CWEPS), commonly known as workfare' (Rose 1995, 132). Without a single coherent strategy, however, workfare programs varied from relatively high-quality and largely voluntary programs to those that emphasized old-style work-for-welfare (Evans 1993). As Laframboise and Kirkham state: 'under O.B.R.A., federal legislation set the guidelines for workfare, however, individual states were allowed to exercise considerable discretion in their implementation' (1994, 1).

Was any real attention paid to this act, or was it just another good idea that became a neglected part of the bureaucracy? According to Rose (1995, 134), training was provided to only 2.3 per cent of WIN

demonstration participants nationwide. Moreover, the formal organizations that have conducted studies on WIN demonstration programs
– the Manpower Demonstration Research Corporation (Goldman et al.,
1985), the Congressional Budget Office (Smith 1987) and the U.S. Government General Accounting Office (U.S. GAO/HRD-87-34) – are hard-
pressed to show any positive results relating to the stated objectives of
moving welfare recipients into the workplace. While these evaluations
support the cause of requiring the welfare recipient to try to become
self-supporting, they provide the usual consultants' recommendations
that more human and financial resources would have increased the
program's success.

After an initial decline in the number of families on AFDC in the
early 1980s, the numbers of women on AFDC continued to rise steadily
throughout the decade. By the mid-1980s, the American government
was still faced with constant growth in welfare caseloads and public
concerns about program costs and beneficiaries' long-term dependence. Things were getting worse. It was time to look for another good
idea. In 1988, the new idea came, again in the form of workfare. In fact,
as we will see, workfare is continually being reintroduced as the same
policy under new titles. Certainly the OBRA workfare experience seemed
to have accomplished little, if anything, in the war against welfare.
How was it that welfare reformers in 1988 once more promoted workfare
as the 'good idea'?

As it happens, the rise in welfare rolls was so acute by the mid-1980s
that both the Republicans and the Democrats began scrambling for
solutions. Each party publicly deplored existing welfare programs,
criticizing the passive receipt of cash assistance central to the AFDC
program and the absence of any incentives designed to help welfare
recipients find work and become independent. However, as Hogan
(1995) recounts, the two parties disagreed on what exactly should be
done about the problem. Republicans, arguing that welfare recipients
lacked discipline, called for mandatory programs requiring recipients
to engage in workfare, that is, to work in exchange for their welfare
benefits. Congressional Democrats, on the other hand, led by Senator
Daniel Patrick Moynihan, stressed low skills as the primary obstacle to
employment for welfare recipients and advocated expanded funding
for education and training programs.

Coincidentally, then Governor Bill Clinton, chair of the National
Governors Association, offered to break the impasse between the two
parties. The compromise, which was ultimately engineered by the fu-

ture President Clinton and accepted by then President Reagan, combined the mandatory workfare advanced by the Republicans and the specific training programs supported by the Democrats. Thus emerged the 1988 Family Support Act (FSA), which created the famous Job Opportunities and Basic Skills (JOBS) program, which in turn required states to enrol an increasing proportion of their adult AFDC recipients (primarily women) in the education, training, and employment-related activities they were deemed to need to become independent. The Family Support Act, a new social contract, mandated each state to establish a specific JOBS program to integrate welfare recipients into the workplace. In the words of Senator Moynihan, welfare would no longer be 'a permanent or even extended circumstance' but a 'transition to employment' (Hogan 1995, 2, 3).

The actual way in which each state decided to name, design, and implement its JOBS program was left up to the state itself, as long as the following federal JOBS requirements were met: increase the number of participants in JOBS (once selected, participation is mandatory) provide education, training, and employment services; target resources to long-term and potentially long-term AFDC recipients; help teenage recipients complete high school; provide child care and transportation to participants (MCSS 1996, 9). An individual could typically choose from the following list of JOBS components: job club, CWEP, subsidized employment program (SEP), on-the-job-training program, high school education, vocational rehabilitation/English as a second language (ESL), mini-refresher (interview preparation and self-esteem) and pre-employment counselling.

Reagan's 1988 Family Support Act (FSA) took his earlier 1981 OBRA one step further in that it increased participation requirements and emphasized the provision of employment services. It also imposed obligations and sanctions on both the states and the recipients if either failed to comply. As well, under the FSA, all teenage parents were required to pursue some form of education. Despite the public image of a full-fledged workfare plan, the 1988 Family Support Act's JOBS requirements were far from applicable to the total AFDC caseload. In fact, FSA regulations required each state to achieve a JOBS participation rate of only 7 per cent of AFDC clients by 1990, increasing to 11 per cent by 1992 and 20 per cent by 1995. (Exempt from participation in JOBS were those who were ill, incapacitated, or of advanced age; those caring for an ill or incapacitated family member; those with children under three years of age, or younger at state option, employed thirty hours or more a week; and those in the second or third trimesters of pregnancy).

Reagan's 1988 Family Support Act (FSA), which created the JOBS program, required every state to have a workfare program in operation by 1993. And on this occasion the program involved not only the usual politicians and policy-makers. Social workers, welfare recipients, and taxpayers were all witnesses to workfare's implementation. The language and logic of the JOBS program were communicated through welfare channels both formal and informal. Media reports and lobby groups against workfare all contributed to the growing perception of workfare as an immutable part of the new reality. The federal government was to provide $1 billion annually and the states were required to allocate matching funds. Using these federal FSA guidelines, the states began to set up a wide variety of welfare-to-work programs, and by 1993 all states had set up state-wide JOBS programs. Evaluations of these JOBS programs show that the effort had little impact, if any, on moving recipients into long-term jobs. By 1993, according to the U.S. General Accounting Office (U.S. GAO/PEMD-95-26), the states had served only one-quarter of those clients who, according to the guidelines, were required to participate; in other words, the program reached barely 25 per cent of its already low target numbers. Despite the revolutionary rhetoric surrounding the introduction of the JOBS program, nothing really came of it. Despite the tremendous investment of time, people, and money, results (U.S. GAO/PEMD-95-26) show that it achieved little beyond a handful of success stories. Indeed, the workfare jurisdiction that is constantly cited as a success story, the jewel in the crown, is Riverside County, California, where a closer inspection reveals that administrators actually skipped the tedious business of training and making work placements, instead choosing to match welfare recipients directly to the labour market (regardless of how little the job might pay).

By the time that Bill Clinton was preparing for his 1992 presidential election campaign, almost every state was operating its own version of the JOBS program, in whose design Clinton had been so instrumental back in 1988. During his campaign, facing crowds who knew full well that welfare rolls were swelling faster than ever before, Clinton told voters that eighteen thousand people had come off welfare in his state of Arkansas because they had found work. If elected, he proposed to institute a national workfare program to force recipients off welfare and to limit welfare benefits for younger recipients in order to encourage them to find employment. It was during this campaign that Clinton first used his now famous promise to 'end welfare as we know it.' According to Carney (1997, 72), it was Bruce Reed, a Clinton adviser, who wrote that line for the then presidential candidate in the fall of 1991, with the hope that the president would follow through on it in his first term.

By 1993, the year Bill Clinton was inaugurated as president of the United States, the AFDC program covered about 15 million individuals and had reached the unprecedented annual cost to federal and state governments of $25 billion (Nightingale and Haveman 1994, 1; U.S. GAO/PEMD-95-26). However, instead of beginning his first term with welfare reform, Clinton indulged his liberal instincts with a plan to overhaul the nation's health care system. According to Carney, 'That left Reed, a boyish 36 year old, sitting in a luxurious office across the street from the White House waiting for the day when the President would turn his attention back to the issues that had gotten him elected' (1997, 73). After two years, Reed and other aides began to worry that if Clinton didn't do something about welfare, he would be accused of inaction. The Republican Party now had control of Capitol Hill after the midterm elections, so there was some concern that a tough road would lie ahead. Reed felt that the Republicans would try to ruin Clinton by throwing his own campaign pledge of welfare reform in his face. As Carney (1997) describes the story, the welfare waivers obtained by each state (to engage in their own particular style of experimentation with welfare reform and time-limited welfare) were pitched to the press as a 'quiet revolution,' as welfare reform that was taking place without the help of Congress.

In the meantime, the Republican Congress was preparing a welfare reform bill, which they eventually presented to Clinton. The Republicans' proposed reforms were so harsh that Clinton could not bring himself to sign Congress's first two attempts at welfare reform. By July 1996 the Republicans had put a third welfare bill on the table, and it didn't look as though Clinton was going to sign that one either. It was apparently still too harsh for his liking. But by now Clinton was rapidly facing an election, and desperate aides tried to soften up the bill. They worked with allies on the Hill to force as many changes as they could, so that the president would be able to finally sign the bill while still preserving his carefully constructed image as a values-driven moderate. Carney provides a colourful account of how Clinton came to sign the welfare reform bill, officially called the Personal Responsibility and Work Opportunity Reconciliation Act of 1996:

> On July 31 [1996], the President called a meeting of cabinet officers and White House aides. He asked everyone in the room what they thought of the bill and whether he should sign it. Veto proponents dominated. Reed did most of the talking for the minority, who believed the President should sign the bill despite its flaws. This was a historic opportunity to reform the system, Reed argued, and it was worth taking the risk. Health and Human Services Secretary Donna Shalala insisted the bill would harm children and expand poverty. The President himself, according to *Time* magazine, called it a 'decent welfare bill wrapped in a sack of shit.' Emmanuel told the President to go with his 'gut.'
>
> After the meeting, Vice President Al Gore, Chief of Staff Leon Panetta and just two others retreated with the President to the Oval Office. One of them was Reed. Earlier in the day, he had drafted a statement for the President to make after a decision was reached. Perhaps out of superstition, or perhaps because Reed sensed which way Clinton would go, the statement assumed the President would decide to sign. He did.' (Carney 1997, 74)

So what was so drastic about the Republican Congress's welfare reform bill that had made Clinton so reluctant to sign it? The Aid to Families with Dependent Children (AFDC) program – the core federal cash welfare program in place since the mid-1930s) – was to be replaced by Temporary Assistance for Needy Families (TANF), a system of capped block grants to states. The highlights of the Personal Responsibility and Work Opportunity Reconciliation Act relate to work requirements and time limits. The new law reinstates the work requirement and penalizes states financially if they don't put a rising portion of their welfare recipients to work (states are given six years to put at least half their caseloads to work). The law came into effect on 1 October 1996. Each state had eleven months to put its plan in place. The changes ushered in by Clinton's 1996 act are described by Richard Berke, writing in the *New York Times* (August 1996):

- Ends a sixty-one-year-old guarantee of federal aid. AFDC and smaller programs are folded into an annual block grant that states can use to operate their own welfare plans.

- Reduces spending by $55 billion over six years, mainly by cutting food stamps and aid to legal immigrants.
- Imposes a five-year lifetime limit on welfare benefits. States can exempt up to 20 per cent of their caseload for hardship reasons and set shorter time limits. The 20 per cent exemption is assumed to be those who are permanently unemployable because of disabilities and other serious problems, and single parents with children younger than five years of age.
- Requires unmarried mothers under the age of eighteen to attend school and live with an adult, except if otherwise exempted.
- Requires recipients to begin working two years after receiving welfare and mandates that half of all single-parent families work thirty hours a week by 2002 (i.e., workfare).
- Reduces spending on food stamps by $28 billion over six years and allows able-bodied individuals without children to receive food stamps for only three months in any three-year period, unless they are working part-time. Applicants can get another three months if they are laid off.
- Bars most federal aid including Medicaid and cash welfare to future legal immigrants for five years. Current immigrants cannot receive disability payments and food stamps during their first five years.
- Makes it more difficult for children to receive federal disability due to mental problems.
- Sets tough new rules to crack down on parents who do not pay child support.
- Provides $14 billion for child care.
- Requires states to maintain their present levels of welfare spending.
- Denies a portion of welfare block grants to states that do not meet the goals for employment of recipients. The penalty would rise from 5 per cent in the first year to 21 per cent in the ninth year.
- Allows states to allocate money now used for welfare employers as a wage subsidy.
- Preserves the federal guarantee of health coverage under Medicaid.

All the states developed their own plans, many setting stricter targets than those imposed by Washington (for example, most went for two-year time limits instead of five, and, by 1997, nineteen states had already indicated that they would not increase the welfare cheques of women who had additional children while receiving public assistance). The result is the American government's most recent attempt to move away from a system of federal welfare payouts to a system of state-controlled workfare, in which states are required to enrol certain percentages of TANF recipients (previously AFDC clients) in work-related activities for a certain amount of time per week. At the same time, 'work-related activity' still includes education and training programs and has been expanded, since the signing of the act, to include almost anything (see Carl Horowitz's article 'Welfare Reform: Passing Phase? Congress Is Already Opening Workfare Loopholes' in *Los Angeles Investor's Business Daily*, 16 July 1997).

The 1996 act took the JOBS program of the Family Support Act of 1988 one step further by requiring each state to set up a more specific welfare-to-work program, in order to ensure that it had a higher participation rate (e.g., one-half of all single parents were to be engaged in work-related activity for thirty hours a week by 2002). Fourteen billion dollars were allocated for child care, partly so that states could not blame the failure of their workfare programs on a lack of support services. As in JOBS, all unmarried teenage mothers were compelled to attend school, but they were now also required to live with an adult.

Apart from the imposition of a five-year lifetime limit on welfare benefits (down to as low as two years should the states desire), the objectives of Clinton's welfare reform had a lot in common with the JOBS program brought in during Reagan's administration in 1988. Both pieces of legislation, through a system of block grants, required states to enrol recipients in work-related activities in exchange for their welfare cheques. The workfare focus still appeared to be on participation, on enrolment, on increasing the proportion of welfare recipients in the program, not on matching the individual to a permanent jobs. In other words, the 'good idea' was still focused on virtual work, rather than real work.

By 1996, workfare formed a recognized part of the welfare landscape. The construction of the workfare reality was now complete. The succession of major welfare reforms from Reagan's 1981 OBRA and the WIN program, to his 1988 Family Support Act, which created the JOBS program, and then to Clinton's 1996 Personal Responsibility and Work Opportunity Reconciliation Act served to move workfare further up the public policy agenda and to complete the reality of workfare in the mind of the American people. The 1996 Personal Responsibility and Work Opportunity Act requires most recipients of the Temporary Aid to Needy Families (TANF) to be engaged in a work-related activity after two years in which they have received cash assistance and limits the total amount of time benefits may be received to five years. States have the option of limiting benefits to as little as two years. In twenty states, as of 1998, the time period during which one may receive welfare is less than five years; in thirty-three states, welfare recipients who fail to comply with a work program lose their cash support, and some seven hundred thousand Americans surrendered their welfare cheques during 1997 alone (Jeffrey Simpson, 'Everywhere, Welfare Systems Are Getting a Dose of Tough Love,' *Globe and Mail*, 21 January 1996).

By 1996, the American public had become accustomed to the idea of workfare. The controversy surrounding workfare in earlier reforms had all but disappeared. Workfare was here to stay. But it was the JOBS program that represented the real implementation of workfare in America. Any workfare idea after 1988 is just more of the same. For example, Clinton's 1996 welfare reforms were variations on earlier reforms: higher participation rates (a requirement as high as 50 per cent in 2002), mandatory education, an increase in the number of hours a recipient must work, more money allocated for child care, stricter sanctions, etc. It was really the 1988 JOBS program that established workfare in America.

As Rose points out, by the time Clinton came on the scene, the moral debate over workfare was over. The anti-workfare advocates who had worked so hard before the 1981 WIN program and the 1988 JOBS program had lost the battle: 'By the 1990s mandatory work programs had become an accepted part of AFDC. There was no longer much discussion of the various programs' merits. Instead, debates concerned how to get recipients off welfare and into wage labor more effectively. Consistent with the emphasis on punitive policies instead of incentives, this was primarily done through sanctions' (Rose 1995, 166). The rather uncritical acceptance of workfare evidenced in the run-up to the 1996 legislation suggests that the concept, and its effectiveness, had finally achieved wide acceptance. What is perhaps more important is the high profile that was given to the term 'workfare' and the anecdotes in the media about people clearing highways and sweeping streets, giving the public the illusion that armies of welfare recipients were becoming work ready. To a certain extent, the acceptance of time-limited welfare is likely to have been made all the easier because of people's beliefs that workfare was really established, and that it really did work. Through workfare, the government does provide the illusion that we have had success and are continuing to shepherd people along toward independence (that is, until their time runs out). Without faith in the effectiveness of workfare, would it not have been impossible to decide to drop people from the rolls after a certain arbitrary period of time?

But what of this good idea and its repeated reincarnations – was the good idea that the politicians convinced us to accept really all that good? Might it not be the case that work experience programs provide the public with the illusion that something is being done about the welfare problem when, in fact, nothing positive is being accomplished? When Clinton signed the 1996 welfare reform bill, the message that 'now we're going to have mandatory workfare' was again beamed to the public. But the act itself seemed to go beyond workfare, to formalizing time limits on welfare. Was the good idea of 1996 really workfare, or was it, in fact, one about time limits (shifting the thinking from 'permanent' entitlement to 'temporary' reciprocal deal). The American public's belief that workfare was a success is likely what allowed the public to swallow the notion of time limits, a harsh concept that might otherwise have seemed too terrifying. Moreover, Clinton's sweeping re-election victory in 1996 would appear to confirm the public's endorsement of his good idea regarding welfare reforms. In 1999, Clinton boasted that the welfare rolls had been cut in half since he took office in 1993, shrinking from 14.1 million to 7.3 million. He also quoted figures from the Federal Department of Health and Human Services that showed that 'all 50 states have moved the required number of people' into work-related activities, making up, on average, 35 per cent of the nation's welfare recipients (*Los Angeles Times*, 2 August 1999). The percentage of Americans on welfare, 2.7 per cent, is the lowest figure in three decades, when it was 2.5 per cent under Lyndon Johnson (Derrick Jackson, 'Former Welfare Recipient Stuck at Bottom,' *Boston Globe*, 19 August 1999).

Workfare in Canada

The workfare movement has been much slower to take hold in Canada than it has in the United States. This is partly due to Canadians' general support for a more comprehensive cradle-to-grave social welfare system – reflected, as suggested earlier, by the arguably generous inclusion in the welfare pool of single/married employables with no dependants, in addition to sole-support parents. It is also worth noting that the concept of workfare itself went against the long-standing 50 per cent federal-provincial cost-sharing agreement known as the Canada Assistance Plan (CAP), which came into effect in 1966. CAP clearly dictated that the only condition for welfare eligibility was financial need. In other words, once an individual has met a provincial needs test, nothing can stand in the way of that person receiving welfare. Any introduction of workfare was forbidden under the long-standing CAP agreement because it would impose certain other conditions upon the welfare client or potential client and impede access to assistance. From 1966 to the dissolution of the CAP agreement in 1996, the concept of working in exchange for welfare was not a recognized criterion for eligibility (unless a province wished to fund the program under some other heading besides welfare). Thus, Canadian provinces have been reluctant to implement workfare because to do so would threaten their funding from Ottawa (Hess 1987). This does not mean that workfare has not surfaced under some guise in the history of the Canadian welfare system, either before CAP or following its demise.

Soon after World War II, for example, work programs became part of the government's strategy for dealing with the postwar recession. In 1945–6, $150 million was allocated for work projects, but only $54 million was used for this purpose, allegedly due to a shortage of planning staff and an overburdened system (Pal 1987, 45). By 1949 the Canadian government had abandoned the work projects. Other fitful efforts at work-for-relief programs were made in the country, most of them in Ontario. In 1958, when the able-bodied unemployed became eligible for social assistance, some Ontario communities required such individuals to participate in public work projects in exchange for their relief cheque. Activities such as shovelling, bush clearing, and road work were common, but this program did not last long. As the jobs of local workers were replaced by work-for-relief participants, the federal government became concerned over the mismanagement of public funds, claiming that the unemployment problem was not being resolved by costly programs to subsidize cheap labour for municipal projects. In 1961, after the federal Auditor General's Office investigated the Ontario work-for-relief programs, Ottawa told then Ontario Premier John Robarts that welfare benefits were no longer to be distributed through work-for-relief programs (Struthers 1994, 188). Following up on the Auditor General's criticism of Ontario's work-for-relief programs, the federal Department of National Health and Welfare also informed Ontario that any local communities implementing work-for-relief programs would be ineligible for 50 per cent federal cost sharing (Struthers 1994, 188). Faced with the risk of losing federal dollars, Ontario soon gave up its work-for-relief programs.

In addition to the early adoption of various, usually mild, forms of workfare, Canada has also been slowly moving towards a greater acceptance of workfare. The 1970s and 1980s saw the federal government confronted with the fiscal challenge of balancing demands for expanded public services with the reality of limited revenues. It was a time when a number of broad reforms were attempted by the federal government to control ever rising costs. Contributions to both health and unemployment were lowered, family allowances and child tax credits were partially de-indexed, a tax clawback on family allowances and old age security benefits was introduced, and the costs of Unemployment Insurance were transferred from the government to employers and employees themselves. With the 1990s came the trend toward greater selectivity and a possible dismantling of 'universality' (e.g., health care). In October 1990 the federal government cut Unemployment Insurance by limiting eligibility, reducing periods of benefit, and raising waiting periods. Welfare in the provinces was affected by the federal government's decision to put a 'cap on CAP,' thereby reducing the federal share of the costs of social assistance. CAP was replaced by the Canada Health and Social Transfer on 1 April 1996, which left the provinces with more discretion as to how they might manage their welfare system and also made workfare perfectly legal in Canada. The dismantling of CAP had a financial impact on the provinces since the 50 per cent costs sharing arrangement no longer existed. In Ontario, the federal share of the cost of social assistance was reduced from 50 per cent to 28 per cent (Evans 1995).

With swelling welfare rolls and less money coming from the federal government to pay the costs, some provinces became desperate to cut their social assistance spending. In a study of welfare caseloads in Canada's four largest provinces, David Brown examined the 'sole-support parent' category and found that 'The increases between 1983 and 1993 for these four provinces were 6.8 per cent in Quebec, 22.6 per cent in British Columbia, 34.0 per cent in Alberta, and an astounding 144.5 per cent in Ontario' (1995, 57). A federal government Green Paper also shows that in March 1981 there were 1.4 million Canadians on welfare, compared to 3 million in the same month in 1993 – a doubling in just twelve years (Canada 1994b, 19–20). How did this come about? What was happening in Canada that made the welfare numbers rise so sharply? John Richards (1997, xiv–xviii), a Canadian expert on welfare reform, provides an interesting set of explanations for the increased Canadian reliance on social assistance. Specifically, he divides the problem into two categories, the first being causes that arose in civil society (e.g., technological change, globalization, decline of family values, decline of stigma attached to receipt of welfare) and the second being causes which arose in public policy (e.g., emphasis of macro-economic policy on price stability, perverse incentives in labour-market-adjustment policies, perverse incentives in welfare programs, and insider/outsider effects abetted by labour laws). Brown (1995) offers a simpler explanation, suggesting a 'destructive syndrome' among poor Canadians over the last two decades that provides the following mathematical result: among those with limited skills, the relative reward from work declined, while the relative reward from 'non-work' increased.

Whatever the reasons, the number of Canadians on welfare was becoming a highly publicized public issue in the early 1990s. Each province wondered what to do about it. What, if any, expectations should be articulated for persons on social assistance? Everyone knew that the restrictive federal CAP agreement more or less prohibited work-for-welfare programs, but they also knew that the thirty-year-old cost-sharing agreement was due to expire in March 1996. After that date, federal cash transfers could no longer be held back if workfare was implemented, and provinces would have a freer hand to impose work and/or training requirements on social assistance recipients. Questions began to arise regarding eligibility. Was social assistance intended more for employable persons who were temporarily unemployed or for persons who had dropped out of the labour force altogether because they saw no employment prospects? Reform strategies varied across the provinces. Some provinces (e.g., Alberta, British Columbia, Ontario, and Quebec) increased resources for caseload monitoring and fraud detection, mounting well-publicized campaigns to cut down on welfare abuse; between 1993 and 1995 some provinces (e.g., Alberta, Quebec, Prince Edward Island, and Ontario) cut the amount of welfare recipients' benefits (MCSS 1996, 2). Certain provincial experiments began to catch the public's attention, for example, that of New Brunswick, a province with an extremely high unemployment rate that introduced an allegedly successful 'learnfare' program in the early 1990s, called New Brunswick Works. Some provinces have shied away from workfare measures while others, such as Alberta and Ontario, have been heavily influenced by the the workfare programs in the United States. Nevertheless, the concept of mandatory workfare – by which employable welfare recipients must engage in some type of work-related activity in exchange for their welfare cheque – is gaining ground in Canada. The mood of the Canadian people toward the concept of 'reciprocity' is reflected in a highly publicized 1994 Gallup poll in which 86 per cent of the Canadians who responded said that they were in favour of making people who receive welfare work.

There are other indications that Canada's interest in workfare will be long term. After its first big political win in the 1995 election, the Ontario government of Mike Harris removed the aged and persons with disabilities out of the welfare system and into a guaranteed income scheme so that the welfare client base would be fit to comply with the new workfare regulations. Also, Evans (1995, 84) discovered that some provinces (e.g., Quebec and Alberta) had moved to categorize employable welfare recipients according to their willingness to participate in work-related programs. She also found that provinces were directing more voluntary work experience programs at welfare recipients and that recipients were being encouraged to commit themselves to 'action plans' or contracts to enhance employability. Specifically, Evans claims the following: 'As Canada continues to grapple with deficit reduction and social program reform ... the issue of "workfare" will remain firmly on the agenda. Workfare, in the sense of increasing the obligations of social assistance recipients to take up education, training or community service as a condition of their entitlement, resonates in a political and economic environment that has identified social programs, rather than unemployment, as a major culprit in increasing both individual "dependency" and the deficit' (1995, 96).

It appears that workfare will be a permanent addition to the social policy armamentarium. The reform of the welfare state in Canada saw a transformation from a system based strictly on financial need to one that is, in some cases, conditional on the performance of some voluntary or mandatory work-related activity. The history of workfare in Canada, like that of the United States, tends to reflect much of the time in which it was located. Workfare in the United States has provided Canada with some valuable programming models. At another level, workfare has developed as a field of discourse, a living element in the process of producing yet another good idea.

Workfare's appeal is broad and varied, and difficult to explain. The introduction of workfare measures in several provinces has prompted extensive debate and controversy. These quarrels are not the major interest here. I am more interested in the meaning of the term 'workfare' and in its concrete manifestation, as illustrated in the six case stories. Some Canadian provinces have been more attracted to workfare than others. Could it be that the very word 'workfare,' with its negative image of controlling the marginal, the ignored, the decentred, those deprived of power, explains differential attraction within the Canadian provinces? Because 'workfare' has come to represent controversy and criticism, many politicians and policy-makers avoid the label, referring to their program in less contested terms, such as 'learnfare.' This brief overview of the history of workfare in the United States and Canada shows that workfare, as a social policy concept, has indeed taken hold in both countries. In each of the following six chapters I tell six workfare stories, each one unique, but each one starting out the same way: Once upon a time, somebody had a 'good idea' ...

4.

California's GAIN Program – The Operation Was a Success but the Patient Died

Summary

California's GAIN (Greater Avenues for Independence) program served as a model for the design of the federal U.S. JOBS program. GAIN was a mandatory workfare program that was based on the belief that long-term training and education were the appropriate vehicles to move welfare workers into the workplace – into not just jobs, but careers. GAIN began in 1985 and lasted thirteen years, to 1998, when it was replaced by the new workfare program that operates under the name of CalWORKS. Thanks to generous formal evaluations, GAIN was widely perceived to be a testament to the value of 'long-term investment in human capital.' But GAIN was particularly unsuccessful in moving welfare recipients into the paid workforce and in reducing California's welfare rolls – in fact, they steadily increased: 'From the start of 1993 until September of last year [1996], California experienced an increase of 6 percent in its caseload of those on Aid to Families with Dependent Children – the core welfare program. It was the only one of the 10 most populous states not to reduce its caseload' (L.A. *Investor's Business Daily*, 21 January 1997). In 1997, in a population of over 30 million, there were almost one million welfare cases, representing 2.2 million people (California Department of Social Services [CDSS], Sept. 1997). Until Clinton's 1996 welfare reforms, California's politicians, policy-makers, and welfare administrators clung firmly to their belief in the long-term benefits of education and training rather than work placements. It was only Clinton's legislation (which included higher workfare participation rates, time limits, and sanctions) that seemed to spark California counties to switch their workfare philosophy from one of 'education first' to one of 'work first.' What is amazing about California's GAIN program is that evaluators praised it for so long as a model U.S. workfare program, when it actually accomplished so little.

California's Good Idea: Background and Context of the Reform

Workfare is not new to California. Experiments in welfare reform along the lines of workfare have been around since the 1970s when Ronald Reagan was the Republican governor of the state; they continued in the 1980s under George Deukmejian and then into the 1990s with Pete Wilson. Although the word 'workfare' has been used by a wide variety of politicians, California never really engaged in hard-line welfare reform in the manner of Wisconsin or Illinois. Despite its Republican governors, the state legislature has often been controlled by the Democrats; and although the legislators did enact reforms with a definite work requirement, as Waste has noted, these reforms were 'tempered with relatively generous assistance levels, work training programs, and exemptions for single mothers with young children' (1995, 55).

The story of workfare in the state of California is of broad relevance to the study of welfare reform because California has the biggest welfare caseload – it is more than twice that of any other state – and the largest and most ambitious state-wide workfare program in the United States (Rose 1995, 167). California has 12 per cent of the country's population but almost 20 per cent of the country's welfare caseload (CDSS 1997). As of June 1996, about 8.5 per cent of the state's total population (2.8 million people) were receiving Aid to Families with Dependent Children (AFDC; soon to become Temporary Assistance to Needy Families [TANF] under Clinton's 1996 reforms); more than ten thousand families in California have been on welfare for seventeen years or longer (Liu, 1997).

California is often associated with innovative social policy. Almost anyone who has had anything to do with welfare reform has heard of the Greater Avenues for Independence (GAIN) program. Established in 1985, GAIN is California's 'highly-successful, nationally-recognized, welfare-to-work program' (LADPSS 1997, 4). GAIN was, and still is today, touted as California's major accomplishment in the field of social welfare reform. As Rose observed, 'GAIN was hailed as a success ... Front-page stories in one of the state's leading newspapers claimed that "GAIN not only moves recipients into jobs but, once employed, they steadily earn more, reducing the need for government assistance"' (1995, 167). This is despite the fact that less than 20 per cent of California welfare recipients ever participated in the program; and of the less than 20 per cent of recipients who did participate in GAIN, 85 per cent remained on welfare (MDRC 1994). Despite dismal results and huge public expenditure, formal evaluations of GAIN remained either optimistic or outright positive. Following President Clinton's 1996 legislation, which handed over responsibility for welfare to the states and imposed financial sanctions and time limits, California subsequently changed the name of its welfare-to-work program from GAIN to CalWORKS (California Work Opportunity and Responsibility to Kids), with the state maintaining that the principles of GAIN have been incorporated into the new program. This chapter focuses on GAIN, since it represents a thirteen-year-long example of workfare in action prior to the imposition of the federal legislation of 1996.

That the story of workfare in California is complex is due not so much to the components of the GAIN program itself as to the smoke and mirrors of its successful public relations effort. In short, GAIN didn't work. Of the fifty-eight California counties in which GAIN operated, only one was declared a success – Riverside County (MDRC 1994). Paradoxically, Riverside elected to ignore GAIN's core philosophy of 'long-term investment in human capital through education and training,' choosing instead to pay private employment agencies to move welfare recipients directly into available jobs (even if those jobs paid only minimum wage). Somehow, California's GAIN program came to be touted as a success.

What is the historical context of GAIN? How did the program come about, and why was it considered such a success? Greater Avenues for Independence (GAIN) was an initiative aimed at increasing the employment and self-sufficiency of welfare recipients. The GAIN program was an extension of a series of earlier welfare-to work programs. According to senior California Department of Social Services (CDSS) staff, the historical roots of workfare and GAIN date back to 1967 when Congress created the Work Incentive (WIN) program, which required states to provide job-related services that would help welfare recipients find work. Then, in 1971, Governor Ronald Reagan introduced California's 1971 Welfare Reform Act, which established an early workfare program known as the Community Work Experience Program (CWEP). After Reagan was elected president, he passed the 1981 Omnibus Budget Reconciliation Act (OBRA), which encouraged individual states to develop alternatives to the existing WIN program to reduce their dependence on the federal Aid to Families with Dependent Children (AFDC) welfare program. In response to Washington's challenge, California designed an education and/or job-training program that included employment supports such as subsidized child care, and presented its idea to Washington. Under Senator Magent, the state obtained the necessary federal waivers, and GAIN was established in California in 1985. Each of the fifty-eight California counties was given the flexibility to design its own version of the program. GAIN staff involved in the early days of the program claim that their workfare project caught Washington's eye and that GAIN was the model for the national Job Opportunities and Basic Skills (JOBS) training program, introduced by then President Reagan under the 1988 Family Support Act (FSA). In 1988, GAIN in turn developed into California's version of the JOBS program, and was given additional funding to support and expand its activities.

When asked about the difference between GAIN and previous California welfare-to-work programs, Raul Ramirez, one of the original designers of GAIN, explained in a telephone interview on 20 February 1998: 'A person could no longer just receive welfare benefits without going out to look for a job. The government would assist with education, training, support services, transportation funds and ancillary expenses. The federal government and other states came out to see the program, they liked it so much ... In fact, JOBS is modelled after GAIN in California. By the time that JOBS was introduced in 1988, GAIN was already in place, so it was hard to change it. We only had to make very minor changes to align it with the Family Support Act.'

According to Ramirez, GAIN was based on 'a decision to invest in human capital.' GAIN's strong emphasis on education remained much the same from the program's inception in 1985 until President Clinton signed the Personal Responsibility and Work Opportunities Reconciliation Act of 1996. Clinton's welfare reforms affected each state's welfare-to-work program because the new federal regulations now required states to achieve certain set levels of participation in their respective workfare programs and to establish a lifetime welfare limit of five years for most families (this limit could be lowered to two years should the state so desire). In 1996, when Clinton ended the sixty-year-old federal welfare program known as Aid to Families with Dependent Children (AFDC) and replaced it with a program entitled Temporary Assistance to Needy Families (TANF), states such as California could no longer get away with having low participation rates in their workfare programs without suffering financial sanctions. Either California started moving thousands of welfare parents into work-related activities or it risked losing millions of dollars in federal aid. By 2002, adults in half of all TANF families (mostly single mothers) are required to be performing work-related activities (twenty hours a week for the first two years, twenty-five hours for the third year, and thirty hours a week thereafter) for the state to continue to receive its block grant; 90 per cent of two-adult families will have to have an adult in work-related activities at least thirty-five hours a week (California State Senate Report 1996).

In response to the need to have a higher percentage of its welfare population participate in workfare, California decided to make some adjustments to its GAIN program. In order to bring its welfare-to-work program into line with the federal requirements, state policy-makers redesigned GAIN to incorporate more rigorous work expectations and time-limited welfare into its philosophy. The new workfare plan, which came into effect on 1 January 1998, is called CalWORKS. Program staff claim that the philosophy and principles of GAIN have been incorporated into CalWORKS. It would appear, however, that the reality of higher participation targets, financial sanctions, and time-limited welfare has caused the emphasis to shift from a philosophy of 'education first' to one of 'work first.' When CalWORKS was launched, there began to be some public admission that GAIN was perhaps not all that it was made out to be. Criticisms of GAIN went beyond the custom of denigrating the old social policy to help introduce the new one. California's Governor Pete Wilson, for example, expressed his opinion of GAIN's shortcomings. In a 9 January 1997 speech introducing CalWORKS, Governor Wilson made the following disparaging remark about his own employees who administered the GAIN's program: 'They thought no one should be moved to work until they spent at least two years in the classroom' (Virginia Ellis and Josh Meyer, 'Study Praises County's Welfare to Work Tactic,' in the Los Angeles Times, 26 February 1997). Other negative comments started to emerge in the popular press. For example, the Los Angeles Investor's Business Daily (30 January 1998) makes the claim that 'California has made less progress in welfare reform than most other states – even though one in five Americans on welfare lives there.' An earlier editorial in the same Los Angeles newspaper also commented on California's poor progress: 'From the start of 1993 until September of last year, California experienced an increase of 6 per cent in its caseload of those on Aid to Families with Dependent Children – the core welfare program. It was the only one of the 10 most populous states not to reduce its caseload' (21 January 1997). Prior to these slowly emerging criticisms, however, GAIN had always been touted as a great success in moving people from welfare to work. How did California give the entire nation the idea, for at least thirteen years, that its good idea was actually good? The following section illustrates how the attractive design and language of GAIN go some way in helping us to understand the long-term appeal of this 'good idea.'

How Was the Program Designed?

The Greater Avenues for Independence (GAIN) program is a large-scale welfare-to-work initiative that operates throughout the state of California. Every such program, no matter how big, must operate with some theoretical notion of cause and effect. In the case of California, with the highest welfare rate of any state in America, the core philosophy is education. Policy-makers in California were concerned that large numbers of welfare recipients had never finished high school, and, as a result, education was made the key priority. But the same policy-makers were also concerned that many welfare recipients had little or no access to affordable child care or reliable transportation and that they had little or no work experience. So GAIN was also designed to eliminate these perceived barriers to employment, offering welfare recipients free education, child care for children under the age of twelve, training, personal counselling, transportation, and work placement opportunities. The underlying theory of GAIN, therefore, was that if these barriers could be eliminated, welfare recipients would become self-sufficient. Those who designed GAIN also wanted to make the program consistent with local needs, to integrate it with other local programs and to use local provider networks (private enterprise, the faith community, community services, etc.).

A key feature of GAIN, which supposedly distinguishes California's program from most other welfare-to-work, or JOBS, programs in the United States, is that it uses educational and basic skills levels to sort registrants into one of two service streams: those judged to be in need of a basic education and those judged *not* to be in need of a basic education. Those who fall into the first stream or those in need of a basic education have available to them an array of activities ranging from Adult Basic Education, to high school diploma preparation, to English as a Second Language instruction, to participation in job-search activities.

According to a California State Senate Report, 'GAIN was established in 1985 to require AFDC recipients to participate in work or job training, with the help of a comprehensive array of tools, including basic education, to prepare them to find and retain employment' (1996, 5). GAIN was designed to increase the employment and self-sufficiency of recipients of Aid to Families with Dependent Children (AFDC), the nation's largest cash welfare program. Until 1988, those who could be required to participate in GAIN were all single parents on AFDC (mostly mothers) with no pre-school-aged children and heads of two-parent AFDC families (mostly fathers), for as long as they received welfare. In 1989, the participation requirement was extended to single parents with children aged three to five. The program was mandatory for the above-mentioned groups, if they were required to participate, but voluntary for the balance of the AFDC caseload. Recipients' welfare grants could be reduced if they were 'required' to participate and refused to do so (MDRC 1994, 3). The following excerpt from a GAIN pamphlet shows how GAIN was presented to welfare recipients:

> GAIN stands for Greater Avenues for Independence.
> The purpose of the GAIN program is to teach, train, counsel and help you find a job. When you become self-supporting, you and your children will enjoy a higher income and a better way of life.
> GAIN was designed with you in mind. It's not just another government program. It's much more than that.
> GAIN is with you every step of the way, providing you with such important supportive services as child care, transportation and work- or training-related expenses.
> GAIN helps you get the skills that are needed in today's work force. You could become a technician, salesperson, assembler or any one of hundreds of other professionals ...
> Everyone wins. You gain a job and a future. Private industry and business gain a skilled workforce.' (GAIN Guidebook 1988, 3)

The Manpower Demonstration Research Corporation's (MDRC) evaluation of GAIN emphasizes that the sequence of services depends on the client's educational background and skills. Those who have a high school diploma and pass a basic reading and math test usually start with job-search activities. Most clients who do not have a diploma, or fail the test, enrol in one of three basic education programs. However, they are also expected to participate in job-search activities either before they start basic education or after they finish. Those already enrolled in education and training programs when they enter GAIN may continue if the activity is toward an occupation that is deemed to be needed in the local labour market and if they can complete the course within two years after enrolling in GAIN (MDRC 1994, 3–4).

Participants who are not employed after their initial activities undergo an employability assessment and are then referred to additional training or work experience (MDRC 1994, 3). All GAIN participants are required to sign a two-part contract: the first part tells the client about the program, his or her rights and responsibilities, what good reasons the client must have for not participating, and what the penalties are if the client refuses to participate (e.g., conciliation, a money-management course, financial sanctions); and the second part of the contract advises the client as to which part of the program he or she will be participating in.

The design of GAIN was simple. Administrative refinements took place over the years, but the program remained basically unchanged from the original plan that drew the attention of the nation up to its 1998 incorporation into CalWORKS (California Work Opportunity and Responsibility to Kids). The main change from GAIN to CalWORKS lies in the intensity of the work requirement and the addition of time limits and sanctions, as per Washington's new crackdown. The 1998 level of $565 for a mother with two children was maintained ($538 for those in regions with a lower cost of living). As with GAIN, those under CalWORKS who seek welfare must also seek work; but now, new applicants must find a job within eighteen months; current recipients are entitled to twenty-four cumulative months of aid, and there is a five-year lifetime limit for parents.

Administrative Challenges: Making Workfare Work

From the introduction of GAIN in 1985 to the time of the signing of President Clinton's controversial 1996 welfare reform legislation, the public image of GAIN was one of success; indeed, the program was a model for the nation. Only when Washington started insisting on tangible evidence of its success that people began to notice that GAIN's results were far from spectacular. But before 1996, California was considered to be on the cutting edge of successful welfare reform. Somehow, this illusion was maintained, both within the public service and with the public, for more than a decade. California was proud of its welfare-to-work program, which was built on the back of Ronald Reagan's 1971 welfare reforms, and firmly believed that the long-term 'investment in human capital' theory would produce visible results. Unfortunately, it did not.

It was the administrative culture of California's Department of Social Services that helped to keep the good idea alive for so long. By pretending that there were appreciable results when there were none, or at least by not drawing attention to the poor results, administrators colluded with the policy-makers and the politicians in making the 'good idea' look good. Despite being a mandatory workfare program, GAIN reached only the tiniest percentage of welfare recipients. When this inadequacy was finally admitted, staff blamed a 'lack of money.' GAIN apparently did not have enough money, either at the program's beginning in 1985, or after receiving millions more from Washington in 1989 when GAIN became part of the federal JOBS program. Even after GAIN received its injection of new millions from the federal JOBS program, hardly anyone was required to participate in workfare. When various GAIN administrators were asked why so few welfare recipients had ever been selected to participate in GAIN, they blamed a 'lack of resources,' such as staff and money. True to the GAIN philosophy, staff priority lay in retaining clients on the welfare rolls during lengthy educational stints as opposed to moving welfare recipients off the welfare rolls and into jobs. When asked about job placement, three senior administrators reiterated the long-term gains of investment in human capital and the waste of placing single parents in low-paying jobs that would not fully meet their financial needs. A worthwhile career was clearly the objective of GAIN.

The 1994 Manpower Demonstration Research Corporation (MDRC) study on the effectiveness of GAIN confirms the administrative culture as being very much one of 'education first, jobs later.' In its survey of six sample counties, only one county was found to have achieved any real results. This county, Riverside, was one in which the staff placed much more emphasis on moving registrants into the labour market quickly than did any other of the counties. The MDRC evaluation states:

> The six counties made different decisions about how much to emphasize quick entry into the labor market versus the longer and more expensive process of building registrants' human capital through education and training ... Most distinctive was Riverside's attempt to communicate a strong 'message' to all registrants (even those in education and training

activities), at all stages of the program, that employment was central, that it should be sought expeditiously, and that opportunities to obtain low paying jobs should not be turned down. The county's [Riverside's] *management underscored this message by establishing job placement standards as one of several criteria for assessing staff performance*, while at the same time attempting to secure the participation of all mandatory registrants. In addition, the county instituted a strong job development component to assist recipients in gaining access to job opportunities. (MDRC 1994, 5); emphasis added

According to the study, the Alameda County (one of the six sample counties that had the worst results) GAIN program took the opposite approach to that of Riverside, favouring long-term education over direct job placement. The other four counties fell in between Riverside's and Alameda's approaches but were found to be closer in philosophy to Alameda's: 'Its [Alameda's] GAIN managers and staff believed strongly in "human capital" development – the use of education and training as a path to getting jobs that offer a better chance to get off or stay off welfare. Within the overall constraints imposed by the GAIN model's service sequences, Alameda's staff encouraged registrants to be selective about the jobs they accepted and to take advantage of GAIN's education and training to prepare for higher-paying jobs. Butte, Los Angeles, San Diego, and Tulare, took approaches falling between those of Riverside and those of Alameda, but closer to Alameda's than to Riverside's (MDRC 1994, 5).

But was Riverside really a success? Did Riverside really effect a magical transformation of welfare unemployables into productive independent workers? Even Riverside's success seems questionable – at least as it relates to workfare. Much of Riverside's supposed success in dropping its welfare numbers appears to have lain in its stricter application of the rules, and in the use of sanctions for those GAIN participants who would not cooperate with the program. Lawrence Townsend, Jr., director of the Riverside County Department of Public Social Services, explained that Riverside's success was due to a focus on job placements as opposed to education and training, as well as the aggressive use of sanctions for people who failed to co-operate (Rose 1995, 167). Moreover, lack of participation for selected recipients was not tolerated in Riverside. It appears that Riverside welfare workers, operating within the same GAIN program, decided on a more direct route to moving welfare recipients into the workforce than did welfare workers in the other counties. Despite the claims of GAIN brochures that the county would assist the client with job search and work experi- ence programs, evidence suggests that it was only Riverside that showed any real interest in direct work placement. Not only did Riverside management require the case workers on the front lines to achieve results, but they also instituted controls, such as success measurement instruments and a new staff performance appraisal system that incor- porated these measures. There is no indication that Riverside County was allocated any more money or staff than any of the other counties. What was different about Riverside was its decision to ignore the 'long- term investment in human capital' theory and get people into jobs. When the MDRC discussed the results of the other five counties, it was clearly hard-pressed to come up with evidence of improvement in any standard measurement indicators such as increased recipient earnings, successful job placements, welfare case closures, or welfare savings. California's case story suggests that it was the particular *way* in which the California state administrative culture chose to interpret GAIN, not the lack of resources (as program staff and MDRC evaluations would have us believe), that kept the program's staff from requiring people to participate in workfare.

When rumblings about Clinton's drastic new welfare reform propos- als reached California, each of the state's counties was forced to take a second look at what their program was actually accomplishing. From the subsequent drastic turn-around of various counties, it would ap- pear that some did not feel that the long-term 'investment in human capital' theory could continue to exist in its present form. Los Angeles County (725,000 person welfare caseload), for example, which retained the same name of GAIN, merely began to insist that Riverside-type operations be carried out – downplaying education and training, and encouraging quick job entry: 'Los Angeles County's ability to quickly transform a poorly-performing welfare-to-work program into a dy- namic effort to push people into jobs could serve as a model for the nation as large urban areas grapple with the demands of welfare re- form ... Over a two year period, the county shifted the program known as GAIN (Greater Avenues to Independence) from one that focused on basic education to one that puts jobs first. This demonstrates that mammoth bureaucracies can retool and refocus as states go about re- designing a sixty year old welfare system' (editorial, *Los Angeles Times*, 26 February 1997).

L.A. County shifted gears completely, making a 'jobs first' rather than a 'school first' switchover, while still maintaining the same name, the same literature, and the same staff. Accustomed as it had been for so long to the long-term education/training route, the idea of ushering welfare recipients off the welfare rolls and directly into the job market appears to have struck California as something quite novel, unique, and of great interest to the entire country. California is supposedly in the Washington limelight, and welfare staff in L.A. County are talking about becoming a national model for welfare reform across the United States:

> The dramatic success of Los Angeles County's welfare-to-work program is proving that cities with large, hard-to-employ welfare populations can find solutions by emphasizing jobs over basic education. It's a matter of insisting that recipients find work. *The county program, known as GAIN for Greater Avenues for Independence, is putting more welfare recipients to work at higher wages than welfare's traditional caseworker system* ... The county's welfare rolls still exceed those of 48 out of the 50 states; only New York and California count more people on welfare than Los Angeles County ... Washington is watching Los Angeles, where the challenge is complicated by geography, language and the sheer volume of recipients who have never been employed. The County is a good test. If GAIN's success continues here, the approach should work elsewhere. (editorial, *Los Angeles Times*, 21 August 1998; emphasis added)

It's as though GAIN had not been in effect since 1985! A reinvented GAIN! The fact that some counties like L.A. did make this cultural shift towards the end of GAIN's life also shows how alternative implementation strategies can apply to the same words within the same program plan. In many ways, the freedom to apply GAIN in whatever way the county wished suggests that the way that GAIN was applied in California for so many years (i.e., hundreds of millions of dollars spent with no appreciable results) reflected a choice in GAIN's administration and almost universal bureaucratic support for a philosophy that wasn't working – but a philosophy with which liberal-minded welfare workers were reluctant to part.

Did Welfare Recipients Participate?

GAIN was a mandatory program for sole-support parents with school-aged children and principal wage earners in two-parent families. As mentioned earlier, California has only 12 per cent of the nation's population, but it has 20 per cent of the nation's welfare caseload (CDSS 1997). Of all the studies that have evaluated GAIN (Wiseman 1985; Kirp 1986; Wallace and Long 1987; Gueron and Pauly 1991; MDRC 1994; Riccio, Friedlander, and Freedman 1994; U.S. GAO/HEHS-95-28 1995; Waste 1995), not one can attest to any discernible effect the program might have had upon welfare recipients, either on their behaviour, their attitude, or their ability to secure a job. Welfare recipients registered in GAIN did not seem to have been overly anxious to participate. Gueron and Pauly (1991, 138) found that one of the greatest challenges of GAIN 'was getting people to show up for orientation'; they also discovered that 66 per cent of GAIN participants did not graduate to the education phase and that those who did make it to the education and training phases did not graduate in high numbers.

Welfare rolls did not even decrease. If anything, things only seemed to get worse. A draft welfare reform proposal prepared by the California Department of Social Services identifies certain 'alarming trends' in the profile of its welfare recipients as follows: 'the rate of births to unmarried women has tripled in the past 30 years; approximately half of welfare recipients had their first child as a teenager, and one third of the women had an additional child while on AFDC' (CDSS 1997). According to a survey conducted by the Manpower Demonstration Research Corporation (Riccio et al. 1994), very few welfare recipients in California had anything to do with the GAIN program. Less than 20 per cent of welfare recipients ever participated in GAIN over its lifetime. And of those few who did participate in GAIN, 85 per cent remained on welfare.

The Official Record: What Do the Evaluators Say?

If workfare is supposed to accomplish anything, it seems obvious that it is meant to move people from welfare to work. But in the evaluations of California's GAIN program that particular dimension was, for whatever reasons, neglected. Other elements were measured – how well administrators understood the changes, how well they got along, how often they met, how well they felt the program was being implemented – but not that of how many welfare recipients moved from welfare to self-sufficiency as a result of the hundreds of millions of dollars poured into GAIN. All the exhaustive analytical research conducted by several Manpower Demonstration Research Corporation

(MDRC) studies (Goldman et al. 1985; Gueron 1986; Wallace and Long 1987; Gueron and Pauly 1991; Riccio et al. 1994) and a number of U.S. General Accounting Office surveys (e.g., U.S. GAO/PEMD-95-26) focus on the high levels of success in implementation but are hard-pressed to show how welfare recipients were actually affected by the large investment of time and money devoted to moving them to self-sufficiency. While it is interesting to read about the frequency of personnel meetings, the warm sharing of experiences between GAIN staff members, and the survey results indicating that welfare workers and clients felt positively about GAIN, evaluators sidestepped the main point of the program. What about the fact that so few transitions from welfare to work can be declared? Waste notes the irony in California's workfare evaluations: 'Thus, despite the fact that evaluators, agency officials, and program participants have given the program high marks for implementation activities, if the intent was to provide a cost-effective way to transition large numbers of the California AFDC population to the workforce and to reduce welfare dependency, the program has proved at best a mixed success and at worst a costly and tragic programmatic failure' (1995, 61).

Evaluators repeatedly obfuscated the dismal results and declared GAIN a success, or, when that proved to be impossible, then they praised the program's potential (Riccio et al. 1994). Back in 1985, when California first introduced its major welfare reform legislation in the form of the newly created GAIN program, the state's Department of Social Services wanted to monitor the progress of this exciting new program. They contracted the services of the Manpower Demonstration Research Corporation (MDRC) for this purpose. The MDRC, an independent research corporation that has conducted a number of in-depth evaluations of government services in the United States, was hired to conduct a comprehensive evaluation of GAIN as the program unfolded. An early study showed no measurable results: of the 8 per cent to 20 per cent of welfare recipients who participated in GAIN in the state's fifty-eight counties, 66 per cent did not make it to the education/training phase, and those who did enter work training/education 'do not graduate in high numbers' (Gueron and Pauly 1991, 138–9).

A later MDRC study also showed little in the way of results. The MDRC decided to focus on six of California's fifty-eight counties (Butte, Alameda, Tulare, Los Angeles, Riverside, and San Diego) and studied them for eight years. The six counties selected to participate in the primary study of GAIN's impacts account for more than one-half of the state's welfare caseload. In southern California, the selected counties were Los Angeles, with about one-third of the state's caseload and a welfare population larger than that of many states; San Diego, with the state's second-largest caseload; and Riverside, a county encompassing both urban and rural areas. In northern California, the counties were Alameda, an urban county that includes the city of Oakland, and, further north, Butte, which had the smallest population of the six counties. Tulare is located in the largely agricultural and rural Central Valley.

The MDRC provided its official evaluation of GAIN (authored by Riccio et al.) to the government in 1994. Its findings revealed that only one of the six counties could show anything at all for the large sums of taxpayer dollars poured into the welfare-to-work program, and this was Riverside County. The evaluators presented the overall results of GAIN as positive, using Riverside's extraordinarily high job placement, higher earnings, and return on investment to average out the mostly negative results of the other five counties. Riverside provided a return of $2.84 for every dollar invested, while the average return for 'all six counties together' was only seventy-six cents per dollar. Regardless of the poor overall results, GAIN was declared a success thanks to Riverside, even though Riverside was the only county that chose to skip GAIN's 'long-term investment in human capital' philosophy (i.e., education and training first) and instead set program registrants directly into the labour market (i.e., jobs first). The difference between Riverside's 'job first' mentality and that of the other counties was described in the report as follows:

> Viewing almost any job as a positive first step, with advancement to come by acquiring a work history and learning skills on the job, Riverside's staff placed much more emphasis on moving registrants into the labour market quickly than did the staff of any other county. Most distinctive was Riverside's attempt to communicate a strong "message" to all registrants (even those in education and training activities) at all stages of the program, that employment was central, that it should be sought expeditiously, and that opportunities to obtain low-paying jobs should not be turned down.
>
> Alameda illustrates a very different approach. Its GAIN managers and staff believed strongly in 'human capital' development – the use of education and training as a path to getting jobs that offer a better chance to get or stay off welfare. Within the overall constraints imposed by the GAIN model's service sequences, Alameda's staff encouraged registrants to be

selective about the jobs they accepted and to take advantage of GAIN's education and training and to prepare for higher paying jobs. (Riccio et al. 1994, 5)

The fact that participation in GAIN was the measure of success, as opposed to, say, the number of welfare recipients successfully moved from welfare into jobs, lies at the root of the entire evaluation problem. If Washington required merely participation rates, they could be met without too much work by placing people in the usual training courses. California never had more than 20 per cent of welfare recipients registered in workfare, but the state still met Washington's requirements because participation in the program was the sole measure of success. Even when using such an absurd measuring stick, evaluators still could not claim any great success. Gueron and Pauly note that 'initial findings on GAIN suggest that the more enriched – and more complex – JOBS programs will not necessarily achieve higher longitudinal participation rates' (1991, 138). Another example of the preoccupation with participation rates rather than finding employment can be seen in a California State Senate Report:

California's work force development system has played a key role in moving welfare recipients to work. But the state will be required to *double* the number of families who participate in work activities over the next five years. Most adult welfare recipients will be subject to a five-year lifetime limit on federal benefits and will therefore need to derive long-lasting results from any services received. But education and training will not be the principal focus of welfare-to-work programs, since most recipients must engage in more narrowly defined 'work activities' to meet federal requirement.

... education and training providers will have to reconfigure class offerings so that recipients can meet work participation requirements if they wish to continue offering skill training, adult education classes and vocational education that last longer than three months. (1996, 21–2)

The wording of this Senate Report is interesting in that it reveals California's fixation on education as the answer (seemingly even·for those for whom formal education has not been a success), little emphasis on moving people into jobs, and a lot of concern about how to arrange it so that those in education and training will *still* qualify as fulfilling the new definition of work requirements. In any event, in

1997, Washington itself expanded the definition of work requirements to include almost anything, from schooling that is unrelated to a registrant's job to drug or alcohol rehabilitation.

Did the Public Play a Role?

Because of California's philosophy of 'education first,' the protests against workfare were not as hard-hitting as they had been in other states (e.g., New York). An emphasis on education and training does not provoke cries of 'slavery' from activists as would, for instance, a massive public works program. Also, despite the politically popular mandatory status of GAIN, so few welfare recipients were ever affected that there was nothing tangible to protest. As in all jurisdictions, California has activist groups such as the Coalition of California Welfare Rights Organization Inc., the Fair Share Network and Welfare Parents Support Group Inc., and the local chapter of ACORN that decried the punitive and paternalistic policies that supposedly characterized the GAIN program. However, as California has never been known to take a hard line towards welfare, administrators claim that many activists ended up partnering with their respective county to advise on, or actively participate in, training opportunities. And, as far as the media was concerned, GAIN was a success until the politicians started to engage in a ritual of degradation before implementing CalWORKS.

There is no indication that GAIN lacked public support. As mentioned earlier, California has a lengthy tradition, extending over thirty years, of workfare and welfare-reform experimentation. Until recently, California's welfare politics appears to have involved tough talk on work requirements for welfare recipients but gentle actions; welfare rates were high, education and training were selected over direct job placement, and, mothers were exempt from work requirements, so long as their children were young. Best of all, despite very low transition rates from welfare to work, the public was under the impression that something was being done about welfare – after all, GAIN was a famous program, a model for the entire nation, a source of pride to citizens. GAIN's policies and procedures were studied with great interest, but little attention was paid to the results. From all dimensions, not just that of the government-hired evaluators, bad was presented as good for more than ten years.

The presentation of 'bad' as 'good' can be dangerous. It creates illusions that can be used as the basis for other serious social policy decisions. The perceived success of GAIN created the illusion that a number of generous services were available to all welfare recipients. While we know that the program actually reached very few recipients, less than 20 per cent (and of those reached, 85 per cent remained on welfare), the public's acceptance of the successful operation of GAIN, and of similar programs in other states, is likely to have provided some degree of comfort to those who introduced the concept of time-limited welfare as well as to those who accepted it. California convinced so many people (including its own) for so many years that it had the model welfare-to-work program that it may well have actually paved the way for time-limited welfare, the next 'good idea.' All indicators point to Californians' overwhelming support for Clinton's welfare re-forms which include time-limited welfare and tough sanctions. For example, a statewide telephone survey of 1,008 California adults (in-cluding 724 registered voters) conducted in 1997 by the Field Institute in collaboration with the California Center for Health Improvement found that about two-thirds of Californians thought passage of the federal welfare reform law was 'a good thing.' Californians did believe in time limits and the requirement that families move to find jobs, but appeared to be reluctant to use harsh sanctions. Californians also stated that they believed in education as the path to employability, just as their government had done for so long, and probably still does.

What Happened to the Good Idea?

Everyone kept up the charade, right to the end, but it was the evalua-tors who maintained workfare's legitimacy for so long. California con-vinced the nation that GAIN was a successful welfare-to-work program; it also assured those welfare recipients who wanted to improve their lot in life that they had all manner of services available to them and plenty of time to take advantage of these. The reality, of course, was that there was no intention of moving people directly into jobs, unless the job suited the welfare recipient's desired career path. Welfare recipients were shuffled from training program to training program, but the ma-jority of them never seemed to achieve anything; in fact, throughout the GAIN years, the number of welfare recipients only increased. Califor-nia has a reputation for being 'soft' when it comes to the application of welfare rules. An article in *Policy Review* entitled 'The Shocking Success of Welfare Reform' talks about the nationwide drop in welfare rolls since states began obtaining waivers in anticipation of Clinton's welfare overhaul, but stresses that the way in which welfare programs are administered makes all the difference: 'But sanctions for recipients who refuse or shirk work often vary from county to county and several states (especially California) are lenient with exemptions and impose only a small reduction in welfare benefits for recipients who ignore work requirements ... To be sure, some states, most notably California and New York, which have the largest welfare caseloads, are stumbling out of the starting gate with weak reform plans and lagging results' (Haywood 1998, 8, 10).

While California's politicians, policy-makers, and administrators were philosophically soft on workfare, and few, if any, results were achieved over the thirteen-year lifespan of GAIN, the greatest damage to the good idea was done by the evaluators who claimed that the program had worked, when it had not. Such claims led to many lost years in the area of welfare reform as GAIN was used as the model for the federal JOBS programs that began in 1988. Thanks to misleading evaluations, California continued to pride itself as a progressive welfare reformer. Formal evaluators such as the MDRC, in evaluating a system whose underlying philosophy was 'long-term investment in human capital,' still declared GAIN to be a success, even though it could find signifi-cant positive results in only the one county (out of the six studied) that had sidestepped the GAIN philosophy and matched its welfare recipi-ents directly to the labour market. The nation's demonstration workfare project appeared to all to have been a good idea at the time. Then President Clinton's 1996 welfare legislation required the states to apply a stricter definition of work-related participation rates. In response to Clinton's 1996 welfare reforms, which required each state to reach predetermined work-related participation rates as well as establish time-limited welfare, policy-makers had to get rid of GAIN and design something new. Curiously, in spite of its poor record, GAIN's principles are currently being extended into CalWORKS, California's new welfare-to-work program. As L.A. County's draft 'CalWORKS Imple-mentation Plan' clearly states: 'The primary goal of welfare reform is to provide parent/caretakers with the means to achieve economic self-sufficiency by entering the workforce. To help families in Los Angeles County reach this goal, DPSS will expand its highly-successful, nation-ally-recognized, welfare-to-work program, L.A. GAIN' (1997, 4).

The 'long-term investment in human capital' philosophy in California was then rapidly discarded in the panic to match welfare recipients directly to the workplace. CalWORKS was introduced with all the fanfare that accompanied another good idea. As Carl Ingram and Max Vanzi reported in the *Los Angeles Times* of 6 January 1997:

> Twenty-six years after Gov. Ronald Reagan offered welfare reform in California as a model 'to show the rest of the country out of their problems,' Gov. Pete Wilson and the Legislature are poised to launch another overhaul ... This time, enactment of welfare reform will not be optional for state government as it was in 1971, when Reagan pushed through a massive overhaul of public aid and pronounced it an 'idea whose time has come' [Note: GAIN was introduced in 1985] ... The plan [CalWORKS] will seek broad flexibility for counties and a heavy emphasis on rapid job placement instead of extensive training ... Although virtually everyone agrees that implementing the federal reforms is an immense task that may take years to fully accomplish, *recipient work requirements* shape up as the biggest immediate challenge for lawmakers. (emphasis added)

It is an irony that, twenty-six years later, 'recipient work requirements' made up 'the biggest immediate challenge for lawmakers.' As of 1 January 1998, GAIN (education first) was superseded by CalWORKS (jobs first), California's new good idea. However, without Clinton's call for visible results, it seems unlikely that GAIN would ever have fallen from grace.

The cracks are already showing in CalWORKS. As of 1999, incoming Governor Gray Davis was warned in a memorandum by the outgoing Wilson administration that the state had already been assessed $7 million in penalties (possibly going to $28 million) for failing to meet federal work requirements to move a significant number of its more than 140,000 two-parent families into the workforce. (California has an unusually high percentage of two-parent families, almost one-fifth of the welfare caseload); the state had, however, met its 25 per cent work participation requirement for 'all welfare families' (Virginia Ellis, 'State Fails to Meet U.S. Welfare-to-Work Goal Jobs,' *Los Angeles Times*, 25 January 1999). Policy-makers have been accused of making the rules too complicated for the administrators, the employment community, and the welfare recipients. Problems are emerging concerning the bureaucrats' poor administrative skills. Newspaper headlines reflect that millions of dollars that were funnelled to California to move people into jobs are not being used: 'Welfare-to-Work Effort Awash in Unused Funds Reform: State gets $162 million for job training, has spent only $9 million' (Carlo Rivera in the *Los Angeles Times*, 31 May 1999). Health and Welfare Secretary Grantland Johnson was quoted as saying that the state is 'a long way from being as effective as we can be in putting people to work and utilizing welfare-to-work money, and the state is concerned about that' (Rivera, 'California and the West Welfare-to-Work Program Flawed, State Official Says,' *Los Angeles Times*, 10 June 1999). Bureaucrats and advocacy groups such as the League of Women Voters of Ventura County claim that there is not enough money for child care, affordable housing, job training, and transportation. Some jurisdictions are skipping over their bureaucrats and farming out job training and job placement to private firms. Despite strenuous union objections, two private corporations, Virginia-based Maximus and Maryland-based Lockeed Martin, were granted $23 million in contracts to run part of Los Angeles County's job-training and placement service; the union representing county workers has threatened a lawsuit, claiming that they could do a better job than these private firms (Nicholas Riccardi, 'Supervisors Privatize Job-Training Services Labor,' *Los Angeles Times*, 12 July 2000). The Economic Roundtable, a non-profit, nonpartisan public policy research group, conducted a study entitled 'The Cage of Poverty.' The Economic Roundtable raises a number of questions about CalWORKS's presumed success in Los Angeles County, and claims that welfare workers in the welfare-to-work program bounce from low-wage employer to low-wage employer, have stagnant incomes, and remain stuck below the poverty line, adding to the usual confusion that surrounds evaluations of a social policy intervention (Riccardi, 'Post Welfare Jobs No Cure for Poverty, Study Finds,' *Los Angeles Times*, 7 September 2000). Lynn Bayer, director of the Department of Public Social Services for Los Angeles County, challenged the finding of the Economic Roundtable in a letter to the editor of the *Los Angeles Times* (12 September 2000), in which she claimed: 'Our welfare program has boosted employment and earnings and at the same time has reduced welfare spending. These results were validated by the prestigious Manpower Demonstration Research Corp. study released last month.' It is interesting that the Manpower Demonstration Research Corp. (MDRC), the same organization that praised GAIN so highly in 1994, had been hired again to conduct an evaluation of CalWORKS in Los Angeles County. It is no surprise that the MDRC's glowing report, released in August 2000, concluded that recipients enrolled in Los Angeles County's welfare-to-work program were more likely to get jobs and earn higher wages than those not enrolled in the program (MDRC, 2000).

5.

Wisconsin – Tommy Thompson and His Welfare Miracle

Summary

Wisconsin believes that immediate attachment to the workforce is the best hope that welfare recipients have for self-sufficiency. Between 1987, the year that Governor Tommy Thompson began his welfare reforms, and 1999, the state's welfare rolls dropped 91 per cent. With a population of about 5 million and a relatively low unemployment rate (averaging 4 per cent), Wisconsin went from one hundred thousand welfare cases in 1987 to nine thousand in 1999. Tommy Thompson faced two great dangers in keeping his 'good idea' good. The first was the possibility that the policy-makers would design a blanket policy for a population with diverse barriers to employment. The second was that the reluctant bureaucrats would sabotage his workfare program. Thompson cleverly averted both of these looming hazards.

Over the years, Wisconsin's policy has been guided by the philosophy that people on welfare (the non-working poor) should not be entitled to more benefits and government services than those offered to the working poor (e.g., those who have only three months' maternity leave, do not receive automatic pay increases from their employer for each additional child born, have to pay for college and university courses if they wish to advance, who have to pay for medications, etc.). There is a loan fund for urgent expenses related to finding work, and child-care assistance is also available. Wisconsin's workfare program also emphasizes direct placement of welfare recipients into the labour market (as opposed to classroom training) and, for the most part, caps all training programs at twelve weeks.

Tommy Thompson did not use his social-work bureaucrats to move welfare recipients into the workplace. Instead, he subcontracted that task, for profit, to the bidder with the best offer (Goodwill Industries won two of the toughest inner-city Milwaukee districts). Rather than lay off his social-work bureaucrats, he gave them the new responsibility of managing child care and other supports that would be needed by the single mothers who were joining the workforce.

Wisconsin's Good Idea: Background and Context of the Reform

Wisconsin is the foremost laboratory for welfare reform in the United States. It is also the state with the steepest decline in welfare cases. From 1987 to 1997, while the U.S. Aid to Families with Dependent Children (AFDC) caseload was steeply rising, the caseload in Wisconsin dropped by half, from approximately one hundred thousand families to fifty thousand (Corbett 1995). When President Clinton's 1996 welfare law replaced the sixty-year-old cash safety net with a new program of work requirements, time limits, and sanctions, he required each state to prepare and submit a plan that would incorporate these principles. Wisconsin had already been applying these principles since well before Clinton's welfare reform, but it formally captured them in 1997 in a program called Wisconsin Works (W-2). Since the implementation of W-2 in September 1997, welfare rolls have dropped to nine thousand. In other words, the welfare rolls have dropped 91 per cent since Tommy Thompson, the Republican governor of Wisconsin, began his welfare reforms in 1987. Certainly, Wisconsin has had a good economy. But many other states have also had good job growth, and lower unemployment than Wisconsin, without seeing any decline in their welfare rolls. Something special and apparently effective was happening in Wisconsin.

Central to the state's reform was the idea of getting people off welfare and into a job, and fast. Wisconsin also used a strategy called 'diversion,' whereby applicants were dissuaded from coming on the welfare rolls in the first place (for example, by providing a car loan to enable an applicant to obtain a job further away from home). Applicants were also required to job search for sixty hours before becoming entitled to assistance. The state further provided subsidized child care and short-term customized training (twelve weeks maximum) in areas such as health-care assistance, the hospitality industry, and computers. While these efforts required a considerable up-front outlay of funds and resources, the state claims that it is more than recovering its investment. Wisconsin's efforts have attracted the interest of Washington and observers from other countries. Visitors come from all over the world to see for themselves how the one-stop job centers work, how case workers 'divert' welfare applicants to non-welfare sources of support, and how sanctions are applied to those who attempt to subvert the system.

The welfare numbers in Wisconsin suggest unmitigated success, and thousands of workfare proponents have made the pilgrimage to Wisconsin to look for the magical answers to the welfare problem. Numerous explanations for Wisconsin's success have been given by a wide variety of people and constituencies. Lawrence Mead (1995), an academic expert on welfare reform, has pointed primarily to political factors. He refers to the Wisconsin workfare system as a 'paternalist model for reform' and has this to say about Wisconsin's unique constellation of political factors: 'The state's achievement reflects special political and institutional assets – a reforming governor, innovation in many localities, a tradition of leadership in social policy, limited political divisions, a supportive political culture, and exemplary local government. If welfare reform is a task for government, no state begins with stronger institutions than Wisconsin' (Mead 1995, 1–2).

Jean Rogers, the politically appointed administrator of the Division of Economic Support (the division responsible for W-2), also alludes to political factors and strong leadership factors as a key to success (personal interview, 11 June 1999). She sees 'an energetic Governor who could read public opinion and knew how to act on it.' She claims that 'when Republican leader Tommy Thompson was running for Governor in 1987 he truly listened to people's frustration with a welfare system that wasn't working.' Believing that the time was right to fix a system that was broken, he pursued his cause, contrary to the advice of political advisers (who considered welfare reform too controversial a topic, inevitably drawing dreaded welfare lobbyists and noisy advocates to people's doorsteps). Thompson campaigned on a platform featuring welfare reform. 'Partly because he was championing such a politically unpopular cause, some politically attuned people didn't expect him to win,' claims Jean Rogers. They were wrong. 'He took the chance – it was a big chance, but he won. What he did was establish a vision, then he developed simple objectives, and stated them in people terms.' Since 1987 Thompson has been re-elected governor three more times. His fervent belief that 'everyone can make some kind of contribution' has never flagged. He is the longest running governor in the history of the state of Wisconsin.

The energetic Tommy Thompson saw to it that Wisconsin was first in line, ready and waiting, with a detailed welfare reform 'plan' when President Clinton signed the 1996 Personal Responsibility and Work Opportunity Reconciliation Act (replacing the old AFDC system of national entitlement with a new system of state-managed block grants). One of the benefits of the new welfare bill was to let individual states experiment with better ways to deliver welfare. Wisconsin was the first state to submit its plan, a mere two hours after President Clinton had signed the national welfare reform bill. It was also the first plan to be approved for implementation under the new Federal law (PRWORA). Even before Clinton had made his changes, Governor Tommy Thompson unveiled his proposal in a press release on 3 August 1995 to scrap AFDC and replace it with Wisconsin Works (W-2), a program that would end the welfare entitlement and provide participants with 'plenty of help but not plenty of free cash.' The new program assumes that everyone is capable of some type of work. It also tries to address the problem of teen pregnancy by abolishing the entitlement of teenaged mothers to set up their own households with cash assistance. Under W-2, parents who are minors and who cannot live at home or with a legal guardian have the option of a foster home, a group home, or a supervised independent setting. The plan has a time limit – twenty-four months. According to Governor Thompson: 'No other state has ever eliminated AFDC before ... others will look to Wisconsin as a model for effectively helping people escape poverty through a block grant system. Under W-2, the moment a person applies for welfare, that person is going to go to work ... W-2 is an appropriate name because this revolutionary new program will emphasize work – and most working people receive a W-2 statement of wages. A W-2 is also a symbol of independence, and that's what this program will aim for: independence through work ... The automatic welfare check is history' (press release, 3 August 1995).

Clinton signed Wisconsin's plan in 1996, and it was implemented in September 1997. According to Thompson, W-2 is by far the most ambitious social undertaking this country has seen in decades: 'If I'm successful in this, it's going to be a rage across America' (Craig Gilbert, 'Governor Talks Up "Holistic" Welfare Reform,' *Milwaukee Journal Sentinal*, 15 April 1999). As of the year 2000, Wisconsin still led all other states in the area of welfare reform.

How Was the Program Designed?

Wisconsin's success in welfare reform did not happen overnight. The current system, Wisconsin Works (W-2), represents the end of welfare in Wisconsin. The program is sleek in its design and smooth in its delivery. But it took Wisconsin ten years and a lot of hard work to achieve it. When Tommy Thompson took over as governor in 1987, he introduced a slight reduction in the welfare cash benefit and made a number of innovations that gradually prepared welfare recipients for the new work philosophy and helped to reduce advocate opposition to welfare reform. The public appeared to be supportive of the 'everyone works' concept from the beginning. These gradual innovations also enabled most of the staff to become accustomed to the new orientation of getting people into work rather than providing a monthly welfare cheque. (Where staff in county offices were resistant to such changes, the responsibility for W-2 was taken out of their hands and contracted out to profit or non-profit agencies that had successfully demonstrated an ability to prepare welfare recipients for work (e.g., YWCA and Goodwill in Milwaukee). The gradual nature of the changes also provided the state with the opportunity to work the kinks out of a new computer system geared more to information storage than to the newly necessary functions of information retrieval, tracking, and evaluation.

W-2 was developed from a number of key welfare reform experiments, each of which provided policy-makers with invaluable lessons for its design: Before W-2, the state operated under the national JOBS program mandated by Washington. But Wisconsin often obtained federal waivers and demonstration projects with a view to constant improvement of its own version of JOBS (e.g., Wisconsin could require mothers with preschool children to participate in JOBS for more than the federal maximum of twenty hours per week). This section draws from a number of state documents that describe the key welfare reform steps (many in the form of demonstration projects) that were introduced in the state of Wisconsin in the decade before W-2's implementation. Not all of these initiatives were successful, but they served as valuable learning tools that contributed to the design of what eventually came to be known as W-2.

One of Governor Thompson's first steps, early in his first term, was to obtain a waiver from Washington to provide a twelve-month extension of Medicaid, the state-federal health program, to recipients who left welfare for employment. This helped to reduce one of the barriers identified by single mothers in moving from welfare to work. Another change was the Learnfare program, whose goal was to keep low-income youths in school. Welfare benefits were reduced for the parents of children who did not attend school regularly. In 1990 came the Children First program, piloted in two counties and extended across the state, which compelled absent fathers who owed child support to pay their child support, participate regularly in work or training, or face a jail sentence. A 1994 study showed an increase of 66 per cent of non-custodial fathers paying child support, with an increase of child support of 158 per cent; Wisconsin's child-support collection rate is 33 per cent versus 18 per cent nationwide: paternity is established for 79 per cent of non-marital children, versus 45 per cent nationwide (MCSS 1995). Payment of child support plays a major role in reducing Wisconsin's welfare caseload.

Other early reforms included the expansion of the Child Care in Wisconsin program. While Wisconsin already provided child-care funding assistance to low-income families statewide who needed help in order to work or train for work (since the 1970s) there were waiting lists for the subsidy. Under Governor Thompson the program became guaranteed to welfare recipients entering the world of work; the program grew dramatically from $12 million to over $60 million. The Kinship Care program was also added. Under certain conditions, cash benefits of $215 per month could be paid to caretaker relatives (e.g., grandparents, aunts, uncles of minors). This program was administered by local social agencies. In 1994 Wisconsin introduced the Parental and Family Responsibility (PFR) demonstration (four counties), aimed at extending job training assistance to the fathers of teen families (this program was also known as bridefare). Wisconsin also encouraged all welfare mothers under nineteen and their spouses not to have additional children before they could emotionally and financially care for them. As a condition of AFDC eligibility, teen parents had to attend intensive case-management services that provided them with assessment, parenting skills, family planning, independent living skills, and employability training. Also in 1994, Governor Thompson implemented the AFDC Two-Tier Welfare demonstration project (four counties) to counter the 'welfare magnet' effect of the high rates of welfare in Wisconsin, especially compared with neighbouring states such as Illinois and Indiana. Wisconsin's benefits (1996 figures) were twelfth highest in the country. For an AFDC family of three (mother with two children), Wisconsin compares with neighbouring states as follows: Illinois: $382; Indiana:

$288; Iowa: $426; Michigan: $459; Minnesota: $532; Ohio: $341; Wisconsin: $517.

What two-tier welfare did was restrict benefits paid to families from out of state to what they would have received at their previous location, for a period of six months (there is some controversy as to whether or not this project was constitutional). In January 1995 Thompson refined the state's JOBS program to pilot the Work First program, a program targeting the applicant (not the recipient) population. Under Work First, emphasis was placed on exploring all available personal, community, and work options before enrolling in welfare. This program later developed into one called Self-Sufficiency First, again focusing on 'diversion' of applicants if any other possible resources were available at all. Starting in March 1996 for a five-year period, all adult welfare applicants must (a) meet with a financial planner to discuss alternatives to welfare and (b) subsequently complete sixty hours of formal job training and counselling.

A proactive Fraud Control Program was also instituted requiring administrators to disqualify intentional program violators from AFDC or food stamps. In 1995, Wisconsin also sought a waiver from Washington to raise the AFDC Vehicle Asset Limit so that families could still be eligible for AFDC if they acquired a more expensive (but more reliable) car. The rationale behind this is that the better car would be less expensive to operate and maintain and would improve welfare recipients' ability to transport their children to child care and drive to work or training sites. Eventually, under W-2, the vehicle asset limit was raised from fifteen hundred dollars to ten thousand dollars. Welfare mothers were also allowed to open a special, restricted savings account for the education and training needs of their families (exempt from asset tests, once eligible) under the AFDC Special Resource Account (SRA), a statewide, five-year demonstration.

In 1995, Wisconsin became the first U.S. state to experiment with cutting off cash benefits to recipients after twenty-four months. Under a waiver received from Washington in 1993, Work, Not Welfare (WNW) – Wisconsin's Independence Plan for Welfare Recipients required recipients to work or participate in concentrated job-search and job-training activities. Within thirty days clients had to either have a job or be involved in community service work. After twenty-four months their cash aid would end. Welfare rolls in the two demonstration counties (Pierce and Fond du Lac) plummeted in the first seven months. Childcare, transportation, and job-search assistance were also provided. Work,

Not Welfare also guaranteed one year of child-care assistance to participants who exited the program due to work. Along with these successful demonstration projects, Wisconsin also wanted to eliminate automatic increases to single mothers on welfare when additional children were born. The very first state to receive federal waiver approval for this benefit cap was New Jersey, which received permission under the Bush administration in October 1992. The benefits cap was challenged in court for allegedly violating the rights of mothers or children denied assistance, but the cap was upheld by a judge who specifically argued that 'New Jersey's reform proposal does not attempt to fetter or constrain the welfare mother's right to bear as many children as she chooses, but simply requires her to find a way to pay for her progeny's care ... This is not discrimination; rather, this is the reality known to so many working families who provide for their children without any expectation of outside assistance' (Maximus 1995, II-7).

Wisconsin received its federal waiver from Washington in 1994 but implemented this change, called the AFDC Benefit Cap Demonstration Project, only on 1 January 1996 (for a period of five years). The rationale for this cap is explained in a government document: 'Non-recipient families do not receive increased wages when additional children are born. Equalizing the treatment of income between AFDC recipients and non-recipient families more closely replicates the financial situation of non-recipient families when an additional child is born and eases the transition from welfare to work' ('Wisconsin Welfare Reform' 1996, 17).

In other words, in 1994 Wisconsin had joined a growing number of other states in asking Washington for permission to make welfare cheques invariable when additional births took place after a family began receiving welfare. In 1996 a major welfare requirement was also enacted under a statewide project known as Pay for Performance (PFP). Under PFP, the welfare cheque was paid to the welfare recipient's employer, who in turn used the funds to pay the welfare recipient's wages. Cheques could be reduced in direct proportion to the required hours of community service the recipient failed to perform. Thus, welfare recipients could no longer receive government assistance without working. This important program required the construction of an excellent computer system to track work and/or training and attendance. According to a government report, the turning point of the welfare system was Pay for Performance. One program manager is quoted as saying, 'The revolution is Pay for Performance. It's all over after that. If we can do PFP, W-2 will be a cakewalk' (Mead 1996, 31).

All in all, the welfare changes introduced by Governor Thompson assume that parents, whether welfare recipients or not, are responsible for the care and feeding of their children and must do what is necessary to secure the income required to provide for their children. The innovations made during the decade leading up to the implementation of W-2 were all consistent in their attempts to provide an incentive for getting off welfare while, at the same time, attempting to design a benefit system that replicated the realities of the world of work as much as possible.

Wisconsin Works (W-2) was implemented in September 1997 and effectively represents the end of welfare in Wisconsin. There is a 100 per cent work requirement (except for single parents with newborns under the age of twelve weeks). For those whose contribution can only be limited there is sheltered work. According to a senior policy-maker, W-2 was designed slowly. First Governor Thompson put together a bipartisan group of legislators, both representatives and senators, who, with the research assistance of the Hudson Institute (an independent think tank from Indiana paid for by private funds), gathered information from all imaginable relevant parties throughout the state (e.g., unions, social workers, business). Then he appointed a small group of civil servants and a representative of the Hudson Institute to craft a policy that reflected the findings. According to Jean Rogers (interview), a committee member and the most senior administrator responsible for the successful operation of W-2, they designed the policy to reflect real expectations in the work world :

> Our biggest finding was the difference between the expectations of the welfare system and the expectations of the real world. Here we were asking single mothers to act responsibly by not having additional children until they could afford them, yet paying them more money per additional child. That's not the real world. Why did we say 'we will allow you to choose the type of education in which you would like to engage (up to a four year university degree), in lieu of work, when you are receiving cash assistance to support your family'? What we found was that, upon completion of a university degree, the attachment to the workforce was either minimal, or if the recipient did have a job, it was not related to the degree. There were also a lot of people bouncing from training program to training program with poor attendance and drop out records. The policy for W-2 was designed by constantly going back to our philosophy 'adults are expected to support their families.' Shouldn't we be helping them to

engage in work just the way society is? What are regular working folks having to do to address the need for education while at the same time having to put food on the table? They have to fit education into their schedule.

This is the thinking that helped to shape the guiding principles of W-2. The policy design of W-2 was ready in 1995, and enabling legislation was passed before the September 1997 implementation date. All AFDC cases were required to apply for W-2 in time for the September 1997 changeover from AFDC, or they would be cut off from the system. Administrators insist that, despite initiatives such as large-scale public-information efforts and free dinners and picnics with W-2 sign-up sheets, a considerable number of single mothers decided not enrol in the new program, which would require that they participate in either subsidized or unsubsidized jobs.

W-2 claims to rebuild the connection between work and income and help families achieve self-sufficiency through the consistent application of the following eight principles (they are outlined in the brochure handed to every W-2 applicant):

1 For those who can work, work alone should pay.
2 W-2 assumes that everybody is able to work within their abilities.
3 Families are society's way of nurturing and protecting children,
   and all policies must be judged in light of how well these policies
   strengthen the responsibility of both parents to care for their children.
4 The new system's fairness will be gauged by comparison with low-
   income families who work for a living.
5 There will be no entitlement. The W-2 reward system is designed to
   reinforce behaviour that leads to independence and self-sufficiency.
6 Individuals are part of various communities of people and places.
   W-2 will operate in ways that enhance the way communities support individual efforts to achieve self-sufficiency.
7 The new system should provide only as much service as an eligible
   individual asks for or needs. Many individuals do better with just a
   light touch.
8 W-2's objectives are best achieved by working with the most effective
   providers and by relying on market and performance mechanisms.

As its name suggests, Wisconsin Works is a work-based system of public aid. The name also refers to the W-2 Form that all working citizens receive from their employer, for tax purposes, indicating how much they have earned in the previous year. The implementation of W-2 marked the end of unconditional cash entitlements, substituting a system of services, subsidies, and opportunities to help parents become self-sufficient, first through work and then through long-term 'job retention' assistance. W-2 bears some resemblance to earlier strategies under the previous national JOBS program, but there are significant differences. Child-care and health-care subsidies are still available, but instead of being connected to welfare, they are viewed as employment-support programs. W-2 is administered not by the state's Department of Health and Social Services, but through a redesigned version of the state's labour department, called the Department of Workforce Development. The local W-2 agencies that offer job placement and preparation services are not exclusively administered by government. While in many cases they are operated by the county, they also include multiple county regions and subcounty areas in metropolitan areas. Milwaukee, for instance, which has more than half the state's public assistance recipients, is divided into six regions. Government bureaucrats do not manage W-2 in Milwaukee. This job was contracted out to would-be W-2 service providers, who come from either a profit or a non-profit industry. Each service provider in these six regions was successful in winning an initial two-year contract to provide job placement and preparation services in that region (Region 1: YWCA; Region 2: United Migrant Opportunity Services, Inc.; Region 3: Occupational Industrial Center of Milwaukee; Regions 4 and 5: Employment Solutions Inc. [a subsidiary of Goodwill Industries] Region 6: Maximus).

All W-2 agencies are either located within a job centre or electronically connected to a job centre in each geographic area (job centres are available to all who seek employment, not just those on public assistance). W-2/job centres provide one-stop shopping for employers to meet workforce needs and for job seekers to obtain career planning, job placement, and employment training at the local level (usually a maximum of twelve weeks of tailored courses). Where a private agency is the service provider for W-2, county workers are also employed to provide assistance with food stamps, health care, and child care. In one of the W-2/job centre locations that I visited (Region 5), Corliss Wood, operations manager of Employment Solutions, showed me an on-site job fair that was in full swing, with employers hiring on the spot, and a very active child-care centre (for up to three hours) for parents who were in interviews with counsellors or employers who were on training courses. Classrooms were also on-site (e.g., the Milwaukee Area Technical College), providing direct opportunities for W-2 participants to take high school equivalency or computer courses. Other W-2/job centre locations were just as active and spoke to the merits of one-stop shopping, especially for people with young children.

Another change for the welfare recipient concerns the type of person with whom the single parent makes first contact. Under W-2, the principal contact for the participant is no longer a caseworker whose prime function is to administer and regulate benefits, but a Financial and Employment Planner (FEP), whose prime function is to help families plan their personal finances and find employment. Unlike the rigid rules that had to be followed under AFDC, the FEP has considerable flexibility in helping families design a plan (including supports) that fits their particular needs and abilities. The FEP also has the authority to deny services to participants who do not appear to be making the required effort to become employed. To those in need of immediate income, the FEP can offer temporary community service jobs and job-access loans for immediate job-related expenses.

Under W-2, applicants are presented with four options, and participation in one of these is mandatory. A recipient's monthly cash benefit will depend upon the type of placement and the number of hours worked during the month. Unlike AFDC, there is no family-size adjustment. Both federal Temporary Assistance for Needy Families (TANF) and state W-2 legislation include a lifetime limit of sixty months' eligibility. Participation in any W-2 employment and training position category (Trial Job, Community Service Job, or W-2 Transition) is limited to twenty-four cumulative months. Extensions may be granted in limited circumstances, with state approval. The four available options form part of what is termed the 'self-sufficiency ladder.' They are described to applicants in the W-2 brochure (1998) as follows:

(1) Unsubsidized Employment: This is the highest and most desirable level in W-2. Individuals entering W-2 are guided first to the best available immediate job opportunity. The W-2 agency supports the participant's efforts to secure employment. Persons in unsubsidized employment may also be eligible for earned income credits, food stamps, medical assistance, child care, and job-access loans.

(2) Trial Jobs (subsidized employment): This level is for job seekers who have good work habits, but are having problems getting hired. If the

applicant fails to get a job or the FEP determines that the applicant is not prepared for unsubsidized employment, he or she may be offered subsidized employment in the form of a trial job. Trial jobs are intended to encourage employers to offer on-the-job training to individuals who seem job-ready but have a weak job history. Employers will receive a wage subsidy of up to three hundred dollars per month to cover training costs. The trial job employer must pay comparable wages and benefits received by regular employees in similarly classified positions for every hour worked. These positions have a limited duration of six to nine months.

(3) Community Service Jobs (CSJ): This level is available for participants who need to practise the work habits and skills necessary to be hired by a private business. CSJ work-training sites are expected to offer real work-practice opportunities under supervision in an environment that replicates that of regular employment but which also offers job coaching and mentoring to help the participant to succeed. A monthly payment of $673 will be paid for up to thirty hours a week of assigned work activities and up to ten hours a week in education and training. These positions also have a limited duration of six to nine months.

(4) W-2 Transitions: This level is reserved for those who might legitimately be unable to perform self-sustaining work even in a community service job for reasons such as multiple personal barriers, an abusive relationship, incapacitation, or the need to remain in the home to care for a disabled, sick, or dying family member. A monthly payment of $628 will be paid for up to twenty-eight hours a week of assigned work activities and up to twelve hours a week in education and training.

Wisconsin's government was confident that the policy would meet the expectations of the taxpayers. Time limits during periods of near full employment were considered to be fair. Administrators claim that, on an individual basis, time limits will be extended when unemployment rates rise or in circumstances where there are significant barriers to overcome, such as drug or alcohol addiction. A risk-protection mechanism is included in the performance standards followed by W-2 service providers, and these include a reassessment in the event of changes in the unemployment rate. But the program was designed for the typical welfare mother, not the exception. As Jean Rogers (interview), W-2's senior administrator, says, 'The public is very smart. They know who can and cannot work – and those who can't are very few. When designing public policy in general, make sure that your design fits the needs of 85 per cent of the target population, not 15 per cent. That's the secret.'

According to Rogers, the program's biggest obstacle was in getting the business community to view welfare recipients as viable employees, and hire them. While a lot of selling had to be done at the beginning, Rogers claims that there is now 'a solid and enthusiastic partnership established with the business community, especially through the Community Steering Committees, which each W-2 agency is required to establish. Rogers also believes that another important step lay in 'doing away with the welfare office itself.' All services relating to public assistance are now located in job centre buildings, the same job centres that are also used by the general public. This move has helped to remove the stigma of welfare from applicants who use the job centres' computerized job system, because those receiving W-2 assistance are indistinguishable from any other applicant.

Administrative Challenges: Making Workfare Work

When Tommy Thompson began his reforms in 1987 there were one hundred thousand families on the welfare rolls. A year after the introduction in 1997 of his most recent program, W-2, there were nine thousand. W-2 cut the welfare rolls by 70 per cent in its first year of operation. In an 18 October 1998 *New York Times* article by Jason DeParle, entitled 'W-2 is Bold, Unique, Laden with Red Tape,' Governor Tommy Thompson cited the decline in the number of welfare recipients as compelling evidence of the program's success: 'I'm extremely happy ... We expected about 36,000 cases left on the rolls, and we're down to 10,875. It's exceeded all expectations ... we've had some problems, particularly with child care, but we moved quickly to fix them.'

In an attempt to explain Wisconsin's success, some administrators point to the value of the state's long history of welfare reform and to its 'ten year history of gradual experimentation.' 'It's taken us ten years to get here,' claims Jean Rogers (interview), 'but that doesn't mean that it has to take everyone ten years. Others can build on the Wisconsin experience. It just so happens that, by 1997, when we introduced W-2 and declared a 100 per cent work requirement (with the exception of mothers of children under the age of twelve weeks), we had already put everything together, piece by piece, during the previous decade. During those years we had also built favourable public opinion, and valuable experience and administrative skills in moving recipients into work through the JOBS program.'

The many years of experimentation with welfare reform also assisted the government in another way, by getting the public, as well as public assistance recipients, accustomed to the direction in which the state was moving, and thereby likely minimizing resistance to the changes. There was much emphasis placed on a 'real world' rhetoric – much of it defined by an application of private sector jargon and rhetoric to policy design and delivery. Wisconsin's workfare program was meant to 'mirror the real world of work.' 'We have a "real world" rule,' claims Jean Rogers (interview). She describes this 'real world' logic as follows:

> How else can you honestly claim to be preparing individuals for transition to the real world of work? For example, do employers pay you extra money per the number of children you have? No. Well then, neither should welfare. Do employers expect you to work less than forty hours a week? No. Well, then, neither should welfare. Do low-income families get to go to university and college during the day for free, instead of working to support their children? No. Well, then, why should people on welfare? Do working mothers in low-income families get to stay home with their baby for more than the twelve-week paid time period provided by federal law? No. Then why should welfare mothers have this privilege? When parents who are employed miss hours of work, does their employer not reduce their paycheque proportional to the amount of work they missed? Yes. Then, so should welfare.

Rogers explained that these and other 'real world' principles gradually became expected ways of thinking, so when the time came to implement W-2, the public, including taxpayers and welfare clients, had already bought into the concept that a welfare plan should resemble 'real world' expectations. According to Rogers, the philosophy of making welfare like the 'real world' also took a lot of wind out of the sails of the activists and lobbyists who had been so opposed to the reforms. Moreover, with supports such as subsidized child care, assistance with transportation, and extended health care, it became increasingly difficult for lobby groups to find reasons for welfare mothers not to work, especially as, over time, high numbers of welfare mothers were reaching self-sufficiency.

As a performance-based system, W-2 requires people to monitor and maintain it. An implementation challenge lay in developing staff with the energy and the willingness to oversee clients closely for the performance of their obligations. Tommy Thompson's solution was to create incentives to motivate the welfare bureaucracy. County welfare offices were required to earn child-care and training funds by increasing the number of recipients they placed in jobs or community service work; offices that failed to reduce welfare caseloads dramatically were replaced by outside contractors. This ushered in a new private sector philosophy, based on standard private sector practices such as results-based pay, bonuses, and subcontracting. Under JOBS and, subsequently, under W-2, some counties had already found that to achieve expectations they had to offer a subcontract to an agency that could meet established caseload performance standards.

In addition to making sure that there were willing staff and a capable computer system, another challenge lay in co-ordinating the efforts between county workers and the private agencies hired to deliver W-2. This was most evident in the administrative confusion that took place during the first few months of W-2 over child-care subsidies. Unfortunately, this confusion had serious consequences for W-2 participants in that some mothers whose child care was not being paid on time by the county lost their jobs. The main problems occurred in Milwaukee, where six agencies had taken over W-2 in the six regions. The displaced government social workers and caseworkers, reassigned to child-care support for single mothers (to preserve their jobs), had been given responsibility for directly approving and paying child-care providers. Due to delays and power struggles on the part of the county workers, child-care providers were not getting paid, so they telephoned the mothers to pick up their children. W-2 mothers had nobody to look after their children until the bureaucracy between the county workers and the agency that had approved the child-care subsidy was worked out, and a considerable number of them lost their jobs. The length of time that it took to get the child-care voucher was a huge obstacle that the state had to resolve quickly. The system was amended to force government bureaucrats in the county offices to have the voucher ready within five working days of the child-care provider's application.

When faced with W-2, some counties or tribes opted out of administering the new employment-based program. In that event, W-2 became administered by a private agency under contract, the agency selected on the basis of a competitive process. The initial contracts were set for a period of two years. While rural areas and demonstration projects were faster to embrace work-related reforms and competed with one another to produce the most spectacular results, the city of Milwaukee, which has more than half the state's welfare load, remained resistant: 'Milwaukee, by sharp contrast, suffers from fractious welfare politics. The city and county have fought Governor Thompson's reforms tooth and nail, arguing that they will increase child poverty. Local political leaders wouldn't take responsibility for the reforms, so state authorities cobbled together a consortium of 15 community service agencies to operate the new programs. Some agencies won inclusion not because of their experience or competence – which they sorely lacked – but because they lobbied successfully for a piece of the training and subsidy pie' (*City Journal* 1997, 26).

The subcontracting dimension of the program reached its apex with the participation of Goodwill Industries. William Martin, a Goodwill Industries executive in his early thirties, created a subsidiary of Goodwill called Employment Solutions. This non-profit private agency won bids for two of the toughest of Milwaukee's six regions. According to Jason DeParle:

> Goodwill has become Wisconsin's largest welfare office, with 20 per cent of the state's caseload. The $119 million contract brings the group new money to pursue its central mission of reducing the barriers to work ... The 91st street headquarters of Milwaukee's Goodwill Industries is a 215,000 square foot monument to the organization's motto: 'We Believe in the Power of Work.' Washing machines the size of freight cars fill one side of the factory, and a packing business turns the other into a shrink-wrapped cornucopia of soap, furniture polish, calendars and car locks. But the striking thing about the industrial tableau is the sight of some of the workers. There are people crossing the factory floor in wheelchairs. There are men and women with Down syndrome sorting parts through inch-thick glasses. It is the visual embodiment of Goodwill's quasi-religious belief that labor is a gift that everybody can give. (1997, 35)

In addition, visits to some of the newly created job centres revealed a high level of activity, from the learning labs and the child-care centre to parenting classes to work counselling and training. The bulk of the community service jobs take place at Employment Solutions' training centre. The government's decision to contract-out the job placement function was criticized, however, in some circles, especially since the agencies could make a profit on their work. Gregory Stanford, for example, in his article 'Delay in Tracking W-2 Clients Inexcusable' (*Milwaukee Journal Sentinel* 18 October 1998), raises the following questions:

News item: Drastic drops in caseloads will yield millions in windfall profits for the five agencies running Wisconsin Works in Milwaukee County.

Let's see if we have this right: The fewer cases an agency has, the more money it makes. Less clientele = more $$$$.

What a troubling equation. It adds up to a financial incentive to jettison needy families from the W-2 rolls without regard to where they wind up.

No, we are not saying the agencies in question took that course. They may well have conscientiously striven to attract as many families to the program as possible and then to guide them into self-sufficiency. What we are saying, however, is that there is no money in being so conscientious. The profit's in merely thinning the caseload. The state inexcusably designed the program that way. If the aim of W-2 is merely to reduce the assistance rolls, then rewarding the agencies by the amount they do so makes sense. But state officials protest that fewer cases are not the goal. Rather, they say, W-2 is designed to make needy families more self-reliant.

In other words, Tommy Thompson sought to (at least partially) subcontract the welfare problem to external agencies. According to one respondent, Thompson didn't want to 'waste too much time with resistant bureaucrats of the type who have thwarted welfare reform attempts in other jurisdictions. He just got rid of them.' According to Leonor Rosas DeLeon (personal interview, 14 June 1999), director of the Bureau of Welfare Initiatives, effective human resources training played a very important role in gaining administrator cooperation throughout the years. 'People had a long way to go, from asking "How can I make you eligible?" to "How can I make you employable?" You couldn't take an Income Maintenance Worker and make him or her a Financial and Employment Counsellor. If he or she wasn't willing to change, it just wouldn't work.' Performance standards were set up in such a way that good news could not be reported if there was no good news to give – counties, tribes, and agencies were rated on the number of placements they made in (a) unsubsidized work, (b) trial jobs, or (c) community placements. Very clear standards were established that administrators could not easily misunderstand or misinterpret.

Did Welfare Recipients Participate?

Before W-2, AFDC recipients in Wisconsin were under a certain amount of pressure to find work. But after W-2, there was officially a 100 per cent work requirement. Did welfare recipients participate? The answer is yes. Either they participated or they vanished off the rolls. According to one senior administrator, the welfare population's response to W-2 falls into three groups. The first group is made up of those who 'are happy that they are working, getting raises, able to save for their own home. They are the ones who are feeling good about the changes, who had the courage to overcome their low self-esteem and get back into the system.' Administrators claim that this group represents the overwhelming majority of women. The second group is made up of the 'resisters.' These are the single mothers who are officially signed up, but 'are not interested in working or in preparing for employment.' They are constantly sanctioned for erratic participation. The third group is made up of those who simply vanished. Some welfare mothers simply moved away while administrators claim that others 'may not have found the work requirement to be worth the effort or had money from other undeclared sources.' Others found jobs on their own. Over the years names disappeared from the welfare rolls.

As traditional welfare continued to be phased out, welfare mothers were required to sign up for the new job-oriented W-2, but many did not do so. The deadline for signing up was 15 March 1998, but a 1 December 1997 article in the *Milwaukee Journal Sentinel* by Joel Dresang, entitled 'Agencies Find Many Ways to Spread Word about W-2,' explains how these cases were being handled:

> Yet a few thousand families receiving conventional assistance have not signed up so far for the new regimen. Does that failure stem from lack of knowledge?
>
> Commendably the private agencies running W-2 here are striving hard to spread the word about the new program, so that no family is left out in the cold out of simple ignorance. For instance, Employment Solutions of Wisconsin (a subsidiary of Goodwill Industries), the largest agency, sponsored a pre-Thanksgiving meal at a housing project to gain the ears of the poor. Other tactics include phone calls and home visits.
>
> These agencies' innovative outreach suggests that privatization may pay off. It's hard to imagine the bureaucratic county welfare department going to those lengths.

Apart from the many notices and follow-up phone calls, agency staff have also spoken to church groups, set up information hot-lines, and appeared on local radio and television shows. One fear was summed up by Linda Stewart, secretary of the Department of Workforce Development, who stated in Dresang's article, 'I think people often feel with change that, if they don't do anything, nothing can happen to them.'

In recent years a greater effort has been made to find out what happened to welfare recipients who disappeared from the welfare rolls. For example, one W-2 agency (United Migrant Opportunity Services, Inc.) in Milwaukee has subcontracted the task of finding out what happened to the mothers who did not sign up for W-2. This agency works in conjunction with a welfare advocacy group and consults with this group before ever closing a file, giving them a chance to make sure that all possible means have been used to locate and/or sign up the welfare mother. One concern is with welfare mothers who did not sign up for the job-oriented program but chose, instead, to leave their children with their parents, usually their own single mother. Under the Kinship Care Program (run by county social services, not by W-2 staff), grandmothers and other relatives can receive $215 a month for every child in their care. Administrators admit that this is a possible work-avoidance loophole in the system. The program was meant only for children at risk of being placed in foster care, but there is some possibility that mothers may have children stay with relatives, or make it look as though they are staying with relatives, in order to collect the money. There is some doubt as to whether these families are receiving the required rigorous home visit from a child protection worker. In a *New York Times* article entitled 'As Welfare Rolls Shrink, Load on Relatives Grows – Weary Milwaukee Grandmothers Tell of Strain' (21 February 1999), DeParle writes: 'As Wisconsin drives its welfare rolls to record lows, the number of grandmothers pressed into action is reaching unexpected highs. Unwilling or unable to work for public aid, many of the state's most troubled mothers have lost their benefits, often en route to drug clinics, jail cells, shelters or the streets.'

Thus, in Wisconsin, the reaction of welfare recipients ranged from enthusiasm for a new opportunity to enter the workforce, to reluctant obedience, to dropping out of the system altogether or continuing to receive support (of a different type) by dropping off the kids with their grandmother.

The Official Record: What Do the Evaluators Say?

Probably the most important of all the statistics available on Wisconsin's system of public assistance is this: since Tommy Thompson took over as governor in 1987, the cash welfare rolls have dropped by as much as 91 per cent as of 1999. Each stage of welfare reform in Wisconsin has undergone intense scrutiny, not only by its own state auditors and the United States General Accounting Office (GAO), but also by outside evaluators such as Maximus. Other American states have also analysed and evaluated the reforms in Wisconsin to find out if Wisconsin really has achieved the miraculous welfare reductions that have been reported in the media. In a study of seven states, of which Wisconsin was one, at various periods between 1995 and 1998, the U.S. General Accounting Office concluded that 'most of the adults who left welfare were employed at some time after leaving the rolls, often at low-paying jobs. There was little evidence of increased incidence of homelessness or of children entering foster care after families left welfare' (U.S. GAO/ T-HEHS-99-116). DeParle also found little evidence of family damage due to the introduction of W-2:

> The chairman of the Milwaukee Shelter Task Force estimates that the number of families in shelters rose by about 25 per cent last winter. On any given night that translates into 41 additional families, or about 120 women and children. It's a lot when measured in human terms, but still a tiny minority of the 10,000 families who have left welfare.
>
> The other available data hint at a similar story, of rising but manageable need. Requests for food assistance are up: the Hunger Task Force of Milwaukee saw activity at its food pantries rise by 14 per cent last year. But the increase seems to be leveling off. Reports of child abuse and neglect are up. But they've risen for 12 of the last 14 years, and they are still lower than the 1994 peak. (1997, 47)

A number of multi-state welfare monitoring projects have been initiated to monitor the effects of the post-Clinton welfare-reform plans of selected states. Most of these include the state of Wisconsin and are still in the works. Organizations studying the effects of programmatic changes in the welfare system include the Center on Urban and Metropolitan Policy at the Brookings Institution a private, non-profit think-tank based in Washington, D.C.), the Manpower Demonstration Research Corporation (MDRC), Mathematica Policy Research Inc., Maximus, the National Association of Child Advocates (NACA), and the Nelson A. Rockefeller Institute of Government. Most studies seek to understand what constitutes success and failure, according to each organization's definition of the terms.

It is a great irony that Washington rated Wisconsin poorly in the operation and in the ranking of its JOBS program, which was instituted in 1988, until its replacement in Wisconsin by W-2 in 1997. Because Washington's constant indicator of success is the percentage of welfare recipients participating in work-related activities (which to most social workers means the eternal training belt), and because Wisconsin's efforts had been aimed at actually placing recipients in unsubsidized jobs so that they would be moved off welfare (rather than remaining on welfare but participating in work-related activities), Wisconsin fared badly in the evaluations of all U.S. states. In 1993, for example, Wisconsin ranked only twentieth of all states, because the yardstick of success had nothing to do with depleting the welfare rolls by finding people jobs, and everything to do with enrolling a certain percentage of recipients in job-related activities, a task that was fairly easy to meet by signing up recipients in more training programs (as we saw was perpetually the case in California's supposedly successful decade-long GAIN program).

Wisconsin has been criticized for its efforts in tracking the fate of W-2 clients. The state did conduct a 'Leaver's Survey' (1998), which found that 38 per cent of those who left welfare were not working when they were interviewed. Administrators admit that they need a more complete picture and are currently developing other surveys that will go to greater lengths to document how former welfare recipients have fared since W-2. However, a recent survey conducted by the Urban Institute (1999) provides evidence that families in Wisconsin (including Milwaukee's inner-city areas) did not experience widespread suffering at the outset of welfare's overhaul, and that, compared with national averages and twelve other states in the study, Wisconsin had encouraging rates of employment, income, and benefits. The survey also found that poor families in Wisconsin were doing better than those elsewhere and that Wisconsin's 8.9 per cent poverty rate for residents under sixty-five was by far the lowest among the states studied (Dresang, *Milwaukee Journal Sentinel*, 4 February 1999).

Did the Public Play a Role?

One of the reasons for the success of workfare in Wisconsin was the lack of well-developed activist and anti-workfare lobby groups. At the same time, Wisconsin was not without groups opposed to welfare reform. Those whose jobs were affected or threatened in some way by the proposed or implemented changes usually made up an important organizing force behind the groups and associations that officially took a position against the changes. In Wisconsin, associations such as Welfare Warriors, the Poverty Network Initiative, ACORN (a community grass-roots group with branches all over the U.S.), the Milwaukee Coalition to Save Our Children, and the Milwaukee Women in Poverty Public Education Initiative, were, and still are, very vocal about the damage that might be done by the proposed welfare reforms, especially to children. Anti-welfare reform activities consist mainly of advocacy (i.e., providing women with the know-how to fight their case), demonstrations and marches, and the publication of newsletters. The Welfare Warriors' newsletter is entitled *Welfare Mothers' Voice* and is published quarterly. A recent issue was devoted to seeking a moratorium on the federally imposed five-year lifetime limit on welfare, with as little as a two-year time limit at any one time. Wisconsin's important first two-year-limit date was October 1999. Advocates predicted administrative chaos; the reality was uneventful. Administrators insisted that each case was being reviewed in an orderly way and on its own merits. An office worker at Welfare Warriors told me that one of the problems advocacy groups such as theirs has been having is that W-2 mothers are 'so busy running here and there' that they no longer have time to demonstrate.

According to Corliss Wood, the operations manager of Employment Solutions, at one Milwaukee job centre from which W-2 is run, the ACORN group 'used to picket two to three times a week but this has decreased considerably in the last year or so.' According to the manager, the attitude of groups such as ACORN or Welfare Warriors is 'How dare you force a mother to get skills, work experience, or a job?' or, alternatively, 'Why should we be forced to take a nursing assistant or low-level secretarial job when what we might want is a career?' (personal interview with Corliss Wood, 17 June 1999). The offices of the Welfare Warriors carry a logo on its walls that reads 'Motherwork Is Work.' The organization holds the firm conviction that the state should provide for a mother who is looking after her children at home. Alesha Nicholson, a member of the Welfare Warriors group, was quoted at a public hearing on W-2 as saying that 'it's ridiculous to require women to work for their benefits as soon as their children are 12 weeks old ... It's really not fair. It's slavery is what it is' (qtd. by Joel Dresang, 'W-2 Welfare Worries Aired at Forum with Lawmakers,' *Milwaukee Journal Sentinel* (4 May 1997).

In terms of slowing down or deterring change, welfare activists from

Wisconsin and those who bussed in from other states accomplished little. In the early days of W-2, at a national convention of the Association of Community Organizations for Reform Now (ACORN), protesters petitioned the state to allow more education benefits in W-2. They carried signs and chanted slogans such as 'Hey-hey, ho-ho, Tommy Thompson has got to go,' but to little or no avail. ACORN and the Communications Workers of America also tried to organize W-2 workers to campaign collectively for work protection, again in vain. Possibly the best that can be said about the work of these protesters is that they have helped individuals on a one-by-one basis to fight their case, they have increased community awareness on an important issue, and they have helped large groups of individuals to express their opinion. Some welfare critics have even softened their positions on workfare. John Gardner, a member of the Milwaukee school board, complains of 'an abysmal implementation' and claims that 'In theory, it's a privatized model of efficiency. In reality, it's a politically gerrymandered cartel.' In the end, even Gardner admits that the hassles forced many recipients to find work on their own: 'It works despite itself,' he said (DeParle, 'W-2 Is Bold,' *Wisconsin State Journal*, 18 October 1998). Even Dick Schlimm, another leading advocate for the poor in Fond du Lac County, where welfare rolls have crashed from 791 to 187 in three years, can find little wrong with W-2. Asked how he would design the system, he admitted that he might pay higher wages but that 'it probably wouldn't look too much different than W-2' (DeParle 1997). This softening is also evident amongst religious groups, many of whom had protested the proposed changes. Wisconsin's Roman Catholic bishops issued guidelines urging church leaders and parishioners to help poor families succeed under W-2. In a statement printed in the *Milwaukee Journal Sentinel* of 10 September 1997, Milwaukee Archbishop Rembert Weakland said: 'I would like to encourage the parishes to reach out so that everyone can experience the dignity that comes from work and a stable job, one that supports them and their family.'

The media also played a role in the life of workfare in Wisconsin. Ever since Tommy Thompson began his welfare reforms in 1987, thousands of newspaper articles have been written about them. As Corbett points out, 'Media attention to what has been occurring in the state has been extensive and continuous, and Wisconsin has often been labeled as a laboratory for welfare reform' (1995, 20). According to workfare administrators, the press were originally against almost every reform, but they are gradually becoming converted as they see the results.

The general public also played a role in the life of Tommy Tompson's good idea, in the sense of its overwhelming and enduring support. A poll conducted by the Institute for Survey and Policy Research at the University of Wisconsin–Milwaukee (1998) found that 76 per cent of Wisconsin residents favoured the state's welfare-to-work program, and that even those who personally knew someone in the program gave it 67 per cent support; 17 per cent said they were undecided and 16 per cent opposed it (*Madison Capital Times*, 24 November 1998). Stories abound of citizen-organized car-pooling programs, aimed at finding rides not only for W-2 participants but also for other low-income employees.

Another example of the public's position can be seen in the enthusiastic support of the business community, without whom all work requirement reforms would have failed. The Wisconsin branch of the U.S. organization entitled Welfare to Work Partnership (a national organization that encourages businesses to hire and retain welfare recipients) is particularly active. Apart from the thousands of businesses included in the partnership who committed themselves to hire welfare recipients, hundreds of smaller employers throughout the state have also signed pledges. The state held seminars to help employers understand the details of W-2. The panellists often included employers who had hired welfare recipients and were happy to share their experiences with other prospective employers.

The business community also participates in W-2 in a more formal way in that each W-2 agency is required to establish a Community Steering Committee (CSCs) in order to provide ties to the local business communities. These CSCs help the agency to identify unsubsidized employment opportunities, as well as create wage-subsidized and community service jobs for those individuals who are not ready for private employment. Each CSC consists of between twelve and fifteen members, appointed by the executive of the W-2 service provider.

What Happened to the Good Idea?

According to program staff in Madison, at the beginning there was a real fear amongst administrators that what the protesters were saying would happen might turn out to be true. There were a lot of concerns about a possible rise in social ills such a rise in child abuse, homelessness, and crime. However, these worries proved to be groundless. Studies are still measuring the impact of W-2 on the families who have left welfare, with researchers from such lobby groups as the Milwaukee

Women and Poverty Public Education Initiative (1998) claiming that W-2 has destroyed families who are on welfare and researchers from organizations such as the Center for Self-Sufficiency saying the opposite.

While much points to the success of Wisconsin workfare, it is too early to declare the program an unmitigated success. Whether or not a success in real terms, it has nevertheless been defined that way. Thus, most attention on Wisconsin has been directed towards identifying the reasons for workfare's success. On the political front, it seems that Wisconsin had a political leadership that saw workfare as more than a temporary political lever – a platform that could win an election and then be forgotten. Workfare was Thompson's political platform; he gambled his whole political career on it and in so doing increased the stakes for the successful implementation of the program. His policy-makers never rested on their laurels, constantly amending policy to adapt to different barriers to employment, as these were identified. The subcontracting of workfare administration should also not be underestimated. By subcontracting out the welfare problem, Wisconsin effectively bypassed institutional resistance, past history, and an old, intransigent welfare bureaucracy. Tommy Thompson heeded the hazard lights that flashed warnings to him as he piloted his good idea through stormy weather and, in doing so, averted the disasters faced by so many other jurisdictions.

As for Tommy Thompson, his term was scheduled to end in 2002, and he said that he would not seek re-election at that time. In January 2001 he accepted President George W. Bush's request to head the country's largest federal agency, the Department of Health and Social Services (HSS). This position gives Thompson the ability to continue his reforms at the national level. Apart from continuing the work on improved tracking of welfare leavers, he claims to need flexibility in the rules from Washington (child care, transportation, and job-retention services) in the way that the state spends its block grant money to keep people off welfare. His plans include taking additional steps to help former welfare recipients stay in the workforce, expand child-care programs to address children with disabilities, and provide 'get well' havens for children who are temporarily sick. Thompson has also expressed an interest in expanding access to Medicaid, the national health care program for the poor, by creating a sliding-scale premium buy-in option for working people. At the national level, the Bush administration will be passing work-based welfare and health care reforms with Wisconsin's Tommy Thompson as the chief health and social services policy adviser.

6.

New York City's Work Experience Program – 'Same Shit, Different Day'

Summary

The centrepiece of New York City's welfare reform is a massive program called the Work Experience Program (WEP). New York City's ambitious workfare program, instituted in 1995, is unique in that it hinges on the substantial development of public sector jobs, most of which are manual or menial in nature. More than one hundred thousand welfare recipients have moved through the program, and, according to Mayor Rudolph Giuliani, the program has been an unmitigated success. While many welfare recipients have, indeed, been ushered through the WEP and welfare rolls have dropped dramatically, there are lingering questions about the efficacy of the workfare program. No one seems to know what triggered the drop in the rolls: was it WEP or was it other, harsher elements of welfare reform such as 'finger-imaging,' or new efforts to check and evaluate eligibility? There is also evidence of a conflict between the city and the public sector trade union as a result of the replacement of public sector jobs with WEP participants and a significant WEP drop-out rate.

While the Work Experience Program does appear to have had a positive effect on some, the program was simply too huge for an un-problematic implementation. The sheer numbers involved meant that most participants were simply shuffled through the program, both recipients and community service providers simply going through the motions. In the end, the overriding concern was the ability to report a drop in welfare cases. Whether or not this drop could be attributable to workfare is not known (even though politicians and policy-makers find it convenient to make a direct link between workfare and the significant drop in the welfare caseload).

New York City's Good Idea: Background and
Context of the Reform

For New York City's Mayor Rudolph Giuliani, the goal of the city's workfare program was nothing short of spectacular: 'We're going to end welfare by the end of the century completely' (editorial, 'Ending Welfare,' *New York Times*, 21 July 1998). The old welfare system was to be transformed into a 'jobs-based' system, organized around a 'universal work requirement.' While other workfare programs may have been developed earlier and with more novel approaches, it was the size and magnitude of the New York City program that earned it celebrity status. Certainly, the New York City program was a symbol for reform, and it was to act as a lightning rod for change: if it could be done in New York City it could be done anywhere.

This was not a pilot project. Nor was it a small social experimental lab. Workfare in New York City was a huge program that aimed for massive results. New York stood as a symbol itself, a place rife with poverty and ghettos, all supposedly propped up with public assistance. The numbers on welfare or some form of public assistance in New York are unbelievably large. There are approximately one million New Yorkers who rely on public assistance (HRA 1997). This includes about half a million children who rely on public assistance and translates to 'one out of every three New York City children liv[ing] in a household receiving benefits under the administration of the city's Human Resources Administration (HRA)'s Income Support Program (ISP). For younger children, the statistics are even more sobering: nearly 43% of city children under the age of 12 live in families receiving public assistance' (HRA 1997). According to the HRA, the city was spending more than $2 billion a year in funds, in the late 1990s, to provide public assistance benefits to eligible New Yorkers and was spending approximately $200 million a year to administer the system.

The administrative welfare infrastructure is matched with these massive numbers: there are thirty-three public assistance centres located at twenty-eight different sites throughout the city, employing more than five thousand workers. The 'Income Support Employees' section constitutes one of the largest city agencies and has more employees than the New York City Department of Health, the Department of Parks and Recreation, and the Department of Transportation combined. If there was going to be a miracle of workfare, it was going to be the miracle of making so many (mostly reluctant) administrators move so many (mostly reluctant) welfare recipients through a six-month work placement. Those who favoured and those who opposed workfare alike watched the New York City workfare experience with interest. For Mayor Giuliani, workfare was to be one of his crowning achievements: 'In polishing his achievements in town hall meetings in Brooklyn and fund raisers as far as Arizona, Mayor Rudolph Giuliani always mentions one that sets him apart from other politicians: his creation of the country's largest workfare program, a welfare work force ... who sweep streets, clean parks and answer phones for their welfare checks' (Rachel Swarns, *New York Times*, 19 April 1998).

Workfare results in the case of New York City, however, appear to be mixed. On the one hand, large numbers of welfare recipients *were* transferred into job experience programs, and large numbers of welfare recipients *were* eliminated from the welfare rolls. On the other hand, the content or self-improvement aspect of this program appears to be limited. In no way is it clear that workfare provided a path into the job market. But this does not really matter because, at the end of the day, what became important was the numbers game: how many welfare recipients could be reported to have transferred to workfare job experience programs and dropped from the welfare rolls, regardless of the effectiveness of these programs. In New York City, it appears that the emphasis on numbers served to create a political stir, but, in a strange way, it contributed to the erosion of workfare as a good idea. In fact, a variety of forces served to turn the good idea bad: political expediency, cynicism on the part of administrators and welfare recipients, and evaluator legitimization.

First, as a high-profile jurisdiction, New York was inevitably tied up with politics and the media management of workfare programs. This meant that much institutional energy was expended on the marketing and packaging of workfare policy as a political platform, as opposed to the more difficult detail-oriented phase of design and implementation of the workfare program.

Second, on the administrative side, the legacy of the massive old welfare system was too great to allow the breakthrough of a new workfare model. The sheer size of the old administrative apparatus, embedded in a rich history of standardized routines and competences, meant that a shift to the new would be both slow and problematic. In addition, the welfare recipients themselves contributed to the demise of the program, by only reluctantly buying into it. Once again, the legacy of the old welfare system was so well entrenched that the welfare recipients seemed to cling to the old system as best they could, only passively and reluctantly participating in the rituals of the new workfare model. Who could blame them, as the new programs tended to offer more political sheen than substance? This meant that they went through the motions, a case of 'same shit, different day.' Frustrated by the apathetic reaction to his hard-line mandatory policies, in 1998 Mayor Giuliani turned to Wisconsin for advice and ended up hiring Jason Turner, the architect of the successful Wisconsin workfare project known as Wisconsin Works (W-2).

Third, on the evaluation side, the numbers game figured centrally in the failure of the program. As long as the city was able to report a drop in welfare numbers, the program would be interpreted as a 'success' (whether or not workfare was serving to help people get back to work seemed less important than the dropping caseload numbers). The drop in numbers served to suggest success and clouded the evaluation process itself. The numbers game superseded the original aims of workfare, i.e., providing substantial work experience that would transform the welfare recipient into an independent and self-reliant citizen.

How Was the Program Designed?

The key implementation vehicle for New York City's new workfare program was the well-known Work Experience Program (WEP). It was first unveiled in March 1995, and by the end of 1996 it had become the largest workfare program in the country. By 1997 more than one hundred thousand welfare recipients had moved through the program, in one way or another. WEP is unique amongst America's notable workfare experiments in its huge creation of public-sector job placements. Under WEP, each employable participant is assigned to a structured work assignment as a condition of receiving public assistance. Most of these are city job placements of a primarily manual and menial nature. Unlike some other jurisdictions, New York's work experience program makes little attempt to place people according to their backgrounds, skills, and work histories. Instead the emphasis is on getting people into a job – any job. The key features of the WEP (summarized in MCSS 1996) are listed below:

- participants are placed in a public or non-profit agency, where they must work to earn their benefits
- the hours of work are calculated by dividing their benefit level by the minimum wage

- no incentive is offered to clients to participate, and participation is mandatory
- as of October 1995, districts had to ensure that 50 per cent of their clients on General Assistance were taking part in the work experience program
- the program was phased in so that by January 1997, 95 per cent of clients on General Assistance would be taking part
- there is a penalty of up to 5 per cent of the administration costs that are cost-shared with the state for districts that do not meet their quotas for placing people in welfare-to-work programs
- new legislation was to be introduced to make work for welfare mandatory for single employables receiving General Assistance.

In order to provide the reader with more detail on the content of New York City's workfare program, I include the following summary of the key features of the program as adapted from the *Work Experience Program: Policy and Procedures Manual (1997)*. The Work Experience Program (WEP) places public assistance (PA) recipients into Work Experience assignments at government and not-for-profit agencies for eligible clients. Participants who do not comply with OES (Office of Employment Services) and sponsoring agency rules can lose their public assistance, food stamp and/or Medicaid benefits.

Participants perform tasks that are useful to the sponsoring institutions and contribute to the quality of life in New York City. The Work Experience Program is not regular paid employment and is temporary. Permanent full-time employment is the goal of every WEP participant.

Work Experience Program: The Office of Employment Services' (OES) Work Experience Program (WEP) is a co-operative effort between OES and other agencies throughout New York City. The types of work performed by participants include but are not limited to office services (typing, filing, data entry, photocopying), maintenance services (mopping floors, emptying waste baskets, vacuuming, maintaining grounds), and human/community services (assisting the elderly, working with children, assisting with food programs, street and lot cleaning).

Intake Agencies: The message given by all parties must be consistent: paid work is better than public assistance and there is dignity associated with all work. Even if paid work cannot be found immediately, unpaid work experience provides benefits to the individual and improves the quality of life in New York City. The Office of Employment Services sends out an Initial Appointment letter to employable clients. These clients report to an Intake site where they are interviewed to ascertain their level of skills and work history. Depending upon the assessment of the worker, the client may be referred for participation in the Work Experience Program. The work experience program assigns its clients from the following areas:

OES Intake: Participants are interviewed by a caseworker to ascertain their level of skills, prior work history, and other information such as where they live and their future goals. They are then referred to a sponsoring agency with assignments that best fit their needs and the needs of the sponsoring agencies. Participants are asked to report to the sponsoring agency's orientation, where they will be given a work-site assignment and specific duties.

Begin Sites: ADC (Aid for Dependent Children) clients whose youngest child is aged three or over are assessed at BEGIN Sites. Some will be required to participate in the WEP program as part of their overall employment plan. ADC WEP participants are single parents with children. It is required that child-care arrangements be made.

Job Club: All employable ADC participants must complete six months of WEP. They are then required to participate in a Job Club training program, which lasts four to six weeks. There they participate in a job search. At the end of the program, if they do not find jobs, they will be evaluated to determine the next OES activity that will enhance their skills. In some instances, they will be referred to a WEP assignment.

Employment Centers: Income Support Centers refer employable Home Relief (HR) applicants for public assistance to Employment Centers (EC), where they are interviewed to determine job readiness. Each applicant has to complete a job search program of four to six weeks. If after six weeks the applicant has not found a job, EC staff will assign those individuals, as well as those who have found part-time work, to Work Experience Program work sites. There they will gain valuable employment related skill and work experience that can be added to their resume.

OES Conference and Conciliation Section: Participants who are considered to be out of compliance with WEP policy and procedures will be sent a Conciliation Notice. If a participant responds to a Conciliation Notice and the issue is successfully resolved, the participant will be given a work assignment.

Fair Hearing: Participants who attend a Fair Hearing may be given a WEP assignment depending on the outcome of the Fair Hearing.

Health Services Systems: Clients who claim that they cannot participate for medical reasons and who present proper medical documentation when seen at an intake site are referred to Health Services Systems (HSS) for a medical examination. On the basis of this exam, HSS will determine a client's employability status. Clients who are found employable, with and without limitations, are given an appropriate WEP assignment.

Lloyd Fineburg, director of WEP, states (interview, 15 March 2000) that the aim of New York City's workfare is to 'try to fill up the week with some kind of activity. Work experience is the biggest part, but we also have other departments which assist with job search and training. Work experience is now compulsory ... if you're going to receive a benefit. The city's mandate is thirty-five hours of activity.' Fineburg is also quick to point out the advantages of workfare: 'The program has great value. It gets you out of the house. If you work in the welfare area long enough, you realize that you need something other than a cheque. We're breaking down a long tradition of dependency ... it may be hard, but in the long run I believe we are doing the right thing.' When Mayor Giuliani put forward his idea for a 'universal work requirement' he truly meant it to be universal. In 1999, the Giuliani administration prepared to extend his workfare initiatives to the homeless. The mayor made workfare a condition of shelter for the forty-six hundred families and seven thousand single adults in New York City's homeless shelter system. The change required the city's homeless shelters to use the same system of rules, work requirements, and sanctions that it employed with the other four hundred thousand people it had moved off welfare.

It is important to note that, as in other jurisdictions, workfare is not new to New York City. Its various earlier incarnations include the Community Work Experience Program (about ten years old) and the Public Works Program. Indeed, quick perusal of the history of workfare in New York City reveals a continual use of workfare-related programs. Workfare seems to simply appear over and over again, repackaged and resold as a political platform to help 'resolve the irresolvable.' New York's welfare problem always seemed ripe for the good idea, a simple and all-encompassing solution to an intractable problem.

Administrative Challenges: Making Workfare Work

New York City's workfare program has many champions beyond the popular press. Lloyd Fineburg, director of WEP, sees the workfare program as a 'miracle.' He claims that 'New York City had everything going against it. It had high union density, high levels of unemployment, and a huge old welfare system that didn't want to budge.' Fineburg himself believes that two factors were critical for success: 'a powerful mayor ... who meant business, and the availability of resources committed to the program.' According to Fineburg, Mayor Giuliani 'is a powerful man ... a person at the top who has the clout and will to push through the program. The mayor effectively controls all the city's agencies. If he says "you are going to provide me with the places I need for people to work," there is no question that you provide him with the jobs.' As we will see in other jurisdictions covered in this volume, where the political leader could not or would not command work experience placements, workfare did not get off the ground.

Interestingly, Fineburg also points to computerization as another key to success: 'Much of what workfare is about is tracking and coding the employables. With workfare you need to keep tabs on all of your people. In some ways, we are a time-keeping agency.' Here, Fineburg alludes to the 'control' dimension of workfare programs. For Fineburg, the control function is central if not essential to a successful workfare program: 'at the end of the day much of workfare is about time-keeping and record-keeping ... without a good tracking system, workfare would not work. It's these mundane administrative things that keep a program like workfare ticking.'

The successful implementation of the workfare system also seemed to hinge on breaking down the old administrative apparatus and the old welfare bureaucratic culture. Along with other workfare experimenters, the city of New York has also gone the route of refashioning the welfare administrative apparatus in the image of private sector employment initiatives. The city has introduced experimental job centres (to replace welfare offices) in Greenwood, Jamaica, Long Island

City, and Staten Island. These job centres now require welfare recipients to meet with a 'financial planner' (replacing the caseworker) to discuss job search and retraining possibilities. These changes were not always easy to implement, especially when welfare bureaucrats sometimes themselves turned on their own programs, favouring the automatic safety net of the past. Alison Williams, a WEP trainer, for example, reportedly takes an 'honest' approach when talking to new trainees, informing them that 'the welfare system is using you' (*City Journal* 1997, 24). Other life-skills trainers have been known to join the Welfare Reform Network, a coalition of left-wing Manhattan advocacy groups protesting against welfare reforms.

In other words, the problem of administrative resistance helped stall efforts to make workfare work. The huge welfare bureaucracy was unlikely to change its approach to welfare to accommodate another new program, in particular one with which the bureaucrats so obviously disagreed. Many of Mayor Giuliani's bureaucrats marched in anti-workfare rallies and assisted in the founding of the powerful Workfairness activist organization. While welfare offices could be renamed 'job centers' and 'caseworkers' renamed 'financial planners, in truth, as Rachel Swarns points out in 'Welfare as We Know It Goes Incognito' (*New York Times*, 5 July 1998), 'the same workers still do business in the same buildings.' For workfare to lead to permanent jobs, the job skills and backgrounds of the new 'financial planners,' at the new 'job centres' needed to be transformed. Just as the welfare recipients needed to be retrained, the welfare 'caseworkers' needed to be retrained and just as short-term job retraining for welfare turned out to be a pipedream, so too did the short-term job retraining of the 'financial planners.' As with any innovative workfare program, the Work Experience Program required a sustained commitment from a number of stakeholders. This support appears to have been absent in New York. A 1994 study of California's GAIN program by the Manpower Development Research Corporation (MDRC) made this point about work experience programs in general. The MDRC study concluded that to run a large-scale work experience program required many things, including a 'strong welfare staff commitment,' a 'buy-in from public employees unions and welfare right groups,' and 'sufficient funding and worksite capacity.' In New York there was neither a strong commitment from welfare staff nor a buy-in from other key stakeholder groups. That is probably why New York emphasizes its success in reducing caseloads over that of moving welfare recipients into permanent full-time jobs.

Did Welfare Recipients Participate?

The popular press has provided anecdotal evidence of WEP's success, at least in terms of workfare participation. There is, for example, the case of Nancy Jimenez, described in the *New York Times* as a 'poster girl' for the workfare experience. Her story, almost too well orchestrated, perfectly fits the workfare dream. But according to Alan Finder, in his article 'One Who Has Found Her Job within the System' (*New York Times*, 15 April 1998), she is 'not just selling the company line':

> 'I feel workfare is good,' she (Nancy) says. 'It gives people an opportunity to do something for themselves.' It's been a great experience, she said. 'You meet a lot of people. You learn a lot, it keeps you busy.' Miss Jimenez, who lives on the lower East side, dropped out of high school in 1987 while in the 11th grade after giving birth to the first of two sons. She went on welfare five years later, she said, because her husband was not making enough money. (They are now divorced) ... In 1995 after three years on welfare, she (found a placement). After two years of taking phone messages, issuing car-fare checks to other workfare workers and entering data in a computer, Miss Jimenez worked up the nerve to apply for a full-time job. She was hired – by her boss ... the agency's workfare coordinator.

Then there is the story of Ethan Ward: 'Workfare is good ... People want to work ... but there are not enough jobs out there. People with degrees and years of education are looking for jobs too ... the competition is stiff' (Denise Millner and Chrisena Coleman, *Daily News*, 4 January 1995). The Mayor's Office has consistently presented the workfare program as a huge success, even though there is no evidence that work placements played a role in the large caseload reduction. Looking at these numbers in isolation, the overall welfare reform package (including the tightening up of eligibility requirements) would appear to be have contributed to a decline in the number of public assistance recipients of more than 350,000 (a drop of 30.3 per cent) from March 1995 to January 1998. One group claims that New York City's workfare program was plagued by a high drop-out rate among participants, although these figures are unavailable (Project Team 1999).

Figure 6.1. Public Assistance Recipients

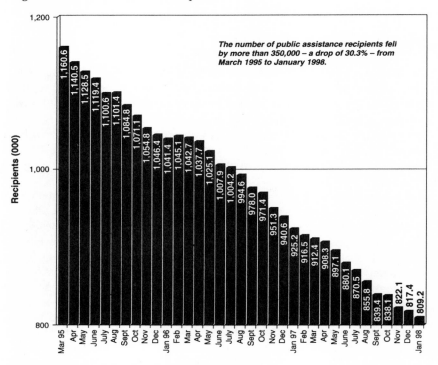

The number of public assistance recipients fell by more than 350,000 – a drop of 30.3% – from March 1995 to January 1998.

Source: *Mayor's Management Report* (1998, 203)

The number of those who left welfare (whether they were in WEP or not) because they found a permanent job after their placement is not known. The drop in New York City's welfare rolls is depicted in Figure 6.1.

The numbers associated with transfers to work activity programs are also trumpeted in each of the mayor's management reports. The 1998 *Mayor's Management Report*, for example, suggests significant success: 'The proportion of Safety Net recipients participating in work activities, as calculated by the State in accordance with its regulations, was 94 per cent during the first four months of Fiscal 1998, compared with a rate of 83.6% for Home Relief (HR) clients during the same period of Fiscal 1997.' On the job-placement front, the *Mayor's Management Report* notes that 'during the first four months of Fiscal 1998 AFDC/TANF-reported job placements increased to 11,645, 31% more than the 11,296 placements reported during the first four months of Fiscal 1997. However, HR/Safety Net Placements decreased to 4,643 from the 6,114 placements reported during the first four months of Fiscal 1997 due to the 33.1 per cent decline in the HR population over the past three fiscal years. A total of 16, 288 public assistance (PA) recipients reported employment during the first four months of Fiscal 1998, a decrease of 6.4% from the first four months of Fiscal 1997, when 17, 410 recipients reported employment' (1998, 204).

Against the popular press's account of successful participation and the stark and clinical numbers from the Mayor's Office there is other evidence of a less robust participation rate. It seems that many welfare recipients either do not participate or simply go through the motions and shortly thereafter disappear from the program. It has been estimated, in fact, that up to 50 per cent of welfare recipients never show up at their first WEP orientation (Kelly Toughill, 'New York Says Workfare Works,' *Toronto Star*, 8 July 1996). WEP seems much like a revolving door. The New York City Parks Department, which has the largest workfare crew in the city, claims that roughly 15 per cent of its welfare workers drop out of the program every two weeks (Toughill, *Toronto Star*, 8 July 1996). Mead has noted this kind of institutional lethargy in many workfare sites including New York: 'The weaker programs are those, above all, that lack control. They have relatively few clients active, and many of those are in education activities often "self-initiated" that are poorly monitored and only remotely connected to work ... In New York, administrators can barely keep up with the recipients they are supposed to induct into the program weekly; monitoring those already on board to prevent drop outs or enforcing job search is out of the question. Staff feel that they are in a bunker, while hordes of recipients pour over the top' (1995, 44).

It is no wonder then, that at the end of the day, both administrators and welfare recipients simply enact a welfare reform illusion, merely going through the motions of the 'new and exciting' welfare innovations. This is the impression garnered by my research assistant. In his first visit to the Municipal Reference Library of the City of New York, my field researcher lost his way to Records and Information Services and found himself facing a small sign providing directions to the second floor of the building where a workfare orientation program for the celebrated 'Work Experience Program' was about to commence. Anxious to experience a WEP orientation meeting at first hand he proceeded to the second floor of the building, passing along the way many busy government workers. At the conference room where the orientation was to take place he encountered two uniformed security guards who kindly advised him that he had arrived at the orientation site. Something clearly important was taking place, because this was the only area inside the building that seemed to be manned by security personnel. Inside the conference room were about fifteen WEP trainees, many of whom were dozing. At the far end of the room was a single television set, the main training device for the session. The impression was one of absolute lethargy.

What had happened to the heralded New York City program? Had all of the energy been drained from the project? Where were the legions of workers ready to be trained and transformed into active workers? Where were the professionals charged with the responsibility of making all of this happen? The apparent success of New York's welfare-to-work program, with thousands upon thousands transferred off the welfare rolls, seemed at odds with the reality of the delivery of workfare. This impressionistic view is very much in line with what Mark Green, Public advocate for the city of New York, has to say about WEP: 'The city's centralized welfare bureaucracy continues to focus its administrative efforts on the speedy reduction of welfare rolls – not on placement of welfare recipients in new jobs. Almost uniformly, line workers and clients report that they are placed in adversarial, rather than supportive relationships. Work conditions are often poor and sometimes dangerous. Training is inadequate and rules are always changing. Staff report feeling demoralized by constant policy shifts and a lack of administrative support' (1997, 4). Welfare recipient participation in the so-called job centres also does not appear to be working. 'While the reconfigured welfare offices known as "job centers" now teach resume writing and interviewing skills, only 256 – or less than 5% – of the first 5,300 job search participants have found work' (Rachel Swarns, 'Welfare's "Job Centers" Bring High Hopes and Thin Results,' *New York Times*, 23 February 1999). Interviews with 'job centre' clients also support this dismal picture: '"All this is big noise about helping you find jobs, it's bull ... They don't get nobody no jobs. Where will that leave me?"' (Jamaican immigrant qtd. in Swarns, *New York Times*, 23 February 1999).

Are New York welfare recipients participating? While the flow-through numbers may be there, much of what is happening seems to be about going through the motions. The program exists, but the combination of the old culture and the sheer numbers of the clients means that few quality programs are delivered.

The Official Record: What Do the Evaluators Say?

Clearly the significant numbers of welfare recipients who dropped from the welfare rolls provide a one-sided and partial proof of WEP's success. To what extent is this drop directly attributable to WEP? Unfortunately, neither the Human Resources Administration (HRA) nor any other agency or group tracks dropped recipients. The drop in numbers of welfare recipients is always presented by the HRA as linked to the welfare-to-work initiative, so that in each of the mayor's management reports the drop is bundled into accounts of the welfare-to-work program. Implicit in this bundling of data is the belief that the program is working. As Vivian Toy wrote in 'Tough Workfare Rules Used as Way to Cut Welfare Rolls' (*New York Times*, 15 April 1998): 'By restoring the luster of the work ethic and providing a path to real jobs, Mayor Rudolph W. Giuliani often says that his workfare program has played a central part in the dramatic reduction of New York City's welfare rolls. The numbers he cites are stark and indisputable: the rolls have dropped more that 30 percent in the last three years, to 797,000 from 1.16 million.'

But is workfare really working? First, on the numbers issue alone, it appears that workfare has not been as successful as some constituencies would have us believe. Testimony from HRA Commissioner Lillian Barrios-Paoli suggests some degree of exaggeration in the numbers: 'Since April 1996, 150,000 AFDC recipients have been called in to participate in work-related activities, and 17,000 of the 38,000 individuals deemed employable have been placed in WEP assignments. Another 17,000 of the AFDC recipients assigned to work-related activities participate in a range of activities that include job clubs, language programs, and education programs' (Green 1997, 12). In other words, while more than 150,000 AFDC recipients were called into the program, only 17,000 actually found themselves placed in WEP assignments. On the important issue of what happens to welfare recipients after they leave the rolls, one survey, commissioned by the State Office of Temporary and Disability Assistance in 1997, paints quite a dismal picture, revealing that the vast majority of people who dropped off New York State's shrinking welfare rolls have not obtained legitimate jobs. This survey represents the first attempt to track statistically the fate of the

480,000 welfare recipients who have left the rolls across New York State (350,000 of them in New York City).

The survey found that of those who came off the welfare rolls in New York City from July 1996 through March 1997, only 29 per cent found full-time or part-time jobs in the first few months they were no longer on public assistance. Of the families in New York City who dropped off the rolls from July 1996 through September 1996, 32.7 per cent showed earnings in the next quarter. Of those who left the rolls from October through December 1996, 32.2 per cent showed wages in the next quarter. And of those who left the rolls from January through March 1997, 22.1 per cent showed wages in the next quarter. The results of this survey were generally interpreted as alarming and suggest that 'people were being knocked off the welfare rolls by a host of new sanctions and rules even though they had no prospect of employment' (Raymond Hernandez, 'Most Dropped from Welfare Don't Get Jobs,' *New York Times*, 23 March 1998). Moreover, Vivian Toy reports that 'At the same time, workfare – or, more precisely, the prospect of having to participate in workfare – has driven many people off welfare without finding jobs. To these people, it is more appealing to rely on off-the-books jobs, to move in with friends or relatives or to otherwise turn to others to get by, say city officials and advocates for the poor' (*New York Times*, 15 April 1998).

Ira Garfinkel, a professor at Columbia University's School of Social Work, has provided his own interpretation of the reality of New York's workfare initiative and the fate of former welfare recipients: 'My guess is that about one third of the people already had jobs and are managing fine without welfare ... Another third are getting jobs, which is the Mayor's story, and the other third can't get it together and the changes have made it impossible to function in the system, and that's the advocates' story' (Toy, *New York Times*, 15 April 1998).

Doubtless there are a variety of different explanations for the drop in the rolls. Joe Sexton, in 'Amid Anxiety, Glimpses of Hope' (*New York Times*, 4 January 1998) provides his own view on the reduction in the welfare rolls: 'Many people have found jobs, or are merely relying on jobs they already had. Those on Home Relief, too, have always been a very fluid population, moving on and off the rolls quickly. Thus as stricter standards for qualifying take hold, an inevitable shrinkage has occurred.'

The answer to the question of what happened to those who are no longer on welfare is unclear, however, due partly to inadequate tracking data, or poor data released for public consumption. Ira Garfinkel made a request to the Giuliani administration for the study of available data on former welfare recipients and was denied access to information. The *New York Times* requested similar access and was also refused information on former welfare recipients. The newspaper subsequently sued, and in April 1998 a State Supreme Court justice ordered the city to release the information, but the city is appealing this decision.

It has also been suggested that workfare contributes to what is referred to as a 'smoke-out effect.' Rather than preparing the unprepared for work, what WEP does is push people who are already working off the books. Because it is difficult to survive on welfare benefits alone, many recipients rely on other sources of undeclared income, and when the 'screws and rules' are tightened on benefit receipts, recipients simply terminate program involvement and rely exclusively on income from already established other sources. Tightening the screws encourages other 'smoke-out effect' responses: 'Many others have either gone out and found work or have turned to friends and relatives for help rather than deal with the stigma of welfare or a city bureaucracy that they believe to be hostile ... Not only has the Giuliani administration's welfare message pushed large numbers of people off the welfare rolls ... the strong economy has allowed some of those who have left welfare to either find work or rely on acquaintances who have benefited from the good times' (Toy, *New York Times*, 15 April 1998).

A tightening-up of eligibility criteria has definitely contributed to the drop in rolls. For example, when finger-imaging was introduced by Mayor Giuliani in 1995, more than twelve thousand people failed to show up for the procedure, saving the city millions of dollars. Some city officials claimed that welfare fraud was also being controlled and spoke of people who showed up for finger-imaging with glue over their hands or an arm strapped behind their back, pretending to be an amputee. The new eligibility checks also found people falsely claming to be disabled: 'One office forgot to clearly mark the disabled entrance to its building. Outside, city social workers discovered people carrying their wheelchairs up the front steps to their appointments' (Toughill, *Toronto Star*, 8 July 1996).

It also appears that the aggressive application of sanctions against those not fully participating in the workfare program is at least partly responsible for the drop in numbers of welfare recipients. An expanded workfare sanctions program, introduced by Mayor Giuliani in 1995, penalizes workfare participants by removing them from welfare benefits for a variety of infractions related to less than full participation in the program. Demetra Smith Nightingale, director of welfare research at the Urban Institute in Washington, has suggested that 'caseworkers are using sanctions more than they used to because time limits mean that there's now more at stake if they don't get people into the job market' (Toy, *New York Times*, 15 April 1998). The numbers associated with sanction-based drops from the welfare rolls are not insignificant and appear to explain much of the magical drop in the welfare rolls. In 1997, for example, about 16 per cent of workfare participants were cut from the rolls for infractions that ranged from showing up late to refusing a work assignment (Toy, *New York Times*, 15 April 1998). As Marc Cohan of the Center on Social Welfare Policy claims: 'Welfare reforms in New York City are not designed to move people from welfare to work' (qtd. in Toughill, *Toronto Star*, 8 July 1996). Given the absence of comprehensive evaluation data, it is not clear whether the drop in numbers of welfare recipients is attributable to WEP or to other factors such as the robust economy and low unemployment rate, to tough new sanctions that remove recipients from workfare activities, or simply to the fact that welfare is now simply harder to get in the first place.

The passage of Clinton's Personal Responsibility and Work Opportunity Reconciliation Act (PRA) of 1996 has had its own impact on New York's workfare program. PRA mandates a lifetime five-year cap on welfare benefit receipt and increases work requirements for recipients each year of the five (PRA Act of 1996, H.R. 3734, Title IV, Subtitle B, Section 405:1 [A]). HRA Commissioner Lillian Barrios-Paoli estimates that nearly 40 per cent of New York City's AFDC population, about two hundred thousand people, will have to move into work-related activities very soon (according to the terms of the PRA, 50 per cent of the city's public assistance caseload must be working or engaged in work-related activities by 2002) (Green 1997, 13).

The city of New York's progress in moving recipients from welfare to work is measured by participation rates in a variety of work and work-related activities (including direct work experience, job search, community service, and unsubsidized employment). Should the city fail to meet these targets, it incurs financial penalties. The specified participation rates are significant; in 1998, 30 per cent of all Temporary Assistance to Needy Families (TANF) recipients had to participate in a work activity, with the rate increasing by 5 per cent for each year until the year 2002, when it reaches 50 per cent. A further important feature of the federal law relates to the employability clause. In the past, only recipients who were deemed employable were included in the participation calculation. Now, all TANF recipients are subject to participation calculations. These added pressures for increased participation will mean that an already stretched workfare system will be processing even more WEP participants, further encouraging the revolving-door syndrome. Some have even suggested that the rigorous job search requirements and emphasis on alternatives to welfare is simply designed to discourage the poor from completing the application process (Swarns, *New York Times*, 23 February 1999). It is worth pointing out that the drop in numbers also has something to do with the front end of entry. It is not just that a variety of programs have been introduced to get people off the rolls, it is also much harder for people to get on welfare in the first place.

A problem with all good ideas is that they are blanket ideas. Their appeal lies in their simplicity, expressed in one-dimensional or narrow policy planks. The world is more complex than that. Deirdre Hussey, in 'Welfare Quotas: Is Workfare the Only Way?' (*Village Voice*, 31 December 1996), refers to this as 'a clear cookie-cutter mentality.' She claims that the thrust of New York's welfare reform is to push most recipients into WEP, restricting entry into education, job training, or job search to the very few. She believes that the HRA is concerned only with meeting the workfare participation quotas established by the 1996 welfare reform legislation. Mark Cohan, of the Center on Social Welfare Policy, concurs and believes that, despite requirements that HRA prepare an employability plan that reflects the recipients' work and training preferences, the plan is rarely designed to move the welfare participant to long-term economic self-sufficiency and rarely reflects their preferences (Hussey, *Village Voice*, 31 December 1996).

Another problem with good ideas is that they tend to get in the way of other good ideas. This is a problem of policy proliferation where we get a number of programs that aim to accomplish a variety of similar goals, but which are not co-ordinated. Program conflict can take place both within a particular jurisdiction and between different jurisdictions. Take, for example, the following example, which highlights program conflict between federal and city programs:

At age 61, Chin had been enrolled in a federal program, Title IV, which provided job training for older unemployed workers. Then he was called to report to WEP. Chin says that at the interview 'they said that under the new law the state and the city say Title IV is not a training program – it's a part-time job. So they counted that as income and took away my rent supplement.

So I was forced back onto Public Assistance. And now I'm a WEP worker.' (Holmes and Ettinger 1997, 27–8)

There is also the problem of competition between policy-makers, wherein policies in overlapping jurisdictions compete with each other for attention, or sometimes simply conflict with each other. A good idea from one jurisdiction may not be interpreted as such by other jurisdictions simply because it deflects attention from home-based policies. This rivalry between jurisdictions seems to manifest itself in the city of New York. As Green notes: 'While CAP (Child Assistance Program, initiated by the New York State Department of Social Services) has enjoyed success in other parts of New York, bureaucratic resistance has prevented it from getting off the ground in New York City. Recent estimates suggest that there were only 130 New York City families in the CAP program – out of 10,000 potentially eligible AFDC households assigned to the three participating income support centres. Advocates and public officials argue that HRA's refusal to devote resources to CAP that would ensure its success has sabotaged the pilot project' (Green 1997, 6).

The problem of competing jurisdictions is not just limited to the loss of potential benefits from the programs of rival jurisdictions. Such competition also impedes the capacity to learn from different workforce experiences, as each jurisdiction must deny the benefits of the others' programs while trumping up its own. In the case of WEP, more intensive job counselling and one-on-one contact over an extended period may have enhanced the program. It might appear that this is a simple problem of implementation, but the co-ordination of different programs involves more rules and regulations, and more such exceptions. Co-ordination thus unleashes its own series of problems. Policy-makers are caught between a rock and a hard place, with no easy way out. The good idea of work experience is thus replaced with the goal of dropping people off the welfare rolls. Whether or not they have left the rolls because of job experience is less important than the fact that they have left the rolls.

It would seem desirable for all programs to have a reliable system of evaluation and accountability in place. Without such a system there is no way of knowing what kind of progress participants are making and what kinds of adjustments are needed to make the program more effective. On the other hand, formalized evaluation systems create the opportunity for gamesmanship and impression management through the manipulation of numbers. New York City is a classic case of goal displacement, where efforts are directed to reducing welfare numbers or fulfilling evaluation goals as opposed to getting people gainful employment. In the case of WEP, little formalized evaluation was built into the process, since the numbers dropping off welfare served to validate the program. But the real success of workfare is always open to doubt. Green's assessment of the system makes this clear: 'there is virtually no accountability built into the system. City officials are unable to provide actual data on the number of welfare recipients who have been successfully placed by the City's welfare-to-work program into the private sector, the average length of employment in those positions, and their wages' (1997, 4–5).

Politics also seemed to derail New York's workfare program. By declaring war on welfare just as he had on crime, Mayor Giuliani raised the welfare stakes to such a high level that his program simply *had* to work. The political dimension of workfare was evidenced in the name-changing (from 'caseworkers' to 'financial planners'; from 'welfare offices' to 'job centres') and the extent to which the Mayor's Office sought to distance itself from the standard vocabulary of welfare. Changing the words was 'meant to carry a politically potent message to voters who will never step into a welfare office but whose discontent with the status quo helped propel an overhaul in welfare policy' (Swarns, *New York Times*, 5 July 1998). As Swarns suggests, 'the words underscore the desires of politicians and officialdom to project a perception of change – even if little actually changes – as they try to curry favor with the electorate.' Robert C. Lieberman, assistant professor of politics and public policy at Columbia University advances the view that 'the name of programs is directed more at voters, certainly on the part of the elected, who are choosing the way they want their policies to be read ... (i)t's a shrewd kind of a move ... (w)ho can be against personal responsibility or family independence or temporary assistance or any of these things?' (Swarns, *New York Times*, 5 July 1998). While name-changing may actually be an important symbolic process in welfare reform, it can also serve to truncate change by creating an illusion that change has already occurred. The simple name change is convenient for politicians, beaming out a message to constituents that the problem has been tackled. It also works for administrators, who might feel that they don't need to go through the tough and laborious process of making real and substantial changes to routines and delivery systems because of the name change. This view seems to be borne out in a draft memo included in a training manual for 'financial planners' describing 'employment as a "secondary goal" at the job centres. The "primary goal" ... is discouraging the poor from applying for public assistance' (Swarns, *New York Times*, 5 July 1998).

From a political point of view, evaluation relates to how many people are coming off the welfare rolls, not how many are being retrained or finding meaningful work. Transition to work thus becomes less important than the transfer of recipients off the rolls, whether it be to work or other forms of assistance. Some welfare recipients are simply transferred to other income support programs: 'financial planners help clients explore "alternatives for independence," telling mothers to seek child support, urging former soldiers to apply for veterans benefits, requiring laid-off workers to file for unemployment benefits and assessing whether relatives or churches can help them' (Swarns, Stiff Rules Cut Welfare Rolls at Two Offices,' *New York Times*, 22 June 1998). This can be likened to a kind of musical chairs of income support.

Did the Public Play a Role?

Mayor Giuliani also had to deal with fierce and determined anti-workfare groups. For example in 1994, a coalition of sixty-eight churches, synagogues, and non-profit groups refused to hire welfare recipients under the workfare program. The coalition said it wanted to use its moral stature to press New York City to treat its workfare employees with greater dignity and pay them far more than they received under workfare. As Greenhouse reports in 'Nonprofit and Religious Groups Vow to Fight Workfare Program' (*New York Times*, 24 July 1994): 'Beside a sign saying "Rudy, We Will Not Be Your Slave Drivers," several clergy members and leaders of nonprofit groups said at a news conference yesterday that they would fight the program by refusing to take any workfare employees, at a time when the city hopes to place thousands of such workers with nonprofit agencies.' Apart from the accusations of 'slavery' by this coalition (Workfairness, ACORN, municipal unions, and others), the central attack on workfare has focused on the issue of 'diplacement,' that is, the practice of sending people out, ostensibly for training, to do unpaid work that was once done by regular employees (who have been laid off or had their own hours shortened).

Over 40 per cent of WEP participants are placed with the city's Parks and Sanitation departments, and many of them are charged with the responsibility of sweeping the streets and cleaning the city's parks (Hussey, *Village Voice*, 31 December 1996). While menial and manual, these jobs cannot be classified as make-work projects. Shelley Eitinger, in 'We Demand Union Rights' (*Workers' World*, 28 November 1996), describes one of the early Workfairness rallies:

> The noontime rally was organized by Workfairness, a young organization that is growing by leaps and bounds. It is made up of people ordered into the Work Experience Program – to work at forced labor in order to keep getting their paltry grants.
> WEP workers labor alongside unionized workers in vital city jobs. But they get neither the pay nor the benefits provided in the union contracts,
> The city gets that same work from WEP workers for a fraction of the cost. The result is not only super-exploitation of the WEP workers, but a steady undermining of the city unions.

Several workers, who were being paid the $4.75 hourly minimum, decided to sue the city, claiming that they were entitled to the same pay and benefits as unionized city workers, who could make up to $10 an hour; a state appeals court unanimously rejected their argument and ruled that New York City could pay its tens of thousands of workfare employees less than regular city workers who do the same or similar jobs ('New York Workfare Jobs Can Pay Less, Count Rules,' *Los Angeles Times*, 19 September 1998). It would appear, however, that in many cases WEP workers have come to displace city unionized labour. Writing in the *New York Times* of 13 April 1998, Steven Greenhouse claims in his article 'Many Participants in Workfare Take the Place of City Workers' that workfare participants, by feeding hospital patients, painting park benches, and translating at welfare centres, have quietly become an important, but unofficial, part of New York City's municipal workforce: 'Workfare participants and welfare experts say many New Yorkers fail to understand a significant fact about the program: the 34,100 people in the city's Work Experience Program constitute a low cost labor force that does a substantial amount of the work that had been done by municipal employees before Mayor Giuliani reduced the city payroll by about 20,000 employees or about 10 percent.

Some union leaders contend that the Work Experience Program violates a state law that prohibits public employers from replacing regular workers with workfare participants. District Council 37 sued the Giuliani administration, charging that it violates state law by using thousands of workfare recipients to do jobs in parks that were once done by city workers (Greenhouse, 'Union to Sue Giuliani Administration,' *New York Times*, 4 February 1999). Mayor Giuliani did agree to hire twenty-seven additional carpenters and painters to settle the lawsuit that accused his government of using workfare participants to replace city employees, but the city did not admit wrongdoing in settling the lawsuit (Greenhouse, in Metro Briefing, *New York Times*, 9 June 2000).

What Happened to the Good Idea?

Just as there are many things that make up a good idea, there are many things that can derail a good idea. In the case of New York's workfare program, workfare's alleged success was not attributable to the program itself, but rather to sanctions and other extra-policy factors, such as the state of the labour market. The numbers game also fit neatly with the political agenda: as long as the city could claim that the welfare numbers were dropping, then it could claim workfare to be a success. The numbers were the perfect political tool, as they could be easily managed. What happened to people when they went off welfare doesn't really matter. What matters is that they are no longer on the rolls.

It must be concluded that workfare in New York was at best only a partial success. The goals of workfare were simply too grand, and the demands of reality too great, for any one policy to wrestle down. It was simply too much to expect that a few training courses, a few months of work experience, most of which was located in low-status, organizationally isolated positions, would somehow transform individuals into ready and motivated workers. Without adequate reports on those who left welfare after workfare, it might be said that workfare provided a satisfactory reason to pull the safety net from under those unable or unwilling to engage in productive work.

7.

'Learnfare' in New Brunswick – Tune In, Turn On, Drop Out

Summary

NB Works was a voluntary 'learnfare' program aimed at single parents (overwhelmingly female) on welfare. The program was based on the assumption that the main reason why single mothers remain on welfare is that they do not have the necessary education to obtain a successful career. Those single mothers on welfare who were selected to participate in NB Works would be financially supported while they completed high school equivalency and then acquired a marketable skill at a community college (this supported education could last up to three and a half years). This good idea was meant to allow the single mother a career, not just a low-paid job. NB Works was designed to accept three intakes of approximately one thousand women per year, in three consecutive years (1992, 1993, and 1994, with the last intake meant to graduate in 1997–8). The more than two-thirds drop-out rate (most dropped out prior to completing the first step, that is, obtaining high school equivalency) from this expensive program seems to suggest that those who signed up for learnfare did not, in fact, share the aspirations held for them by the politicians and bureaucrats. NB Works wound down in 1997, three years after the last intake group had been enrolled. Formal evaluations carried out on NB Works do not admit that it was a disaster, despite the extraordinary drop-out rate. The word 'success' features prominently in the mainly process-related evaluations, yet there is little, if any, evidence of anyone having moved from welfare to work thanks to NB Works. What remains most impressive about NB Works is that the province of New Brunswick managed to get the federal government to pay for this hugely expensive program (estimated to cost between fifty-nine thousand and one hundred thousand dollars per participant).

New Brunswick's Good Idea: Background and Context of the Reform

One man is known for having brought about welfare reform in the province of New Brunswick. His name is Frank McKenna. In 1987, Frank McKenna had his first electoral victory win as premier of New Brunswick. His Liberal Party swept all fifty-eight seats in the legislature. When he resigned as premier, on 13 October 1997, at the age of forty-nine, a number of media reports speculated that he wished be the next prime minister of Canada. As he cleaned out his desk, he told reporters that he was uncertain as to what he would do next, but that he had not ruled out federal politics. Picking through piles of papers and mementos, the man who once wanted to be a professional hockey player showed the journalists the prized possessions that he would be keeping: hockey pucks from encounters with the stars of Canada's national winter game, prized brass baseballs from the Toronto Blue Jays, and a ceramic Holstein (Canadian Press, *Globe and Mail*, 14 October 1997).

The province of New Brunswick is located in Eastern Canada. Of Canada's four Atlantic provinces, New Brunswick is located closest to the mainland, bordered by Quebec to the north, Nova Scotia to the south, and the state of Maine to the west. The population of New Brunswick is roughly 725,000. It is Canada's only officially bilingual province, with approximately 35 per cent of the population French-speaking. New Brunswick is generally known as one of Canada's poorest provinces; a participant in the provincial report entitled *Creating New Options* (1994) remarked: 'There are more soup kitchens in the province than there are McDonalds restaurants' (17). Unemployment seems to remain permanently stuck at very high levels (approximately 10 per cent) and large numbers of the well educated have moved away to find work. The welfare rate is one of the highest in the country. In 1995–6, during the lifetime of NB Works, the caseload was 34,953, representing 66,035 people on welfare (NB Works 1995–6). There has been an increasing proportion of the population receiving social assistance, moving from 8.5 per cent in 1975–6 to 10 per cent in 1996 (Milne 1996).

When Frank McKenna and his Liberals won their sweeping victory in 1987, (having beaten the two other main political parties, the Progressive Conservatives and the New Democrats), they were facing a declining economy and increasing welfare caseloads. In his two terms as premier, McKenna managed to improve the negative image of the province. Soon after his election victory he hired an American image consultant, who helped him to develop ideas to convince investors to do business in New Brunswick. He sold them the rural quality of life, the bilingual workforce, access to the eastern and European seaboards, low taxes, low wages, and low telecommunication costs (Mullaly 1997, 47). Ministry of Tourism brochures cite the province's traditional re-sources as forest products, mining, manufacturing, agriculture, fishing, and tourism. Expanding industries are considered to be in the areas of energy, telecommunications, environmental engineering services, high technology, value-added forest products, software development, and aquaculture. Still, unemployment hovered between 10 and 13 per cent.

Thanks to excellent public relations, during his time as premier, the name Frank McKenna was being heard all over Canada: 'Part of the image-building included McKenna himself. He is presented as a no-nonsense, hands-on, hard-working and business-friendly premier who is obsessed with economic development. Through his cross country tours and frequent news releases he preaches the gospel of self-suffi-ciency, deficit-reduction and the need to get the province's financial house in order. He has been the subject of many feature articles in national magazines and newspapers across the country in which he is sometimes hailed as the likely successor to (Prime Minister) Jean Chrétien' (Mullaly 1997, 48).

McKenna's interest in social reform was very much consistent with his economic principles. Soon after taking over, his government set about making a number of administrative improvements to increase efficiency in a number of areas of government (with the help of the internationally renowned firm of Andersen Consulting). He asked the Department of Human Resource Development (then called Depart-ment of Income Assistance) to begin to work to develop a strategic plan, over the next five years, that would improve New Brunswick's image of a province that was dependent on federal government hand-outs for its survival.

McKenna constantly spoke of his vision of self-sufficiency for the province and for its people. An advocate of human-capital investment, McKenna believed that the large increase in the number of able-bodied people on the welfare rolls that the province was experiencing was directly related to the claimants' lack of education or inadequate job preparation. His philosophy is illustrated in the following statement: 'I have an absolutely dominating belief that in this chicken-and-egg co-nundrum of whether you should have jobs or training first, the answer is that you need training first. If you have the training, the jobs will take care of themselves' (McKenna, qtd. in Swift 1995, 131).

Central to McKenna's vision was the principle that able-bodied individuals should use their time on income support as an opportunity to work toward self-sufficiency, through access to education, training, and work experience. A joint cost-sharing agreement between the federal government of Canada and the province of New Brunswick (first signed in 1987 and extended in 1992) gave New Brunswick policy-makers the financial flexibility to design and implement three large-scale experiments in welfare reform: (1) NB Works (voluntary learnfare/workfare), (2) the Self-Sufficiency Project (time-limited earnings supplement lower taxback rate); and (3) the NB Job Corps (for displaced older workers aged fifty to sixty-five). Each of these three ideas was based on the assumption that there should be greater participation by welfare recipients in education, training, or work.

The best known of the three programs and the one that grabbed the attention of the nation was a voluntary welfare-to-work learnfare program, entitled NB Works. According to administrators, the idea of NB Works originated in discussions between an American consulting firm, key ministers, and management staff. These discussions concluded that the provincial government of New Brunswick was experienced at determining welfare eligibility and dispensing welfare cheques, but that it had limited experience devising ways to help recipients get off welfare. Frank McKenna wanted the government to play a more active role in helping individuals on welfare to obtain the skills they needed to find and maintain a permanent job. McKenna's stated long-term strategy was to use the newly trained workforce from NB Works to attract business to the province. McKenna apparently wanted to make the program mandatory, but the federal government, which was footing most of the bill, was not interested in such an arrangement.

The official reasons given to justify NB Works were, first, the sharp growth in the number of people receiving social assistance in New Brunswick, and second, the perception that existing government training programs were fragmented, too short to be effective (maximum of fifty-two weeks), poorly linked to other programs (Baseline/Norpack Evaluation Consortium 1995). It was in 1992 that New Brunswick introduced NB Works, a six-year national demonstration project (1992–8) that was funded and managed jointly by the federal and provincial governments, with the province in charge of its delivery. The program was designed to receive its first intake of one thousand social assistance recipients (mostly single mothers) in 1992. Participants would take part in an intensive program of education and skills upgrading. Another thousand participants were to be recruited in the spring of 1993, and then again in 1994. It would take participants in each of the three intake groups approximately three and a half years (forty-two months) to go from intake to completion. Over that period they would participate in a two-week orientation, a twenty-week job placement that qualified them for federal training money, two years of high school completion, summer internships, and one year of specialized skills training at a community college.

Some might claim that NB Works doesn't fit the definition of workfare. One such is Elaine Campbell (personal interview, 1 October 1999), an evaluation consultant with the New Brunswick Department of Human Resources: 'I don't consider NB Works to be workfare since receipt of benefits was not contingent upon participation, benefits were not withheld from persons who chose not to participate, nor were they withheld from eligible persons who dropped out of the program.' Others might say that the program would only fit the very broadest definition of workfare, in that it is voluntary. Still others, like Robert Mullaly, a New Brunswick professor of social policy, claim that NB Works does fit the definition of workfare, in that 'workfare simply means engaging in work or work-related activities (including training) in exchange for one's welfare' (Mullaly 1997, 37). In my opinion, NB Works is a voluntary learnfare program that fits a very broad definition of workfare.

Why was NB Works considered to be so innovative? One reason was the program's claim to remove barriers to work participation and training by making sure that child-care and other work-related expenses were paid for. Another unique feature was that New Brunswick managed to shift the cost of training and support for participants to the federal government, for a full three years. Apart from its innovative approach to welfare recipient unemployment, the program had a very high price tag, although opinions about the cost vary. William Milne, an economics professor at the University of New Brunswick, explains why the cost was so high: 'NB Works is very expensive. In gross terms, the project was budgeted to cost $177 million over its six year life span. If a total of 3,000 participated, that would mean a cost of $59,000 per participant. However, this assumes all participants successfully complete the program, which will not be the case ... Attrition has the effect of increasing the cost per successful participant ... Thus the cost per participant rises to the vicinity of $100,000' (Milne 1996, 75).

Patricia Evans, a professor in the School of Social Work at York University for example, also mentions the program's high price tag: 'New Brunswick Works is an employability enhancement program that has attracted wide publicity. With an estimated price tag of $100,000 per participant, it may also be the most expensive. It begins with an individualized case plan, followed by 20 weeks of job placement. Costs then shift because the participant becomes eligible for 156 weeks of training under the UI program (federal unemployment insurance), which could include educational upgrading, job search skills or specialized training, skills and employment counselling and subsidized job placement' (Evans 1995, 92–3).

While Evans estimates the cost at a hundred thousand dollars per participant, the government claims that up to fifty-nine thousand dollars was spent on each participant. According to Tom Blackwell, in '500,000 Welfare Recipients Brace for Ontario Workfare,' published in the *Ottawa Citizen*, 19 March 1996, 'The government says the voluntary program is successful but expensive, and can only handle limited numbers of participants.' The high cost of the six-year (1992–8) program has been one of the main criticisms aimed at NB Works.

The other main criticism of NB Works is its high drop-out rate. By the time that the first intake of one thousand was expected to be graduating from NB Works, more than two-thirds of participants had already dropped out (Mullaly 1997). The majority of participants – both those who completed the program and those who quit – returned to social assistance (NB Works 1995–6). While the subsequent annual intakes had a lower drop-out rate at that same evaluation time, they soon caught up in drop-out levels, and those who quit did not do so to begin work (see participants' reactions at the end of the section Did Welfare Recipients Participate?). The program was basically an expensive failure. Did Frank McKenna really have a good idea when he decided to provide thousands of welfare workers with free education, training, child care, and support services for three and a half years, in a province in which there were already so many well-educated unemployed? It would appear not. In any event, he resigned in 1997, the year before the last intake was to graduate. As of 2001, the government has not released a clear picture of how many participants actually completed the program and how many found long-term employment.

How Was the Program Designed?

The policy-makers responsible for NB Works designed a 'continuum of programs and services' of up to three and a half years' duration that were geared to helping selected participants obtain the skills required to reach 'their personal career goals' (NB Works, 1995–6). Policy-makers faced a number of design challenges. The fact that the NB Works agreement was signed in 1992 and had to be put into operation that same year meant that the project had to be designed and implemented more or less at the same time. The need to implement NB Works relatively quickly led to a number of design problems that caused confusion and inconsistency in administration, not least of which was the absence of a NB Works policy and procedures manual (finally completed in 1994, the year of Intake 3). 'Improvements' to the design of the program were made every year. One such was the decision to select more highly educated participants each year, in an effort to achieve higher retention rates. Another was the provision of a short-term computer course for those discouraged participants who could not complete the high school equivalency (presumably so that they could 'graduate' from something and officially 'complete' NB Works).

Despite the design experimentation that was taking place in policy-making, a Communications Committee for NB Works was established right from the start and a high profile was given to the program in the news media and in government flyers and brochures. The formal stated objectives of NB Works were as follows: (1) To develop the human resource and employment potential of the social assistance recipient caseload, to achieve the goal of a more educated, better trained workforce; (2) To begin to change the attitude that may exist that income assistance is an end in itself, to the attitude that people can increase their employability and job-ready status; (3) To save social assistance costs through the movement of people from the caseload to the workforce.

Every program operates with some theoretical notion of cause and effect. In the case of NB Works, the theory underlying the program was simple. If New Brunswick welfare recipients only had the education and the skills, they would move into long-term employment. This theory of action did not prove to be effective in the case of New Brunswick.

The budget for NB Works was $177 million for a six-year (1992–8) demonstration project geared at three intakes of one thousand participants each in 1992, 1993, and 1994. Because of the high drop-out rate, more participants were added to the third intake, in the spring of 1995. These were the last intakes in the NB Works program. NB Works was managed by three joint federal-provincial committees made up of representatives from the federal Human Resources Development Canada (HRDC), the provincial Department of Advanced Education and Labour (DAEL), and the Department of Income Assistance (this department changed its name in 1994 to Human Resource Development New Brunswick [HRDNB]). Responsibility for the administration of NB Works lay with HRDNB. NB Works was a voluntary program. After completing an achievement test and attending an assessment meeting, the welfare recipient who was accepted into NB Works was expected to take part in the following program stages, according to a government brochure entitled *NB Works* (undated):

(1) Two-Week Orientation: Orientation sessions were contracted out to various institutions and agencies (e.g., Memramcook Institute), although staff from the provincial departments of Human Resource Development and Advanced Education and Labour and the federal department of Human Resources Development Canada were also involved in presenting information to participants. Orientation was devoted to group motivation counselling and the development of individual case plans. Each participant was assigned a case manager. Regular social assistance was received by the participant during this time.

(2) Work Placement: The primary responsibility for developing worksite placements rested with the provincial department of Advanced Education and Labour. In some cases, career counsellors and case managers were also involved in seeking appropriate placements. The initial work placement was of twenty weeks' (five months') duration and, during the placement, the province reimbursed the employer up to $6.25 per hour plus the employer's share of benefits (except Workers Compensation). The NB Works participant was provided with free child care, a clothing allowance, and a health card. After twenty weeks of work, the participant was eligible for years of federal Unemployment Insurance, which allowed participation in the next phases of NB Works.

(3) Academic Upgrading: Nine months of academic upgrading were provided, involving classroom study toward an academic high school diploma. The primary responsibility for delivery of academic-upgrading

programs rested with the provincial department of Advanced Education and Labour, which also made alternative programs for those who could not proceed through their academic upgrading phase at the expected pace.

(4) *Summer Internship*: A host employer provided work experience and training according to the welfare recipient's career goal. No wages were paid since the welfare recipient received unemployment insurance while working.

(5) *Academic Upgrading*: A further nine months of classroom study was provided for the participant to attain an academic high school diploma. The time spent on educational upgrading varied, depending upon the participant's educational attainment and rate of progress.

(6) *Skills Training*: One year of specialized skills training was provided at a community college. Upon completion of the skills development phase it was expected that participants would enter the labour force.

If, however, the participant was unsuccessful in finding work after completing the six phases of NB Works, there were still a number of other provincial government programs available. For example, a program called Partners provided an optional eight-month (maximum) assistance phase for those who could not find work after completing their program at a community college. But this program was available only to those who completed NB Works. Due to the high drop-out rate of NB Works participants, not many would have been streamed into the Partners program.

Administrative Challenges: Making Workfare Work

Drawing from conversations with program personnel and documents such as the NB Works 1995–6 *Annual Report* and the Baseline/Norpack *NB Works Process Evaluation Year-End Report* (23 June 1995), I have tried to identify the major obstacles in implementing NB Works. First of all, the signing of the NB Works agreement in 1992 and its speedy introduction in the same year created some difficulties for program personnel, not least of which was the lack of a formal policy and procedures manual (which staff finally cobbled together in 1994). Another problem caused by the rush to implement NB Works was that the management information system (MIS) was not ready in time. Those who developed the MIS did so incrementally, releasing modules onto the desks of untrained staff as they became ready.

Good ideas are invariably rushed into implementation. Because they promise so much and provide an instant solution, good ideas are often ushered in before their time. And because good ideas are linked to political platforms and careers, extra pressure is placed on them for early and swift implementation.

Administrators also report that the recruitment, selection, and orientation of the first participant intake was done too quickly, without enough emphasis being placed on the criterion of participants' likelihood of success (in subsequent intakes, administrative staff assigned greater importance to this factor). Also, the orientation sessions apparently misled participants, who thought that the first five months of their work placement would take place in jobs related to their career choices – when, in fact, the purpose was to get them into *any* work for five months, in order to qualify for federal training money. Intake participants often had little choice in this first placement. Since the government had secured only a limited range of jobs (for the short time period required to qualify recipients for federal Unemployment Insurance and move them off the province's caseload), participants found themselves assigned to tasks involving manual labour such as cutting brush, to the displeasure of many. (It is worth noting that some Intake 1 participants 'liked' or even 'loved' cutting brush, especially those with rural backgrounds [McFarland and Mullaly 1996].) The distribution for Intake 2 was far more varied. According to Elaine Campbell, an NB Works evaluation consultant, 36 per cent worked for the Department of Education, 29 per cent worked for NB Power, 17 per cent worked for non-profit organizations, 15 per cent worked for the Department of Natural Resources, and 3 per cent worked for other government departments. There was no skills training before taking on these five-month-long jobs. But five months of paid training in these industries surely increased welfare recipients' employability and demonstrated that they already had the necessary skills for some types of work. One has to wonder if they really needed three more years of education and training at the government's expense.

A number of staff changes occurred as a result of the new program, and new staff had to learn not only new practices and procedures, but also how to work together. Case managers and other staff involved with NB Works complained of overwork during the three intakes, claiming always to be in a catch-up position. Some important positions remained unfilled. For example, the most difficult position to fill was that of career consultant, and it was often vacant. While there was no trouble finding instructors for all the new courses that were being offered with federal and provincial dollars, many regions were without career consultants for months on end. Career consultants play a crucial role in welfare-to-work programs, and it is odd that a greater effort was not made to fill these positions. Bureaucrats usually have much experience with training and instructors and are often less familiar with (or possibly interested in) the essential role of job placement. This lack of attention to the need for career consultants shows how hard it is to transform bureaucracies.

In addition to the problems engendered by the need to implement the NB Works program quickly, administrators faced the challenge of standardizing its delivery of services on a regional basis. With different regions to serve, regional variations became apparent in both the delivery of services and in the availability of education, training, and job opportunities. For example, the skills training part of the program, which was mostly offered through the community college system, was limited to the period from September to June. This meant that participants were constrained by course schedules. New Brunswick's specialized campus system also meant that some courses were offered at certain locations only, and many participants were unable or unwilling to move.

Finally, staff expressed frustration at having to operate within the framework of the federal government's Unemployment Insurance legislation. For instance, although federal cheques were distributed every two weeks, welfare recipients were used to receiving their cheques on a monthly basis. Staff indicated that this caused constant money management problems with each intake group. Another problem with operating within federal guidelines was the province's requirement to conform to the three-year time limit (maximum federal training pay-out time). It soon became apparent to NB Works staff that three years was not sufficient time for many participants to complete their academic high school upgrading (let alone their community college skills training). Those who did finish high school over three years found that they had run out of time before the skills acquisition stage had even begun.

In the last few years of NB Works: as it became painfully obvious that learnfare was not working, welfare policy staff seemed to lose interest in the project. Administrators interviewed in 1997 claimed to be 'bored' with NB Works, 'that's in the past ... but we have a *new* welfare-to-work program that's going to be called Jobs Plus.' An evaluation consultant interviewed in October 1997 remarked: 'I'm bored with NB Works. Everybody's bored with NB Works around here. Nobody wants to talk about it.' Before NB Works had even completed its full life-cycle (while the one thousand participants from the last intake were meant to be completing their third successful year and nearing graduation), papers and file covers on desks revealed that the new good idea, an extension of NB Works called Jobs Plus, was the order of the day. Nobody even wanted to *talk* about NB Works any more.

Did Welfare Recipients Participate?

NB Works was a voluntary program. The target population for NB Works were those persons who had been in receipt of social assistance for at least six months; were entitled to higher ranges of income support (e.g., single mothers and two-parent families); had less than a grade 12 education but at least grade 7 (this was later changed to grade 9); had little or no labour-force attachment; and were assessed as having the greatest potential for success in the program. According to project personnel, the province decided to target single parents and two-parent families because 'they were a more expensive group than the single employables.' More than 80 per cent of NB Works participants were single mothers. Eventually, as the extraordinarily high drop-out rate of Intake 1 became evident to the bureaucrats, selection procedures were changed to admit only applicants with at least a grade 9 education and to apply a more rigorous screening for those with the greatest potential.

The primary responsibility for recruitment and selection of participants rested with Human Resource Development New Brunswick (HRDNB). Recruitment of candidates took place from computerized lists. Case managers reviewed lists of welfare recipients who met the NB Works selection criteria and, by means of a letter or telephone call, established contact with the potential participants. Based on interviews and assessments, case managers selected as participants those they thought most likely to succeed in the program.

So, what happened to these participants? In large part, they either quit outright or took much longer to complete the phases of the program than anticipated (other programs, such as the Training and Development Fund and HRDNB, assumed the expenses of participants whose NB Works training allowances had expired before they completed their

TABLE 7.1
Summary of Project Enrolment and Exits

	Intake 1 (May 92)	Intake 2 (May 93)	Intake 3 (March–June 94)
Total enrolments	1,030	959	807
Enrolments as of 2/6/95	318	531	685
Exits to date	712	418	122
Retention rate to date	31%	55%	85%
Months from intake	31	20	10

Source: HRDNB, March 1995

skills training). If we add up the time from the assessment interview, including the two-week orientation period, the five months of work experience, and the three years of education and/or skills training, the total comes to approximately three and a half years, or forty-two months. According to the Baseline/Norpack report, most drop-outs took place during the period of study for high school equivalency: 'The project participant is most likely to encounter problems at the academic upgrading stage and, if the decision to exit is made, it is most likely to occur during academic upgrading' Baseline/Norpack (1995, 76).

It is extremely difficult to extract data from the government figures for those who dropped out of NB Works and those who completed the planned educational/skills continuum. The tracking system, or possibly the reporting system, obfuscates these data. In March 1995, for example, HRDNB provided the summary of project enrolments and exits (Table 7.1), revealing that, at thirty-one months into the forty-two-month-long program, only 31 per cent of the 1,030 participants from Intake 1 were still in the program. The tracking of exits by staff from HRDNB shows that the overall rate of exits declined for each subsequent intake. But these last figures must be regarded as inconclusive, having been taken so early into the intakes.

Administrative staff, observing the high number of drop-outs right from the earliest stages of the Intake 1 group, and ever mindful of the program's status as a national demonstration project, adjusted their selection criteria for Intake 2 to select participants whose academic standing was much higher. According to Baseline/Norpack's *NB Works Process Evaluation Year-End Report* (23 June 1995), no more than 7 per cent of Intake 2 participants required academic upgrading at the Basic level (academic upgrade categories are Basic, Intermediate and Senior).

Despite this adjustment to participant selection criteria, the NB Works drop-out rate for Intake 2 had already reached 45 per cent only twenty months into the forty-two month program. The exit summary for Intake 3, only ten months into the program, shows a drop-out level of 15 per cent. Regardless of the intake year, most drop-outs occurred during the acquisition of high school equivalency.

As for the current status of NB Works participants, we simply don't know. As of 2001, the 'final' evaluation report on NB Works, to be provided by Baseline, had not yet been produced. The NB Works *Annual Report* for 1995–6 provides a summary of the retention rate of NB Works participants as of 31 March 1996. Interestingly, this summary (Table 7.2) does not reveal how many participants completed Intake 1 (even though four years had passed). Exits and completions are lumped into the same category, making it hard to know who quit and who graduated. It is known, however, that by March 1996 more than half of all participants had already returned to social assistance.

HRDNB's decision to mix the exits/quits with the completions makes it impossible to know the real drop-out rate or completion rate for the program. In 1995 a considerable number of participants left the program, but it is difficult to see how many quit and how many completed. For Intake 1 (1992), the 1995 figures show that 712 out of 1,030 participants (69 per cent) had already quit, while the 1996 figures show that 1,029 out of 1,030 participants (almost all) had exited or completed. For Intake 2 (1993), the 1995 figures show that 418 out of 959 participants (44 per cent) had already quit, while the 1996 figures show that 645 out of 959 participants (67 per cent) had exited or completed. Finally, for Intake 3 (1994 and expanded intake from spring 1995), the 1995 figures show that 122 out of 807 participants (15 per cent) had already quit in the first year, while the 1996 figures show that 437 out of 909 (this larger number reflects the expanded intake) participants (48 per cent) had exited or completed.

What does all this mean? It means that we don't know who quit the program and who completed it. This type of summary effectively hides the drop-out rate of the program. Program personnel repeatedly claimed that all relevant data could be found in HRDNB's published documents. But nowhere in HRDNB's reporting procedure, not even in the *Annual Report*, could the quits be compared to the completes.

Moreover, the question should not be, 'Out of the original intake, how many returned to social assistance?' but rather, 'Out of those who quit or completed the program, how many returned to social assist-

TABLE 7.2
Retention Rate of NB Works Participants, 31 March 1996

Intake	Began NB Works	Total exits / completions		Exited and returned to social assistance		Exited but did not return to social assistance		Participation as of 31 March 1996	
Intake 1	1030	1029	99.99%	523	50.7%	507	49.29%	1	.01%
Intake 2	959	645	67.2%	347	36.2%	298	31.00%	314	32.80%
Intake 3	909	437	48.1%	244	26.9%	193	21.20%	472	51.90%
Total	2898	2112	72.9%	1114	38.4%	998	34.50%	787	27.10%

Note: Overall, 61.6 per cent of participants who began NB Works are either still in the project or have not returned to social assistance. Of those who exited the project, up to 998 participants and their families were no longer relying on social assistance as of 31 March 1996.

Source: NB Works Annual Report (1995–6, 8)

ance' (not counting those who were still enrolled in NB Works)? The HRDNB's reporting style makes the percentage of those who quit the program and returned to social assistance appear smaller than it actually is. If, for instance, the numbers for those who returned to social assistance were shown as a percentage of those who actually quit or completed, the figure on the chart would appear as 51 per cent (1,114 out of 2,112 exits and completions) and not as 38.4 per cent (1,114 out of 2,898 participants in the program). Another question concerns whether the figures for those who exited and/or completed the program and who did not return to social assistance included participants who did not finish their academic upgrading in time and were being provided for by the Training and Development Fund (TDF) or otherwise supported or assisted by HRDNB?

Despite the lack of clarity in HRDNB's reporting of the NB Works retention rate, it appears likely that the drop-out rate was more than half. For example, in the 1996 reporting figures for Intake 3, few of the 437 'exits/completions' (out of 909 participants) could possibly have been 'completions' of NB Works, given that the intake date was so recent (and even less likely, since more than a hundred participants had just been added in the spring of 1995).

Government surveys also seem to support the notion that NB Works participants quit the program because they found employment. The first shows the results of an exit survey that tracked those who quit (the word 'completion' was not used in this survey) before September 1994. The second, a tracking survey, gives the reasons cited by those who quit (the word 'completion' was not used in this survey). The findings of these surveys are summarized in the Baseline/Norpack report and are reproduced below because they provide insights into the recipients themselves and the barriers (or at least the stated barriers) faced by volunteer welfare recipients participating in a free training course. The major reasons cited by those who quit before September 1994 include health reasons (18 per cent); too low an income (11 per cent); personal or family problems (10 per cent); conflicts, problems with program/project staff (9 per cent); and inadequate financial support (9 per cent). The major reasons cited for quitting NB Works after September 1994 (and up to June 1995) include applicants finding the program too stressful/difficult (21 per cent); health reasons (12 per cent); personal or family problems (10 per cent); administrative termination (10 per cent); inadequate financial support (9 per cent); part-time employment (9 per cent); and full-time employment (3 per cent).

Clearly, few participants quit NB Works because they found employment. This list of reasons for quitting suggests that, with all the money that was poured into NB Works to provide free child-care and employment supports for those applicants most likely to succeed in the program, the government failed to address these single mothers' key barriers to employment.

The Official Record: What Do the Evaluators Say?

The inability to measure the effectiveness of a demonstration project such as NB Works is one of the significant problems with the program. Milne is right when he states: 'Perhaps the most serious design problem with NB Works is the difficulty, if not the impossibility, of serious evaluation. Since caseworkers choose participants based on their potential success in the program, there is a self-selection bias. It is impossible to know whether the results from NB Works can be generalized to typical welfare recipients. Second, there is no experimentally designed control group to use as a basis of comparison' (Milne 1996, 75). The idea behind NB Works was to provide education and training for single mothers on welfare so that they might enter the workforce at a higher wage than would otherwise have been the case. Did this happen? Could evaluators gauge whether participants entered the workforce at all as a result of NB Works? It would appear not, although this is only a guess, drawn crudely from the massive drop-out rate. The design of demonstration projects poses significant problems.

Although the policy-makers who developed NB Works stated their objectives for the program, they did not disclose its results. Did NB Works help over the long term to get people off welfare and into careers? While the answer must be no, the evaluation reports commissioned by the government (preliminary and interim evaluations) dazzle the reader with the word 'success' again and again. Reading the official evaluation reports, one would never guess that the program had been an expensive boondoggle. In fact, the evaluation reports made the project look extremely relevant and important. But extracting information about NB Works from HRDNB is not an easy task. Curious individuals who wish to track the fate of participants enrolled in NB Works are handed a 1995 evaluation conducted by Baseline/Norpark Evaluation Consortium and a copy of the NB Works *Annual Report* (which contains a summary of the Baseline/Norpack Evaluation Consortium report). We are also informed that Baseline is still under contract to provide a 'final' evaluation report of NB Works, but, as of early 2001, the report was not yet ready. Others have complained of the New Brunswick government's secrecy. McFarland and Mullaly, for example, make the following complaint about the way in which the government witholds information about NB Works: 'Politically, there is the question of the communications strategy which seems to be deliberately misleading. It highlights the successes but appears to operate under a "gag order" on problems and failures. This is possible because the evaluations are compiled by a joint government committee that can (and has) delayed the release of results. We have been told that job placement outcomes may not be made available until after the year 2,000. Also, case study data have been collected and not released' (McFarland and Mullaly 1996, 216).

In New Brunswick, evaluators raved about the wonderful way in which 'the different committees got along with each other' and the 'high rate of participant satisfaction' with the orientation program and the 'excellent course instructors.' Such observations do go a certain way toward legitimizing a program's $177 million price tag. But what about actual results? How many NB Works participants graduated from this three-and-a-half-year program? Of those who graduated, how many secured employment? For some reason, neither the government nor official program evaluators could get to this elusive bottom line.

The New Brunswick government selected the consortium of Baseline Market Research and Norpack Research Associates Inc. to produce, first, a 'process' evaluation report on NB Works (three years into the program) and, later, a 'summative' evaluation once the program was completed. What did it get for its money? From Baseline/Norpack's 1995 *Process Evaluation*, the government received a glowing report of a model project. One of the fascinating aspects of implementation evaluation is that evaluators can produce a glowing report on the behaviour of dedicated bureaucrats while avoiding key questions about the program's effectiveness; meanwhile, anyone can plainly see that the program was a failure. In the formal evaluation of NB Works, what we are presented with is not quite a case of 'the operation was a success, but the patient died'; rather, the NB Works evaluation process suggests something more along the lines of 'the operation was a success, but we don't know whether the patient is alive or dead.' Or, possibly, 'we do know, but we're not telling.'

What did the *Process Evaluation* have to report, three years into a hugely expensive program aimed at removing barriers to employment from the path of already highly motivated welfare recipients? We know that approximately two-thirds of Intake I had already dropped out of the program by the time of the *Process Evaluation* and that Intakes 2 and 3, which already had significantly high drop-out rates of their own, would likely fare no better.

The evaluators prepared their report for the NB Works Evaluation Committee, which also played a role in the design of the evaluation framework. The evaluators claimed to develop their findings on the basis of a review of project-related reports and manuals; findings from several surveys of participants and former participants; results from a survey of employers responsible for the initial work placements and internships; discussions with thirty-seven case managers and five focus groups with sixty participants; analyses of thirty case studies; and a review of the NB Works management information system (MIS).

Having spent all this time, energy, and money studying the first three years of NB Works, what did the evaluators conclude? Apart from a few snags with the MIS (claimed to be understandable because of the quick start-up), 'there were no real problems.' Committees functioned smoothly. Participants showed high satisfaction with staff and instructors. Interestingly, the evaluation report makes no connection between the supposedly effective government processes and the already well-known high drop-out rate of the program. The 1995–6 *Annual Report* contains a summary of the *Process Evaluation* team's findings. These are reproduced below, in full, to demonstrate the evaluators' capacity to focus on the irrelevant while sidestepping what is important about the program. Note how evaluators ignore the fact that two-thirds of Intake 1 had already quit and blindly heap generous praise on workfare administrators. The following excerpts from *Highlights of the* NB Works *Process Evaluation Report* reveal a preoccupation with bureaucratic process and behaviour and little interest in how many welfare recipients were reaching self-sufficiency:

> *The NB Works Partnership*: Over the course of the project, extraordinary cooperation has developed between NB Works federal and provincial government staff. The NB works Operations Committee, comprising staff from all partner departments, is able to find a solution to most questions.

> *The Recruitment Process*: The overall retention rate for NB Works participants has improved over the course of the three intakes or groups of participants. Although the recruitment process for NB Works remained rushed, without enough time for a thorough assessment of participants, a

more standardized selection process was in place for the second and third intakes, including improvements in the information given to potential participants and improved testing.

Orientation Sessions: There was increased standardization in the orientation sessions given to potential participants over the three intakes. Most participants (97 per cent) were 'very' or 'somewhat satisfied' with the information they received during these orientation sessions.

Initial Work Placements: Over the three intakes, participants were better informed about the purpose of the initial work phase and the type of work they would be doing. The variety and the quality of the jobs participants held during the initial work phase also improved over the three intakes. The evaluators noted that participants needed more counselling and information on how to adjust to their new financial arrangements.

Academic Upgrading: The demand for Basic Academic Upgrading (BAU – less than grade 7) decreased as a result of the improved selection process for NB Works participants.

The environment and the atmosphere in the classrooms and the buildings where academic upgrading was delivered presented a challenge for some participants. Ninety-six per cent of participants were very or somewhat satisfied with the academic upgrading programs they received. While a high rate of absenteeism was a problem for some participants, the overall attendance rate was good at 87 per cent.

Skills Training: In a tracking survey of NB works participants, over 98 per cent of respondents reported being satisfied with skills training, although 25 per cent of those in skills training said they were not well prepared. Career counselling helped NB Works participants to choose careers expected to be in demand in the future.

Participants were not moving as quickly through the NB Works continuum as had been expected. This may be a result of the hurried selection and recruitment process.

Internships: Participants were very satisfied with their internship work experience placements. Internship employer-hosts were also generally positive about their experiences with NB Works participants.

Case Management: Eighty seven per cent of the participants were satisfied with the case management process and 90 per cent were satisfied with the career counselling process, even though contact between the case managers and participants was less frequent than the evaluators expected.

NB Works Information System: There were concerns expressed by senior staff about the NB Works Information System, for example, they found the tracking features to be poor. Case managers did think the system, with some modifications, could be a useful tool but currently found it to be cumbersome and time consuming.

Operations: The evaluators found that some of the operations were affected by current federal and provincial administrative policies. This included: the funding arrangements under social policy and Unemployment Insurance legislation, the structure of the community college system and the management structure involving three government partners. (NB Works 1995–6, 14–15)

Having provided a glowing interim report of NB Works, the same Baseline/Norpack Evaluation Consortium was selected to provide the final summary evaluation of NB Works. Evaluation programs that heap praise on civil servants and develop charts that lump intake 'quits' with 'completes' obfuscate the fact that few participants, if any, acquired the skills, and subsequently the jobs, that made them self-sufficient. Systems (e.g., MIS, community college arrangements, legislative time limits) may be criticized, but the architects and administrators of the program appear, in effect, to be off limits. As with so many government evaluations, if it is determined that the program was an expensive failure, the poor administrators will be judged to have done their best with the meagre resources available to them. Since both the federal and the provincial governments were involved with NB Works, the evaluation stakes were all the higher and the need for delicacy was perhaps greater.

The consultants' glowing evaluation may be seen as another aspect of the sophisticated public relations strategy that accompanied all phases of NB Works. New Brunswick academic Robert Mullaly studied the communications strategy surrounding NB Works and found that, consistent with McKenna's efforts to portray the province as a good place to invest, the image of NB Works as an innovative, progressive, and effective social reform experiment was 'carefully manufactured and marketed':

A communications committee for NB Works has been established ... A full time communications officer has been assigned to NB Works, a newsletter entitled *NB Works Update* is published quarterly and a NB Works video has been produced for distribution. The message is always the same: NB Works is an innovative program containing substantial opportunities for its participants to become self-sufficient, is efficient in its delivery and is a model of co-operation between two levels of government. The method used to get its message out is also always the same: to publish glowing testimonials from program staff and from 'selected' participants as to how NB Works has turned their lives and those of their families around ...

The communications strategy of NB Works is misleading. While it publicizes anecdotal successes, it does not tell of any problems or failures. (Mullaly 1997, 53–4)

New Brunswick academics Joan McFarland and Robert Mullaly conducted their own study of NB Works and found that the information that they gathered 'contrasts sharply' with the image of NB Works that was beamed out from the Communications Committee. In an article entitled 'NB Works: Image versus Reality' (1996), they reveal the results of a survey of sixteen NB Works participants who were interviewed to find out their views of the program with respect to its case management approach, job exposure, upgrading, skills training, potential for finding a job, and the impact that the program had on their own lives and that of their families. While the authors recognized that sixteen is a small sample size and that their means of locating participants could possibly lead to bias, they indicated that they did not wish to use participants referred by the program for fear of being sent 'the "stars" who are being used in the communications strategy' (McFarland and Mullaly 1996, 209).The authors also encountered problems accessing NB Works data, especially regarding whether any participants actually obtained a job at the program's end. The authors complained of the secrecy surrounding the real results of NB Works and program staff's refusal to release to them the results of a recently carried out case study of thirty participants. McFarland and Mullaly's survey included participants from each of the three main intakes and the later intake of spring 1995. Fifteen were female, one was male, and they represented each of the provinces's major centres: Fredericton, Moncton and Saint John. Almost all were single parents with minimal experience of the labour market, fitting the target group profile for NB Works. McFarland and Mullaly's key survey findings are reproduced below:

- Case management: While the program advertised itself as a case management approach, 'almost all felt that they had no "plan" and had had no such discussion with their case managers. For them, the case manager was just like their worker under social assistance.'
- Work experience: Despite the public criticism received by the twenty-week work experience (e.g., poor planning, unsuitable and poorly supervised jobs – mainly cutting brush for NB Power – sexual harassment, and dangerous working conditions – one NB Works participant supposedly drowned while working on a dam, although program staff denied any knowledge of this) the participants were relatively satisfied with this phase of the program: 'A number of them "liked" or even "loved" cutting brush, especially those that had a rural background.'
- Academic upgrading: Studying toward high-school equivalency proved to be the most problematic phase. Some complained of not being able to complete the upgrading in the time allotted, and others complained of getting more upgrading than they really needed, especially those who already had a high school diploma when they started, but whose academic competence had been found to be lower than their credentials suggested.
- Skills training: While not many reached this stage in the survey or in the overall program, complaints focused on the community college system, which provides certain programs at different locations, often making it impossible to access one's selected course without moving.
- Jobs: None of the surveyed participants were ready to look for a job. The authors attempted to find out how many NB Works participants had actually reached the level of looking for a job. In January 1995 they were verbally informed by program personnel that 'thirty-nine of the 3,000 original participants were at the job search phase and that sixteen were "job ready."'
- Impact of the program: While NB Works literature promised that the participant would be no worse off financially while in NB Works (because of the free child-care and support systems for which the government was paying), 'the women we talked to felt that being on NB Works was a considerable financial sacrifice for them.'
- Impact on children: 'The picture painted in the publicity surrounding NB Works is that the program is great for the children in the families involved. Again we were provided a somewhat different version. Some women did describe their children as being "proud"

of their mothers and the program as "having mostly a positive impact" on their children. However, many felt that the program had been "hard" on their kids and "hard" on them as mothers.'

- Impact on self-esteem: 'In general, self-esteem was related to the amount of time that the participant had been in the program. Just after acceptance to the program, self-esteem was very high. After that, self-esteem was related to successful completion of each stage of the program ... However, if the experience of university graduates in the current New Brunswick job market is any guide, this phase could be the ultimate self-esteem destroyer.'
- Drop-outs: 'What we found was that "drop-outs" are, in fact, of two kinds: those that drop out themselves and those that are expelled or dismissed. The drop-outs we spoke with did so because of insurmountable barriers in terms of their personal circumstances, almost always family related, that the program could not accommodate. The reasons given to participants for their expulsions or dismissals were "too many absences" sometimes combined with "an attitude problem."' (McFarland and Mullaly 1996, 210–13)

The McFarland and Mullaly survey provides us with a better feel for what NB Works was all about, and how little it did to actually get people into long-term jobs. McFarland and Mullally asked the interviewees what they thought of the concept of NB Works: In general their responses to the concept were positive: "good idea," "wonderful if people can get off welfare." However, when the researchers asked participants if NB Works was a success, their responses were different. According to interviewees, NB Works "would have been good" but for reasons such as the following: "It needs more organization"; "We need more help with career goals"; "It needs a more realistic time frame"; "The program should screen better"; "Upgrading was a waste"; "Participants are not getting enough reward"; "It needs to recognize people's family problems"' McFarland and Mullaly 1996, 213–14).

McFarland and Mullaly conclude that, for participants, the image was better than the reality: 'the participants approved of the program as it had been presented (the rhetoric of NB Works) but had quite a different view of its reality' (213–14). It would appear that the image left in participants' minds is largely a negative one. Under NB Works, recipients did not appear to be sufficiently motivated to remain with the program. And although some graduates of NB Works are probably gainfully employed, information HRDNB gave to McFarland and

Mullaly in 1995 ('thirty-nine of the 3,000 original participants were at the job search stage and sixteen "job ready"') makes one doubt that there are very many successful completions to show for the public money invested in the program.

Did the Public Play a Role?

Anti-poverty groups and special interest groups constantly criticize New Brunswick for paying the lowest welfare rates in Canada. What did the same lobby groups think of NB Works, one of the most generous social welfare policies ever administered in Canada? The program was criticized for being one step along the slippery slope to American-style workfare, blaming the unemployed for their own fate. As Mullaly and Weinman point out: 'This government has been receiving much attention for its so-called social experiments such as NB Works. The fact of the matter is that these experiments are not new as they too are based in Poor Law practices. The Americans have tried a number of workfare and learnfare programmes over the past two decades. All serious studies of these projects have shown that they are dismal failures in getting people back into the labour market' (1994, 6).

The media helped to build up Frank McKenna's reputation as an innovator in human resources, a believer in the value of education who gave three thousand welfare mothers the opportunity of a lifetime. When the program was first announced, the press flocked from all over Canada to New Brunswick, a poor little maritime province with a visionary premier who had a new take on welfare. But soon other stories beckoned, and in the absence of any results, nobody went back to see what had happened. Like the bureaucrats, the local media got bored with NB Works after the initial fanfare. To the general public, the television commercials full of wonderful NB Works promises probably seems like a long time ago. It is unlikely that any complained that their tax dollars were being used to educate those who *already* had the skills necessary to manage at least five months of work, paying $1.25 higher than the minimum wage.

What Happened to the Good Idea?

We have seen that the top politician of the province resigned in 1997, one year before NB Works officially ended. Policy-makers began work on Jobs Plus, a new 'self-sufficiency' program for welfare recipients, which had a very short shelf life. Administrators don't know or won't tell us how many people actually completed NB Works. They are bored with NB Works, since, 'after all, it did start in 1992'. The earliest and most definitive statistics suggest that at least two-thirds of the 'highly motivated' participants in Intake 1 quit NB Works. But New Brunswick's welfare-to-work program did pay political dividends. Learnfare provided the perfect opportunity for Premier Frank McKenna to gain a high public profile. Merely by introducing an American idea to a ripe audience, McKenna attracted national media coverage. The political benefits happened early, in fact at the very announcement of this modern, human approach to single mothers on welfare. There was hardly any need for the good idea to be implemented – what more was to be gained? The visiting media had all gone home, and nobody came back to find out that the program had been a failure.

The government, by introducing a blanket education and training program in an economy with high unemployment, took a gamble on high participant motivation and an improved economy. In the political sphere, Frank McKenna moved from NB Works to Jobs Plus, singing the praises of the next new welfare reform that provided (again) just the right amount of subsidized work to requalify welfare recipients for federal Unemployment Insurance and reduce the provincial welfare rolls as fast as possible. The belief that welfare recipients needed only to complete high school and gain a marketable skill at a community college to achieve self-sufficiency constituted the philosophy of NB Works. However, despite a generous array of child-care and transportation supports, the vast majority of recipients did not even complete the first stage of achieving high-school equivalency. In spite of this, preliminary and interim evaluation reports remain favourable, and charts of numbers, undecipherable. (One ministry staff member confided that the numbers provided in the interim reports made no sense and that a group of staff *had asked* the evaluators to be more clear and understandable in their final report. NB Works program staff were allegedly told by the contracted evaluators that the numbers were presented incoherently at the government's insistence.) This mismatch between results and evaluation appears to be part and parcel of the unfolding of good ideas everywhere. Because so much is at stake with the implementation of good ideas (careers, political platforms), and because good ideas are presented as solve-alls, good ideas rarely go out with a bang. Instead, they quietly retreat from centre stage, as the next good idea is ushered in.

8.

Alberta's Mandatory 'Voluntary Opportunities'

Summary

Alberta's welfare caseload declined more than 60 per cent (from a monthly caseload of 94,087 in 1993 to 34,464 in 1998). This decline can be attributed to a number of reforms introduced by Progressive Conservative Premier Ralph Klein, including tighter eligibility criteria, technical adjustments to the system, and philosophical changes to the administrative culture of Alberta Family and Social Services (e.g., turning the welfare caseworker into an employment counsellor). Among these reforms were three supposedly 'voluntary' work experience programs. Able and employable welfare recipients (except parents of small children) must participate in either training or employment. The work experience programs were designed in such a way that, upon entry, a welfare recipient is taken off welfare (unless the wage does not meet their financial needs) and paid a government employee wage to work for a limited time, either within (a) the government, (b) community or volunteer organizations, or (c) directly with the Department of Human Resources and Employment, which obtains contracts in areas such as trades and construction. By expanding government work-placement and training opportunities, creating temporary government employment programs and transforming social workers into employment counsellors, Ralph Klein ushered a lot of people off welfare and into the workplace. Approximately 75 per cent of work experience graduates move from the program to a full-time job and, at the twelve-month post-graduation checkpoint, remain outside the welfare system (Alberta Family and Social Services, 1997–8).

Alberta's Good Idea: Background and
Context of the Reform

According to car licence plates, Alberta is 'Wild Rose Country.' Alberta is also known as a bastion of political conservatism – and the provincial premier who has made the most drastic changes to the welfare system, Ralph Klein, is the most conservative of a long line of conservative premiers. Alberta (population 2,847,006) is the Canadian province that most closely resembles the 'Wild, Wild West.' It is oil-rich prairie land and, as the millions who have visited the famous Banff Springs Hotel know, it is also home to some beautiful mountains. Premier Ralph Klein is popularly portrayed as a 'ride 'em up, shoot 'em down' cowboy who, since his 1992 election victory, has made drastic changes not only to welfare, but also to the province's systems of health and education.

Ralph Klein's first step in his publicly declared 'war on welfare' was to name Mike Cardinal, a Métis from the traditionally welfare-dependent community of Calling Lake, as minister of Family and Social Services. Mike Cardinal is the first treaty Indian to have been appointed to an Alberta Cabinet post. At the time, the welfare budget was $1.6 billion and the welfare rolls were swelling out of control. It is widely conceded that naming Cardinal, who came from a poor family himself and was vehemently opposed to welfare, was a very smart strategic move. Cardinal was able to make sweeping changes to the way that welfare was administered and, in just the first year of his term, he dropped the welfare caseload from ninety-three thousand to sixty-eight thousand, a 27 per cent cut (Ted Byfield, 'The Cardinal Rule: Povery Means Not Working,' *Financial Post*, 16 June 1993). Welfare caseloads have been dropping ever since. A number of interest groups, bureaucrats, and various media pundits were shocked and appalled at the rapid changes made to welfare. But, as Jonathan Murphy, an anti-poverty activist and then director of the Edmonton Social Planning Council said about Mike Cardinal's appointment: 'He's been dumped with the government agenda. The fact that he's aboriginal, that he's lived the life of adversity means the government feels he's in a strong position to push this agenda. It's no accident he's in this portfolio. It's a clever move' (Corinna Schuler, 'Special Report: The Boss,' *Edmonton Journal*, 2 October 1993).

Joe Blyan of the Wood Buffalo Metis settlement believed that the government was taking advantage of Cardinal to do its dirty work: 'The government is using him because he's an Indian' (Schuler, *Edmon-*

ton Journal, 2 October 1993). Ted Byfield, a well-known conservative reporter, pointed out in the *Financial Post* (13 June 1993) that, for people in the media, and especially the more left-wing journalists, Cardinal was a 'tough target to hit' ... because he's from a minority group, and therefore (it has always been tactfully implied) can't do anything wrong.' Earl Mansfield, a retired assistant deputy minister, saw Cardinal's background as an advantage to the job: 'He could bridge the white and native community. He was respected by both. And that was something not many could do' (Schuler, *Edmonton Journal*, 2 October 1993).

In many of his early speeches and press conferences as minister of Family and Social Services, Cardinal declared that welfare was a debilitating disease, responsible for drunkenness, family breakup, suicide, child abuse, and other social evils. He claimed that his own home town had been wrecked by welfare. Writing in the *Financial Post* (13 June 1993), Ted Byfield captured some of the flavour of Cardinal's sentiments toward welfare in the following editorial:

> Cardinal, 52, makes no secret of the passion that motivates him. He hates welfare, he says. All his life he has seen the despair that overtakes people who depend on it. At least 40 of his friends have committed suicide or died violently because of this despair.
>
> In his childhood, he said, Calling Lake was a poor community that paid its way through trapping, logging and commercial fishing, 'We were happy,' said Cardinal. 'Everyone worked hard. Everyone had dignity.' ... In the 1950s, welfare came to Calling Lake. Soon 80% of the community was on it. Nearly all work stopped. Drunkenness, wife beating, child abuse – things that were hardly known before – became a norm. His home town, he said, was wrecked by welfare.
>
> 'Poverty activists,' said Cardinal, 'have lost touch with reality. They think the solution is more welfare. They're wrong. Poverty means not working. People want work. They want to be proud and independent. They want to participate in the future.'

In other words, Mike Cardinal's objective was not actually to improve welfare, but to eliminate it altogether. Welfare was the 'curse of the poor,' especially for native communities. He had definite views about the welfare system and often made statements such as the following: 'Nothing should come for free ... When there was no welfare, the native community was completely self-sufficient. They were living off the land. There was no alcoholism, no family breakdown. They lived in harmony with nature prior to 1950' (Schuler, *Edmonton Journal*, 2 October 1993).

So what exactly did Mike Cardinal do to achieve drastic reductions in the number of welfare recipients? Not only did he institute a number of administrative and structural changes to the way in which welfare was delivered, he also convinced the social services bureaucracy that there was the political will to move people from welfare to work. Although this chapter focuses on the innovative employment programs used in Alberta to reduce the numbers of welfare recipients, the administrative and structural changes that took place were also important in reducing the welfare rolls. The net effect of these changes was to reduce the welfare caseload by 29 per cent in the first nine months of the 1993–4 fiscal year and to reduce actual expenditures by 15 per cent – approximately two-thirds of those who left the welfare caseload at that time were single people and couples without children (Alberta Family and Social Services, 1993–4). By 1997, Alberta's caseload had fallen by more than 60 per cent (Don Thomas, 'Welfare Caseload Down to '82 Levels,' *Edmonton Journal*, 4 October 1997).

Canada's National Council of Welfare (NCW) claims that most of this drop took place in the first year. According to the NCW (1997), '172,176 cases left welfare sometime between September 1993 and October 1996.' (The number of cases appears high compared with the average monthly caseload of any one year because a large number of people go on and off welfare each month; the average monthly caseload for Alberta in 1995, for example, was 50,620, but the number of different cases that went through the system over that year totalled 103,750.) Apart from facing an improved economy (although the 1993–4 drop in caseloads was much sharper than the drop in unemployment), what did Mike Cardinal do? The following explanation of how this drop occurred is drawn from a report by the NCW (1997).

Cardinal first moved about eleven thousand students out of the welfare system, shifting them to a grant system under the provincial Students Finance Board. He then tightened eligibility criteria so that some eighteen thousand cases were dropped from the welfare rolls. Another eleven thousand cases dropped off the rolls as a result of three 'special initiatives': (1) recovery of cheques that were left unclaimed at residences, (2) more investigations of suspicious circumstances, and (3) targeted home visits. Cardinal also transferred about two thousand 'permanently unemployable' cases from welfare to a new program called Assured Income for the Severely Handicapped (AISH).

Meanwhile, Alberta Family and Social Services (AFSS) was also trying to minimize the number of new people who would come onto the welfare rolls. Structural and philosophical changes in the intake and treatment process of the department had the effect of making access to benefits more difficult. The number of new welfare cases was much lower by the middle of 1993, either because of tightened eligibility criteria (Boessenkool 1997) or the tougher application of existing criteria. In March 1993, all fifty-two district welfare offices across Alberta were asked to develop their own initiatives to cut caseloads. While there was some variation between offices, most of the suggestions made by caseworkers stressed the need for more intensive reviews of new and existing cases, for people to attend information sessions before the processing of their applications for assistance; for clients to follow through on mutually agreed-upon case plans; for the establishment of waiting periods for non-emergency applicants; and for information-sharing among different governments. Intensive case reviews were conducted on 67,385 cases in 1993–4 and 11,048 were closed (out of these, 367 charges of fraud were laid).

There were other changes that made life tougher for welfare recipients. In October 1993, Mike Cardinal cut the maximum basic allowance by twenty-six dollars a month per adult and the shelter allowance part of the welfare cheque by fifty dollars a month. The reason given for these cuts was that rates had to be brought into line with the earnings of the working poor. Other changes included the province no longer paying rental damage deposits (except in the case of family violence) and reductions in the amount of money given out for moving, telephone connections, laundry costs for infants, prescription drugs, dental and vision care, and funeral services. Employable recipients were cut off welfare immediately when they refused or abandoned a job without stating a valid reason. One-time emergency assistance went only to people who had used up all their savings. 'Spouse in the house' policies began to be enforced, with the result the people who claimed to be single but were actually in a common-law relationship and had not declared their partners' earnings were cut off welfare. Welfare recipients who were living with parents or relatives were no longer provided the shelter allowance part of their benefits. Since 1994, welfare recipients who reached the age of sixty were required to apply for an early retirement pension from the Canada Pension Plan.

Cardinal also developed a 'work incentive program' that allowed people to keep more earned income to top off their welfare cheque (for a single person working full time at minimum wage the earnings exemption of $245 per month was raised to $303 per month). Previously, single parents with children under the age of two were exempted from the job search requirement. As of 1993, the age exemption dropped to six months.

Discussions with three senior staff members of Alberta Family and Social Services (AFSS) reveal that not all changes were of a technical nature. The very philosophy behind administering welfare had changed, and the new philosophy was implemented because it came straight from the top. Training sessions for caseworkers were held at all district offices to reinforce the new philosophical principles that (with the exception of those who were severely disabled or were single parents with children below the age of six months) (1) entitlement to welfare should be viewed as transitory; (2) benefits should be available only after all other sources – including family members – have been exhausted; and (3) persons in receipt of welfare should not be better off than the working poor (Klein 1996, 134).

Cardinal also developed job creation programs that gave wage subsidies to groups that hired welfare workers. Officially, the employment and training programs in Alberta are *voluntary*, but AFSS staff agree that, in practice, they are effectively *mandatory*. In the area of retraining, Cardinal's message was simple: 'If eligible people refuse to study or join the "job corps," they'll be cut off' (Jeff Harder, *Edmonton Sun*, 2 May 1997). Mike Cardinal's famous slogan 'Any job is a good job' resounded throughout Alberta Family and Social Services and was posted on a number of department pamphlets and brochures. Writing in an article entitled 'Welfare Beats Minimum-wage Job – Except in Alberta' (*Calgary Herald*, 17 December 1993), Andy Marshall quotes AFSS spokesperson Bob Scott as announcing: 'We've changed from a passive welfare system into an active re-employment system. That's made the difference. Alberta is leading the way.' Alberta's employment training programs have been hugely successful in that twelve months after job placement, over 70 per cent of participants are no longer on the welfare rolls.

How Was the Program Designed?

The key innovation of Alberta's welfare reform was a type of workfare. While welfare recipients were not officially required to work in exchange for their benefits (such a requirement would have been forbidden in Canada before the Canada Assistance Plan expired in 1996), they were cut off if they did not participate in the newly designed welfare program. Alberta's welfare program is called Supports for Independence (SFI). The province streams welfare recipients into one of four categories: (1) employables, (2) low-wage earners who require a top-up, (3) persons who are temporarily unable to work or who have a child under six months of age, and (4) persons in the assured-income category (those who cannot work because of a severe disability or illness). This chapter concerns itself only with Alberta's treatment of the first category, that is, the employables. For employable welfare recipients, the process is generally as follows: an intake worker sees the client in an initial interview and makes sure that no other sources of money are available to him or her. If all is satisfactory, a client service worker then does an assessment of the client and helps him or her to develop an Employment Plan. Approximately 70 per cent of clients are judged to be employment ready; for the other 30 per cent, some kind of training is considered a necessity (Klein 1996, 135). Clients are assigned a Financial Benefits Worker only after they complete an employment session and have an Employment Plan. Refusal to agree to the conditions of the Employment Plan results in ineligibility for benefits. Once the Employment Plan is signed, clients are then streamed into one of the following programs:

1 Formal education and training: the client moves under the provincial student assistance program, a separate non-welfare category;
2 Employment preparation programs: the client may take a short course (less than nine weeks in duration) in skills for work or self-employment, or do on-the-job training, or be referred directly to a job-placement agency (the placement agency receives $150 for each client assessment, $300 for each client who stays in a job for three months, and $500 for each client who stays in a job for six months); or
3 Work experience programs: the client becomes a participant in one of Alberta's three employment programs, either the Employment Skills Program (ESP), the Alberta Community Employment (ACE) program, or the Alberta Job Corps.

In other words, once the welfare recipient is deemed to be employable and an Employment Plan is signed, the recipient will participate in one of three categories. The first category is straightforward, in that recipients can choose to go to community college or university (in which case they are no longer on welfare, but, rather, under the provincial student assistance program). The second category is in which the recipient usually works closely with a private employment agency for direct entry into the competitive labour market. The third category is the focus of the rest of this chapter in that it involves the three programs that the province of Alberta runs directly, each of which aims to provide welfare recipients with work experience that will render them employable. These three work experience programs are unique and appear to be highly effective in moving welfare recipients into the workplace.

Each program is tailored to a different population group. The Employment Skills Program (ESP), the oldest of the three, is designed for people who are considered ready to work, but who could benefit from recent job experience and references on their résumés. The twenty-six-week employment placements are located entirely in busy provincial government departments, and the population group is mostly single mothers. The second employment program, entitled Alberta Community Employment (ACE), was introduced by Mike Cardinal. This program is an extension of the earlier Employment Skills Program. Unlike under ESP, the participant works not in a provincial government department but in non-profit community organizations such as nursing homes and school boards. People selected for participation in ACE often require slightly more supervision than those who are operating at a full competence level in the provincial government departments. Alberta's third employment program is the Alberta Job Corps. This is an extension of the Northern Alberta Job Corps, which had so impressed Mike Cardinal when he was growing up. Traditionally an employment program developed for remote rural areas, its concept of hands-on learning was brought south to urban areas, reaching Edmonton and Calgary in 1995 the concept is expected to spread throughout the province. The population group served by this program is generally those for whom formal education has not been a success and whose barriers to work are so severe such that they would normally be considered unemployable. Welfare recipients participating in this program become employees of the Alberta Job Corps under the supervision of government staff. Most jobs are in construction and trades in work projects sponsored by local communities, non-profit organizations, and the private sector.

The innovative aspect of these work experience programs is that, for their duration, recipients are no longer on welfare but instead receive an hourly wage, paid for by the government through the agency involved in overseeing the participants' work experience. While this 'salaried' component does not really match the standard definition of workfare (wherein the concept of reciprocal obligation requires the welfare recipient to train in exchange for welfare benefits), the requirement of actual work experience is Alberta's singular innovation to workfare. The participant who is selected for one of the three employment programs becomes an 'employee' of the Alberta government, or of the non-profit community organization, and earns a wage that is at or slightly above the provincial minimum wage of five dollars per hour (1998), plus benefits. Thus does the 'welfare recipient' become categorized as an 'employee.' This relabelling process is considered by policymakers to be an important component in assisting the client to make the transition from welfare to the competitive labour market. Once the participant has been deemed to have attained his or her maximum skill set, employment counsellors with experience in marketing participants' strengths work closely with the participant and local employers until employment is found.

The success rate for all of these programs is impressive. According to Diane Paul, manager of Employment Programs for Alberta Family and Social Services (in an interview on 27 October 1998), the following statistics represent the number of participants who remained off welfare twelve months after completing the program:

- Employment Skills Program (ESP): 71 per cent are totally off welfare (an additional 11 per cent are working, but their earnings are being topped up by welfare).
- Alberta Community Employment (ACE): 71 per cent are off welfare (an additional 10 per cent are working, but their earnings are being topped up by welfare).
- Alberta Job Corps (AJC): 74 per cent are off welfare (an additional 8 per cent are working, but their earnings are being topped up by welfare).

All three employment programs are similar in that they require a work placement to offer the participant a skill in preparation for entry into the Alberta job market, but they differ in their administration, client group, and implementation. Because of the high success rates that these programs appear to have achieved, a more detailed description of each one (adapted from the government literature) is provided below:

1 Employment Skills Program (ESP)

Established in 1980, ESP is a public service work experience program that is geared to welfare recipients who have no major attendance problems or lifestyle issues that would prevent them from working in a provincial government department. The largest number of participants are single parents.

Objective: To assist social assistance recipients in securing work experience and training to refine or relearn work-related skills and attitudes. Participants will obtain recent work records, which will help them to secure ongoing employment.

Eligible Employers: Eligible employers include departments of the government of Alberta, the Public Affairs Bureau, Public Safety Services, and the Personnel Administration Office.

Eligible Employees: Employees must be unemployed provincial social assistance recipients who are available for work but have been unsuccessful in finding employment.

Key Components: Positions must be new, full-time positions that provide transferable skills and career development opportunities for the employee. Additional training suited to the participant is an option. Positions are twenty-six weeks in duration. These positions must not displace or replace existing employees. There must be a two-month break between similar positions.

Financial Assistance: Alberta Family and Social Services (AFSS) will pay 100 per cent of the wage costs of six dollars per hour, plus employer contributions for UIC, CPP, statutory holiday pay, and vacation pay. The department will also pay up to one thousand dollars for additional training costs based on the employee's assessed need.

Comments: A job description of the employment placement is forwarded to AFSS and the request is assessed. If the placement meets certain criteria, candidates are selected for an interview with the potential employer department. Once a match is made, the amount of six dollars per hour is transferred over to the employer department. The employer department pays the participant's benefits and paycheque. The participant is not an employee of AFSS, but rather of the employing government department.

2 Alberta Community Employment (ACE)

When Mike Cardinal took over as minister of Family and Social Services, he brought with him the argument that people really want to work, and that it is up to the community to create opportunities. In accordance with this belief, he announced that his department would be introducing a new community-oriented employment program. Policy-makers were given six weeks to design Alberta Community Employment (ACE). This they successfully accomplished, developing procedures, application forms, employer contracts for a simple, straightforward community work program that would not displace volunteers or employees. While the program was originally based in Edmonton, it gradually became decentralized, leaving front-line regional staff with the responsibility to review the appropriateness of the ACE project proposal.

Objective: To assist municipalities, publicly funded organizations, and not-for-profit organizations to expand their workforce through the cost-shared hiring of new staff. The projects funded by ACE will help social assistance recipients to develop or enhance skills that they can use in the competitive job market.

Eligible Employers: Municipalities, Indian bands, Métis settlements, school boards, post-secondary institutions, health authorities, hospitals, auxiliary hospitals, nursing homes, and not-for-profit organizations.

Eligible Employees: Employees must be unemployed provincial social assistance recipients who are available for work but have been unsuccessful in finding employment.

Key Components: ACE offers project-based funding to provide work experience for social assistance recipients while meeting community priorities. Positions must be new full-time positions that will assist the ACE employee to secure long-term employment in the competitive labour market. These positions must not displace or replace existing employees. Projects are twenty-six weeks in duration. There must be a two-month break between similar projects.

Financial Assistance: Alberta Family and Social Services will contribute six dollars per hour to offset wages and benefits. Employers are encouraged to top up the salaries of ACE employees. The employer may apply for one thousand dollars to defray training costs if the ACE employee is retained for six months beyond the completion of the ACE project.

Comments: Employment workers oversee the administration of the grants. While the government provides funding for the wages of ACE participants, the employer provides the equipment, materials, supervision, training, and project administration. The project must provide the ACE employee with thirty-two to forty hours of work a week. A person cannot participate in the ACE project or other job-creation projects more than once. The ACE brochure clearly states: 'You are encouraged to top up the employee's wage from your own organization's funding sources.'

3 Alberta Job Corps (AJC)

The Alberta Job Corps is geared to the long-term welfare client for whom classroom learning has not been a success. Work placements are mostly in construction and in the trades, primarily carpentry. Wages are $5.00 to $7.50 per hour, depending on responsibilities, plus benefits. The AJC is the most expensive of the three employment programs, running at approximately ten thousand dollars per participant. The 1995–6 budget was $5.2 million. While the temporary employment is designed to a maximum of six months, the participant remains an employee of the AJC until, with the aid of employment counsellors, he or she is able to successfully transfer to the competitive job market. Seventy-four per cent of those who have commenced on the payroll of the AJC are no longer on welfare twelve months after they have left the program. An additional 8 per cent, although working, need to have their incomes supplemented by welfare. When asked to explain the spirit of the Alberta Job Corps, Diane Paul, the manager of Employment Programs for AFSS, stated the following in an interview on 27 October 1998: 'Formal education is not the answer for a lot of people. Of course, there are a lot of studies that show that the higher the level of education, the greater the level of earnings and success for the individual. But often there are *reasons* why people have not succeeded in school. The population group that most surprises us, in terms of success, are those whose lifestyle issues and personal habits are so far from workplace values that they learn best by "doing." With the Job Corps, participants can see themselves as "workers" rather than as an adult student *still* struggling along and having trouble in the classroom. Through the Job Corps they learn how to be a good employee.'

Objective: To assist welfare clients to develop employment skills through participation in shop projects, community projects, and work opportunities. The range of services varies according to district and community priorities. The essence of the AJC is skills development through work experience. Employees go through a formal performance-appraisal process with their supervisor every two weeks. Clients get in the habit of working for a wage and managing money. They receive paid work experience, employment counselling (and the chance to experience different types of jobs), life-management skills development (e.g., anger management), basic skills development in a variety of areas (e.g., home and automotive repair and maintenance, cooking, office work) the opportunity for certification in skills such as First Aid, assistance with their résumé, job-search assistance, and follow-up support. They receive a welcome package and draw up a formal work contract.

Partnerships: The AJC actively seeks partnerships with public, not-for-profit, and private sector employers. Community involvement is essential and is a key ingredient in determining project suitability. Together, local businesses, community groups, and the AJC develop essential job skills for the participant, under the guidance of prospective employers. AJC staff work closely with each partner to design, administer, and evaluate the success of the partnership.

Eligible Employees: Employees must be unemployed welfare recipients who are available for work but have been unsuccessful in finding employment.

Key Components: Positions are full-time positions that will assist the participants to secure skills for long-term employment in the competitive labour market. These positions must not displace or replace existing employees. Participation is normally up to twenty-six weeks. When employed under AJC, participants become wage employees of Alberta Family and Social Services.

Financial Assistance: AFSS pays the wage costs of $5.00 per hour, plus benefits, to AJC employees, and $7.50 per hour to lead hands on AJC projects. Participants can compete for positions of lead hand, and supervise other participants and serve as role models for skills and work habits.

Comments: Valuable work experience is gained while community groups and non-profit organizations are able to complete work projects that otherwise may not get done due to lack of resources. Examples of recent projects in the north of the province include the construction of twenty-five houses for low-income families, assistance to seniors with yard work, and environmental clean-up. In Edmonton, the capital of the province, Ken Gurski, the manager of the local AJC proudly shows off the upholstery, carpentry, and welding workshops and the full operation of an on-site canteen where all food is made from scratch by participants and sold at cost. Outside, he points to some of their moving trucks, which are contracted to the Victims of Family Violence Program. In an upstairs warehouse, furniture is also stored for the use of this same group in emergencies. One work team has just finished painting a skating rink for children with disabilities. Tiny picnic tables line one wall, waiting to be shipped to a day-care centre. Bigger ones are being made for the Department of Parks and Recreation. The Edmonton AJC has just landed a big contract with the Salvation Army to build and paint dressers, beds, and night tables for people in need. Since it opened in May 1998, over 550 people have been trained by the AJC in Edmonton over a two-year period.

The atmosphere at the Calgary AJC is dynamic. Managed by Donna Daniluck, this AJC is home to many of the same projects that are going on in the other AJC in Edmonton, to the north. Open only since 1996, almost two hundred people were trained in the Calgary location in the first two years of operation. Daniluck's work teams also have short-term contracts with churches, aboriginal centres, group homes, and other community groups. Daniluck has added a little personal motivational twist to the office. In the reception area of the Alberta Job Corps in Calgary there is a large, wall-sized cork bulletin board littered with paper stars of different colours. In the centre of each star is the first name and initial of participants who have left the AJC and the name of companies for whom they are working (e.g., 'Sam A., Budget Rent-a Car.' On another wall hangs a second huge cork board, and it is already half full of stars. According to Daniluck, since the local AJC opened in

1996, there is not a single graduate who has not returned, on their lunch hour, or at some other time, to take a look and make sure that their own star has been pinned onto the Wall of Success. Daniluck also claims that participants have usually made good friends during their stay at the AJC and that they often call her staff when they want advice or need to get their résumé updated. She also claims that follow-up and support after placement is essential to AJC success, confiding, 'we take them back if it falls apart.'

Administrative Challenges: Making Workfare Work

Alberta's monthly caseload declined from 94,087 in 1993 to 34,464 in 1998. What went into making these changes happen? How were such large reductions in the welfare rolls achieved? In contrast to a number of other workfare experiments reviewed in this volume, Alberta's welfare transformation did not happen overnight. While central to the Conservative platform, political expediency did not triumph over concerted, methodical action. The key to much of Alberta's success lay in its long experience with welfare reform. The administrative groundwork for welfare change was already well laid out early in 1990, beginning with the landmark 1990 Alberta Family and Social Services conference (held under the previous Progressive Conservative regime of Premier Don Getty). For example, the word 'welfare' had already been replaced by Support for Independence,' and new computers had been purchased well in advance of the workfare programs, in anticipation of the need to issue cheques and track recipients under a stricter, more performance-based system. In addition, recipients had already been recategorized according to their relationship to the labour market (as opposed to labels such as 'single parent'), and tougher eligibility criteria were put in place, even though initially they were not being applied by front-line caseworkers.

While these essential administrative supports had been in place since 1990 and were there to greet the new Klein administration in 1993, welfare was still being approached in the same old way by front-line administrators, and little else had changed. While new language in welfare brochures stated that welfare was now only to be seen as a last resort, welfare rolls actually rose steadily from 1990 to 1993. So what subsequently happened to transform the welfare system? According to staff in Alberta's department of Family and Social Services, what had been missing prior to the election of Ralph Klein and the appointment of Mike Cardinal as minister was the 'political will ... to bite the bullet ... to take the political backlash' that would follow many of the reforms. Asked to explain what occurred back in 1993, Yolanda Stojak, director of Assured Support Programs, put it this way in an interview on 29 October 1998: 'Insiders knew that there were serious problems, but there was nothing we could really do. And caseloads kept increasing. There were so many things that we just couldn't do. For example, we couldn't reduce benefits, we couldn't compel people to participate in work programs, we couldn't insist on the completion of an employment plan at intake, there were no incentives to reduce the caseload. Mike Cardinal's greatest contribution was that he supported internal staff to get things done. He just said "do it."'

According to Stojak, 'most social services staff supported all the changes that were made by Mike Cardinal except for the reduction in benefit dollars [which had been a Treasury decision] ... I think that they feel that the philosophy is the right tone.' Stojak pointed out, however, that it was the change in the mentality of both clients and caseworkers, that has had such results. Both clients and workers had always thought along similar lines of entitlement. With the reforms, however, people had to take responsibility for their own lives. Welfare became a last resort, not a first resort. As Stojak admits, it is not so much the formal rules of welfare that tightened up, but, rather, the way of applying the rules: 'The manual makes welfare look easy. It's the actual practice that makes it hard.'

The administrative culture of Alberta also experienced the stresses and strains of systemic transformation and organizational restructuring. Staff in social services were very worried about what the proposed departmental reorganization would mean to their jobs, and representatives of the Alberta Union of Provincial Employees Local 6 protested at Government House and buttonholed politicians on issues of job security. At the same time, one hundred social workers opted for the government's voluntary severance package, adding to the concerns about heavy workloads. According to Paul Marck, in an article entitled 'Cardinal Tries to Calm Angry Social Workers' (*Edmonton Journal*, 7 May 1993), Mike Cardinal said that his department's number one priority was to look after people on welfare, children, the handicapped, and the elderly, and he insisted that he would not allow staff cuts to undermine the process. The new minister also asked the union for patience while 'he becomes familiar with the concerns of all concerned.'

When large numbers of social workers complained about the welfare reforms introduced in 1993, the public gave them no support. Margaret Duncan, executive director of the Alberta Association of Social Workers, called the changes regressive: 'It's a lousy way to address the issues of your budget ... by punishing people. But Jason Kenney, executive director of Alberta Taxpayers (a private, twenty-thousand-member lobby group), said that the province needed to make these changes: 'If people run into difficulties through no fault of their own, then of course the system should do what it can, but sooner or later you have to say "Everyone has troubles" and give the person some responsibility for getting off welfare. Kenney said he would support a work-for-welfare provision so able-bodied clients would have to work on various public works projects for their cheque ... "These are painful cuts and there will be a lot of dissatisfied people, but unfortunately this is the type of pain everyone is going to have to share over the next few years, and it will get worse"' (Allyson Jeffs, 'Welfare Crackdown Ordered,' *Calgary Herald*, 27 March 1993).

At a national social work conference held in Edmonton in 1998, there were still some rumblings about social workers' inability to speak out because of the implied criticism of their employer, but senior department officials maintain that the administrative culture is currently in line with the department's objectives.

Did Welfare Recipients Participate?

While Alberta's work experience programs give an impression of astounding success to the extent that they moved welfare recipients into paid, long-term employment, the introduction of Klein's welfare reforms (including the tightening of eligibility requirements) was not altogether welcomed by welfare recipients. The media reported at the time that large numbers of welfare recipients were fleeing Alberta and seeking welfare refuge in nearby British Columbia. British Columbia's angry outcry over their arrival gave some substance to the report. Doug Ward, in his article 'Welfare Stats Prove Alberta's Loss Is B.C.'s Gain' (*Edmonton Journal*, 27 December 1993), provides an interesting summary of the feud between the two provinces:

> When he was mayor of Calgary in the early 80s, Ralph Klein complained about creeps and bums from Eastern Canada coming to cause trouble in his town. Klein is now premier of Alberta and new figures from B.C.'s social services ministry indicate he has few qualms about exporting his

poor to British Columbia. Social Services ministry official Peggy Herring said people arriving from Alberta are consistently 27 per cent of all out-of-province welfare applicants. That level is high considering Alberta's population in relation to other provinces.

There were 754 applicants from Alberta in August, 691 in September, 785 in October and a projected 610 in November, according to ministry records. B.C.'s basic monthly welfare cheque is $141 more than Alberta's ...

Harcourt (Premier of B.C.) has attacked Alberta for providing welfare recipients free bus tickets out of the province. Alberta officials have countered that B.C. also hands out tickets.

It would appear that some Alberta welfare recipients did leave because of the welfare reforms, which included rate cuts and work programs. It would also appear that, as Kenneth Boessenkool (1997) argues, Alberta's welfare numbers dropped so drastically not so much because people were pushed off welfare, but more because they could no longer get on welfare in the first place. Boessenkool suggests that early changes to the administrative culture at AFSS tended to restrict eligibility and eliminate any possible misuse of the system. In addition, intake workers required applicants to exhaust all other alternatives before they could qualify. Boessenkool also points out that administrators addressed the issue of welfare fraud and reduced benefits so as to bring them more in line with the earnings of the working poor, thereby eroding the incentive to collect welfare instead of earning employment income. Together, 'these reforms appear to have contributed to a nearly 50 per cent decline in Alberta's welfare caseload in the subsequent three years' (Boessenkool 1997, 10). In other words, large numbers of welfare recipients did in fact leave the welfare rolls, but for a variety of reasons.

The Official Record: What Do the Evaluators Say?

In his 1994–5 *Annual Report*, the provincial Auditor General declared that there was no proof that the thousands of people who had left welfare since 1993 had actually found work: 'To measure the impact of initiatives, the Department needs to gather information on why clients leave or return to the Supports for Independence program. For example, the Department should know how many, or what percentage of, clients leave the program because they find employment due to the training they have received. If they later return, the Department should know how long they were employed, and why they have returned.

Information of this nature would enable the Department to assess the effectiveness of the Province's training initiatives, and evaluate their cost-benefits.'

In response to this report, the provincial government of Alberta in 1997 commissioned the Canada West Foundation (at a cost of $120,000) to conduct a survey of former welfare recipients to find out what had happened to the estimated 172,176 people who had stopped receiving assistance between 1993 and 1996. Despite some methodological flaws, the Canada West Foundation's survey, *Where Are They Now? Assessing the Impact of Welfare Reform on Former Recipients, 1993–1996,* provides the most in-depth look at what happened to former welfare recipients in Alberta. Out of a total of 1,096 people contacted at random, there were 769 responses, 693 of which were telephone interviews. The study, released in June 1997, concluded that 'the majority of clients had found employment and ... were better off working than they had been on welfare,' although it did recognize that some former clients earned low wages when they re-entered the workforce. The socio-economic profile of the survey respondents is as follows: 'Not only are most respondents single, about half have no dependents under 18 years of age. Only one-fifth of the sample reported growing up in a family that received welfare at some point ... Over four-fifths of the sample (83.1%) were born in Canada ... About 40% of respondents reported an education level below grade 12 ... Most respondents to the survey are under 45 years of age (74.1%)' (Canada West Foundation 1997, 37–8).

All of the people in the survey had gone off welfare, but some (15 to 20 per cent) were back on welfare by the time they were interviewed. Their reasons for leaving welfare are summarized in Table 8.1.

While the main reason given (53.3 per cent) for going off welfare was to find a job, a number of doubts have been raised about the quality of the jobs to which welfare recipients went. One critic, Gerald Boychuk (1998), claims that the Canada West Foundation survey methodology exaggerates the positive post-welfare experience of participants as well as the number of recipients who left welfare for jobs. Apart from the small survey sample and the telephone and mail survey technique, Boychuk claims that the study excludes the initial period of caseload reduction (more than one-third of all caseload reductions) and also 'ignores the most important component of caseload reduction in Alberta which has been the decreasing number of people allowed on social assistance' (Boychuk 1998, 1). Jonathan Murphy (1997) also points to the difficulty in evaluating provincial welfare reform measures due

TABLE 8.1
Reasons for Leaving Welfare

Reason for Leaving Welfare	Total %
Found a job	53.3
Found a better job or able to put in more hours	2.6
Spouse or partner found a job	2.1
Spouse or partner found a better job or able to put in more hours	0.8
Now supported by a spouse, family member, etc.	3.4
Health improved	2.6
Moved out or person with more income moved in	1.5
Child or other person left household	0.1
Entered job training program	0.5
Transferred to students finance board or received student loan/grant	7.8
Received or became eligible for UI, Workers' Compensation, etc.	7.8
'Rate cuts' or benefits were insufficient	0.3
'Cut off'	7.3
Went to school	2.9
Other	6.0
Don't know or refused	1.0

Source: Canada West Foundation, *Where Are They Now?* (1997, 7)

to the lack of proper project monitoring and secrecy on behalf of the provincial government. He further claims that direct cuts in benefits were equally important in reducing the welfare caseload, in many cases driving welfare recipients out of the province entirely.

Another survey, conducted by Richard Shillington of the University of Alberta, examined more closely the types of jobs obtained by former welfare recipients and concluded that only two-thirds of these were full time, and that most were relatively low-skill jobs:

Comparing incomes from social assistance and paid employment for sample members who had held jobs, the pay level was about the same as the social assistance benefit level in only 18 per cent of all cases. For about one in four cases (24 per cent) the average pay level was less than the average social assistance level. Thus, for almost half of the social assistance recipients surveyed in this study, the jobs they held (when employed) did not provide more income than the social assistance they received (when on welfare).

Only 13 per cent of the jobs reported by sample members provided paid health insurance, and even fewer offered other benefits. In contrast, for the

Canadian labour force as a whole, about 59% of paid workers have Extended Health Benefits, and about 40% have a pension plan. (Shillington 1998, 5–6)

While Shillington found that Alberta training programs for welfare recipients did enhance the employability of welfare recipients and that recipients' participation in employment increased dramatically over the period from 1993 to 1996, he points out that employability for the population in general also rose at a similar level during that same time. Shillington's findings clash somewhat with Ralph Klein's objective of making minimum-wage work an attractive alternative to collecting welfare. However, by changing the structure of welfare (lowering welfare rates and allowing welfare recipients to keep more of their earnings), Premier Klein's reform package does seem to have achieved its desired result of providing a financial incentive for a large number of welfare recipients to go to work. As Ross Klein observes: Before April 1993, most social assistance recipients would not have improved their financial situation significantly by taking minimum-wage work; since then, with reduced rates of social assistance and an allowance for a larger proportion of wage income to be received before social assistance benefits are reduced, minimum-wage employment has become attractive – if not necessary for subsistence – to social assistance recipients in that it was the only means by which they could maintain the same level of disposable income that they had before April 1993' (Klein 1996, 136).

Alberta's work experience programs have been criticized as make-work programs that lead nowhere. An early editorial in the *Calgary Herald* of 15 January 1993 illustrates this attack on Alberta's workfare programs: 'Cleaning up camp sites and working on public works projects hardly qualifies as a comprehensive skills and training program in this, the information and technology age. Like thousands of other Albertans, some welfare recipients could benefit from government-initiated training programs that would leave them with marketable skills – and the ability to be truly self-supporting.'

According to the government, Alberta's three hands-on work experience programs do assist people to move directly from welfare into paid employment. In fact, the job-placement rate for these three programs is very impressive (the placement and retention rates for each of these programs was noted earlier in the section entitled How was the Program Designed?). While the government does not monitor the fate of those people who leave welfare or who are cut from the rolls, it does make an attempt to track the performance of graduates of the three work experience programs. While these programs are small in size, participants benefit from a very dedicated staff who work hard to place graduates of 'hands-on' training in permanent jobs.

Did the Public Play a Role?

Alberta is unique in that its citizens offered little resistance to the drastic changes that occurred in 1993. Unlike jurisdictions such as Ontario and New York City, for example, whose special interest groups are very powerful and persisted in their attempts to block workfare, Alberta's special interest groups made little commotion. An *Edmonton Journal* (28 August 1993) editorial laments the inactivity of those affected and those who should be helping:

> What would you do if you are poor, dependent upon government funds to stay alive, and under attack from that same government? Or what should you do if you are one of the many 'helping agencies' for the poor, dependent also on the government for funds and facing a slow death as a result of the gradual withdrawal of those funds?
>
> Perhaps, just perhaps, you should get together and fight back.
>
> One disheartening aspect of the recent Alberta government assault on welfare payments is the virtual absence of protest. The province's poorest people, forced to bear a disproportionate burden of spending cutbacks, are voiceless in response.

One of the most prominent protests was a September 1993 march organized by Albertans United for Social Justice, a coalition of dozens of organizations representing labour, aboriginal groups, churches, the disabled, and community social agencies: 'more than 2,000 people marched on the legislature Saturday to voice pain, fear and anger directed at the sweeping cutbacks made to the province's social programs' (Florence Loyie, 'Marchers Decry Social Cutbacks,' *Edmonton Journal*, 19 September 1993). Current criticism of welfare revolves around concern over the increase in the number of children being taken into care over the past few years. Some, such as Brian Bechtel, executive director of the Edmonton Social Planning Council (ESPC), have suggested that this increase is directly attributable to the harsh welfare strategies being applied by the Alberta government. Bechtel also claims that the number of children using food banks has been on the rise.

These claims cannot be shown to derive directly from Premier Klein's welfare reforms, however, a paper by the ESPC and the Edmonton Gleaners' Association entitled 'Two Paycheques Away' (1996) does make a forceful argument for this connection. Although there has been concern over child poverty in Alberta, no one group has emerged with the specific aim of reversing welfare reforms in the province.

A study of the print media's coverage (more than one hundred newspaper articles) of the major changes to welfare suggests that Alberta journalists favour the 'long-term investment in human capital' approach to welfare. The media objected to the government's plan to move welfare recipients into the workforce immediately, preferring that recipients be fully supported in their quest for meaningful careers rather than be forced to take dead-end jobs. There also appears to be media curiosity regarding the whereabouts and activities of the large numbers of people who left the welfare rolls. By and large, the media is not satisfied with the Canada West Foundation's survey conclusion that most people left welfare because they found work. The media wants to know more.

The general public in Alberta, though, appears to be in agreement with the direction of welfare reform. Linda Goyette paints the following profile of Albertan's attitude towards welfare in her article 'Alberta Heartless Towards Its Poor' (*Edmonton Journal*, 29 August 1993):

There are thousands of things to love about Alberta and one thing to regret. The citizens of this province hate poor people.

This is a harsh assessment, and I would love to be contradicted, but I've gradually become convinced of it.

Albertans bear a colossal grudge against the minority of people in their midst who depend on social assistance. They can't think of a punishment too severe, a humiliation too deep, for people on welfare.

Whenever a Conservative government cuts welfare payments and benefits – a regular indulgence for two decades – the sadists in the crowd call out: 'More! Deeper! Make it hurt!' Alberta's moderates look on in embarrassed silence, like witnesses at a public caning, afraid to speak up. And then they look away.

So why are we like this? There are plenty of theories. Alberta feeds itself on a mythology of self-reliance. The Ten Commandments of Alberta require that its citizens pay their own way, never ask for help, never complain about tough times, never admit weakness, and always accept personal responsibility for every rotten experience that life throws their way. This is admirable thinking, but it can get twisted into an ugly judgement of the unemployed ... The Alberta ethic, if you can call it that, sanctions the persecution of the poor.

This portrait of Alberta folk, should it approach reality, suggests that Mike Cardinal's welfare reform package remains popular with the majority of Albertans.

What Happened to the Good Idea?

Before 1993, Alberta lacked the political will to support the new, tough changes that had already been written into the policy manuals. Ralph Klein (the new leader of the long-reigning Progressive Conservative Party) provided that will. He reduced the political backlash against reforms by appointing Mike Cardinal, a Métis who loathed welfare, as minister of Family and Social Services. Cardinal not only changed the structure of Alberta's welfare program, but he also changed the administrative culture of Family and Social Services from a cheque distribution office to an employment-directed centre. His ultimate goal was to move welfare recipients into the job market through a series of measures, some developmental and some coercive. The formula was simple: if eligible people refused to train or participate in one of the three employment programs (Employment Skills Program, Alberta Community Employment, Alberta Job Corps), they would be cut off. At the same time, he also made sure that hands-on training opportunities were provided by the community and that dynamic staff would be available to assist program participants, in a direct and personal manner, to find a permanent job. The Wall of Fame bulletin boards are a testament to the success of these programs. Cardinal was well aware of the limitations of job creation programs, and he challenged critics to come up with something better. During an announcement about the expansion of the Alberta Job Corps, he admitted 'I don't think it's the whole answer; the answer is to have enough jobs for everybody in the private industries' (Gordon Kent, 'Minister Sees Public Works Jobs for Welfare,' *Calgary Herald*, 4 January 1993).

While Mike Cardinal resigned as a Cabinet minister in 1996, his reform package (that is, his good idea) did not go away; his emphasis on employment for clients who are able to work set the tone for the management of welfare in Alberta today. The provincial welfare caseload has dropped since welfare reforms began in 1993. The caseload declined by 63.4 per cent over a period of five years, from 94,087 in March 1993 to 34,464 in March 1998. The reduced caseload resulted in savings of $56 million from 1996–7 expenditures, and this money was redirected toward such high-needs areas as Services to Persons with Disabilities and Child Welfare (Alberta Family and Social Services *Annual Report*, 1997–8). Starting in January 1997, program funding for seniors also went up by $14 million, benefiting about fifty-eight thousand seniors and increasing the popularity of social reforms.

The idea of forcing people to 'volunteer' for one of three hands-on work experience programs is still a 'good idea' in Alberta. It would appear that the culture of dependency was changed through a variety of reforms, including expanding government job placement and on-the-job training services as well as transforming welfare caseworkers into employment counsellors. It is the work experience programs that stand out, mostly because of their extraordinarily high job placement and retention rates. But, according to welfare officials, the job is not over yet. The new challenge lies in dealing with clients who face a broader set of barriers to entering the workplace. As welfare rolls have declined, those who remain on welfare, or those who have constantly returned to welfare, have become more readily identifiable. Those clients are often the longer term and more difficult welfare cases whose behaviour or personal habits are serious barriers to getting or keeping a job. According to AFSS staff, emphasis will in future be placed on developing more vocational rehabilitation services for those clients who are only marginally able to work. For example, in June 1998, Kathy Lazowski, spokesperson for AFSS, announced that an interdepartmental framework was put in place to co-ordinate and measure the effectiveness of various support programs for the psychiatrically disabled (Ed Struzik, 'Social Net Leaving Mentally Ill Adrift,' *Edmonton Journal*, June 24 1998).

9.

The Ontario Works Program – Mutiny on the Bounty

Summary

The history of workfare in Ontario is the story of trade unions and special interest groups that were resolved to never permit the proposed 'community service' aspect of workfare to be implemented, regardless of how well or badly workfare was designed (and it could have been better designed). Thanks to government bureaucrats who never bought into the idea of workfare in the first place, the 'work placement' (as opposed to job search or training) dimension of workfare never really materialized. The social-worker culture in Ontario, supported heavily by activists and lobby groups, favour classroom training over work experience.

The welfare rolls declined by almost 50 per cent in the five years since Mike Harris's 1995 landslide election victory (many attribute this victory to the popular workfare initiative), but this reduction cannot be directly linked to workfare. Rather, the reduction in caseload is more attributable to an administrative overhaul (e.g., tightening eligibility requirements, moving students and persons with disabilities to a different system) than to the effectiveness of workfare. In fact, those responsible for administering workfare estimate that only 2 per cent of eligible welfare recipients are engaged in community placements. This participation rate is low compared with the government's original mandated rate of 15 per cent (in 2000 the rate was raised to 30 per cent). But the government is not giving in, at least not yet. Mike Harris has reiterated his government commitment to workfare and recently solicited the private sector to provide work placements for welfare recipients. In 2000 he demonstrated his willingness to continue to tackle welfare bureaucrats' sabotage of his workfare plan by tying the amount of money that each municipality receives for welfare directly to the numbers of welfare recipients engaged in work placements. In Ontario, the battle to make workfare happen is not yet over.

Ontario's Good Idea: Background and Context of the Reform

Ontario is Canada's largest (population approximately 10 million) province, and it is also one of the wealthiest. In 1981, Ontario had 83,000 General Welfare Assistance recipients (single, able-bodied employables) and 117,503 Family Benefits Assistance recipients (single parents and persons with disabilities) on the welfare rolls. By January 1995, the General Welfare Assistance caseload had risen to 340,500 and the Family Benefits caseload to 327,473 (Sabatini 1996, 31). By 1995 the Ministry of Community and Social Services (MCSS) was dealing with well over six hundred thousand cases. With these swelling welfare rolls, Mike Harris, the new leader of the Progressive Conservative Party, began to see welfare reform as an important political lever for his political campaign. In the 1995 election campaign, Harris proposed to make welfare recipients perform some kind of community service in exchange for their welfare cheques. This proposal is thought to be a contributing factor in the Progressive Conservative Party's overwhelming provincial election victory of June 1995. During his campaign, Mike Harris would hold up a 'Blue Book' containing his list of platform promises, and one of the key planks was welfare reform. The Blue Book attacked welfare at its most basic level – its cost: 'Ontario pays the highest welfare benefits not only in Canada, but anywhere in North America. This is one of the reasons our welfare caseload has swollen to record levels. The simple fact of the matter is that we can't afford it. Our plan will set welfare benefits at 10% *above* the national average of all other provinces. This initiative is fair to all involved' (*Common Sense Revolution* 1995, 11).

The public's overwhelming support of Mike Harris and his fabled Blue Book provided justification for the newly elected government's various welfare reforms. Once in power, the Harris government moved quickly to cut provincial welfare benefits by 21.6 per cent (excepting those for the aged and persons with disabilities). The government kept its election promise to bring down Ontario's welfare pay rates to a point no higher than 10 per cent above the average for all the other Canadian provinces, despite the uproar from anti-poverty groups. This cut alone promised the government almost $2 billion dollars in projected annualized savings. The government also installed a Welfare Fraud Hotline to 'catch people who were ripping off the system' and tightened up eligibility requirements (for example, cutting off the welfare payments of tens of thousands of people in jail). Apart from these immediate reforms, the government focused on replacing the existing system with one that centred on client responsibility rather than entitlement.

In order to be able to introduce workfare, it was necessary for the government to review all the different categories of persons who made up the overall caseload, in order to evaluate which groups would, or would not, be required to participate in workfare. For example, persons with disabilities, single parents of children under the age of three, and seniors were to be exempt. This review was in itself a significant bureaucratic undertaking. A great deal of house-cleaning was done in the area of recategorizing welfare recipients so that, when the time came for mandated workfare, it would be clear who would be eligible for participation in Ontario Works and who would not.

An effort was also made to simplify Ontario's complex, two-tiered welfare system by merging the General Welfare Act (mostly relating to single employables) and the Family Benefits Act (mostly relating to single parents of children younger than nineteen and persons with disabilities). The government also set about removing persons with disabilities from welfare, redirecting them to a (more generous) guaranteed income plan, called the Disability Support Program, which was introduced in June 1998. The merger of the two previous acts resulted in a new piece of legislation called 'Ontario Works,' Ontario's version of workfare.

How Was the Program Designed?

The Ontario government's intentions regarding workfare were clearly spelled out in the 1995 campaign Blue Book:

> The best social assistance program ever created is a real job, and this plan (the Common Sense Revolution) will generate hundreds of thousands of those. In the meantime we must move to control costs and help people return to the workforce.
>
> The facts are staggering. In the recession of 1982, just a dozen years ago, total welfare costs in Ontario were $930 million. Coming out of the current

recession, we have four times as many people in the welfare system, and our costs are more than 6 times higher – an astonishing $6.3 billion a year ...

Ontario can do better than the status quo. You have told us that you want to replace welfare with a work, education and training social policy that rewards individual initiative and demands responsible behaviour from recipients of social assistance ...

We should prepare welfare recipients to return to the workforce by requiring all *able bodied* recipients – with the exception of single parents with young children – either to work, or to be retrained in return for their benefits.

There are no short term cost savings in this, but we believe that for every life we get back on track we are avoiding further costly programs down the road. In the next few months, we will be asking charitable groups and other community organizations to meet with us and talk about ways in which this vision could be realized. (*Common Sense Revolution* 1995, 9–11)

Although the Ontario workfare idea had a large number of supporters, there were, of course, groups in Ontario that opposed the idea. Mike Harris made some dedicated enemies who unfailingly turned out at political events to protest and jeer – not only during the election, but well after his victory. At various anti-Harris rallies, protesters stood in black-and-white-striped prison garb, complete with ball and chain, carrying placards that read No Workfare. Ontario was going through a period of unusually high unemployment (approximately 10 per cent) in 1995, which made critics wonder where the jobs would be at the end of workfare.

But the newly elected Progressive Conservative government, which had ousted the New Democratic Party and swept the province, forged ahead, designing a workfare plan that required welfare recipients to work a maximum of seventeen hours a week in exchange for welfare support (excluding single parents of children under the age of three or people who had been on welfare for less than four months). Critics called this 'unpaid labour' and unions and special interest groups pledged to resist any mandatory plan that required welfare recipients to work or train in exchange for welfare support.

Under Ontario Works, the two groups to which workfare applies are (1) single employables who have been on welfare for more than four months and (2) single parents of older children. The huge amount of work in clarifying categories of welfare participants in accordance with their relationship to the labour market took up much of the government's first year of welfare reform. When the Progressive Conservatives took power, single parents (mostly single mothers) in Ontario who qualified for welfare had always been declared unemployable and automatically qualified for the higher rate known as Family Benefits. From the birth of their first child until their youngest child reached the age of nineteen years (twenty-one if the child was still in school), single parents received Family Benefits with no requirement that they seek employment or be employed. Harris lowered the automatic entitlement to single parents with children of three or fewer years of age. Once the single parent's youngest child reached the age of three, the parent would be moved to Ontario Works. This meant that single parents would join the ranks of those required to conduct job searches every month, and participate in community service or employment training, and accept a job should one be found for them. The province is still working with the federal government to secure a child-care funding pledge to render single parents of young children eligible for Ontario Works. As of 2001, single parents of young children were not included in the Ontario Works requirements since new child-care legislation has not yet been passed. Seniors (people aged sixty-five and over) are also not required to participate in Ontario Works. All of these groups, however, can participate voluntarily.

In 1996, the government also announced a reorganization of ministry employment programs to emphasize getting a job. The government negotiated with private sector or non-profit job placement agencies that, on a fee-for-performance basis, receive up to twelve hundred dollars (referred to by some critics as a 'bounty') for successfully placing a single employable person in a job. Welfare recipients considered to be 'job ready' would be referred to these agencies.

Ontario's workfare guidelines were designed quickly, and only one year after its election victory, the government announced that Ontario Works would be phased in starting in September 1996 and would be province-wide within two years. The then minister Dave Tsubouchi claimed that 'work for welfare will benefit recipients by helping them acquire skill, self-confidence and contacts that will assist them in finding a job' (*Dialogue* 1996). The sites for the first phase were selected from submissions made by municipalities (the welfare delivery level) across the province. While most municipalities were opposed to the idea of workfare, they were still required to submit a plan to the government, showing how they would administer the program. From these plans, the first twenty sites were selected.

In their design of a workfare model for Ontario, policy-makers studied a wide range of workfare programs operating in other Canadian provinces, the United States, and New Zealand. They eventually developed a hybrid design that was hard to understand and even harder to administer. The government devised a policy that required the welfare recipient (except single parents of children under three, seniors, and persons with disabilities) to perform community work or train for a maximum of seventeen hours a week in exchange for welfare benefits. This seventeen-hour formula was calculated by dividing the average single employable recipient's monthly allowance by the provincial minimum wage of $6.85. Under Ontario Works, the welfare recipient has three options: (1) Community Participation (volunteer work); (2) Employment Placement (which includes paying agencies to either place welfare workers into full-time jobs, or help set them up in their own business); or (3) Employment Support (standard classroom training).

Eligible individuals who refuse to participate or fail to make reasonable efforts to participate in an Ontario Works activity risk having their assistance cancelled (where the individual is single) or reduced (where the individual is a dependant or has dependants) for a period of three months. If this happens a second time, this individual's assistance will be cancelled or reduced for six months.

The fact that welfare recipients would have a choice of three categories of activity (only one of which is community participation) seemed to confuse the media, which claimed that the workfare program that emerged was a far cry from the hard rhetoric of the Blue Book. John Barber, in the article 'The Socialist Side of Workfare' (*Globe and Mail*, 26 July 1996), quotes Shirley Hoy, Metro Toronto's social services commissioner, as saying: 'It's a much softer approach, a more humane approach than what people had feared. The workfare label has been so negative, but they're not really approaching it that way.' Central to this softening was the flip-flop between the mandatory and voluntary dimensions of the program. In the development of the workfare program the government moved slowly to the softer side of choice. Philip Gombu captures the public's surprise over this development in an article entitled 'Mandatory Workfare Rule Now Uncertain – Minister's Speech Hints There's a Choice' (*Toronto Star*, 20 November 1996):

What is workfare?
Until now, Ontarians might have thought it was a mandatory program in
which welfare recipients would be required to work for their benefits.

But in a recent speech, Social Services Minister Janet Ecker suggested
that the workfare program promised by the Progressive Conservative
government won't be mandatory at all.

'No single choice within Ontario Works is mandatory, but over-all participation (in Ontario Works) is a requirement for each recipient.'

Thus, workfare in Ontario includes not only work in exchange for
welfare, but also employment placement (through agencies) and employment support (the usual requirements of job searching, résumé
writing, training and so forth). For the Harris government, workfare
had moved from 'something' to 'anything and everything.'

The text describing the three dimensions of Ontario Works is reproduced here at length because its wording provides insight into the
government's commitment to welfare reform. In Option 1, Community
Participation, the private sector was originally excluded from offering
placements to workfare participants, but in 1998, after very slow
work placement results, the government announced that it would develop partnerships with the private sector to provide the necessary
work placement opportunities. In Option 2, Employment Placement,
we learn that the government is not only willing to pay up to twelve
hundred dollars to place welfare recipients in full-time jobs, but that it
will also provide incentives for self-employment. This is an aspect of
Ontario Works that has received very little media attention and about
which the public knows little. In Option 3, Employment Support, we
see that 'referral to education and training should only be made to
support the recipient's shortest route to employment.' The following
description of the three components of workfare is excepted from *A
Summary of the Ontario Works Program* (1996), which was distributed to
municipal agencies in 1996:

Option 1. Community Participation

Community Participation will enable participants to contribute to their
community while receiving social assistance and to build some basic
networks, valuable experience, and employment-related skill to help them
move into the paid labour force ...

Placements can be sponsored by communities and/or public, non-profit or private sector organizations. People receiving welfare can also develop their own community placements under the direction of these organizations.

Private sector organizations are restricted to offering financial or in-kind support such as equipment, materials, and expertise to community placements. They may not directly or indirectly offer, administer or supervise community placements. (Note: The government made the decision to include the private sector two years later.)

Service delivery agents must ensure that Community Participation placements (including self-directed placements) offered by communities and public and non-profit organizations meet the following specific criteria for participants:

- Not more than six months at any one approved placement except where a specific plan of skills training is in place, in which case a participant may spend up to 11 months in the placement;
- Not more than 70 hours a month at community placements (if more than one placement, the time spent at all placements cannot exceed 70 hours a month) ...

Recipients who currently volunteer with community, public or non-profit organizations may propose a self-initiated community placement in these organizations, based on their current activities or newly-defined activities provided that the organization involved agrees to administer and supervise the placement and agrees to be a participating organization and the placement meets all program standards and guidelines ...

Organizations participating are asked to develop and administer on-site placements, where appropriate, develop and administer proposals for financial or in-kind support for placements, and supervise recipients in placements and report non-compliance to the municipality.

There are four specific program standards for community placements: not to displace any paid employment position currently held by an employee or previously held by an employee within a minimum of two years of the organization offering an Ontario Works placement or within the scope of the collective agreement, not to violate the recipient's condition of membership in a professional association or trade union, not to interfere with the recipient's paid employment or a paid employment opportunity such as a job interview and to comply with standards concerning hours of attendance, public and religious holidays, pregnancy and parental leaves, and termination of placement.

Option 2. Employment Placement

Employment Placement supports recipients who are job-ready to find and maintain paid employment and helps those interested in self-employment to develop their own businesses. Job placement and self-employment development agencies will be paid based on their success in helping recipients into employment.

(a) Job Placement Opportunities: Job placement agencies may be paid a deposit or flat fee of up to $200 up front to find a job for a recipient. The deposit would be paid back if they aren't able to place the person. The agency is eligible to receive two additional payments: one after the recipient has been working for three months and another after six months. The payment will be based on a percentage of the welfare savings generated by the recipient being placed in paid employment. The maximum fee payable for a single employable placed in six months of paid employment is $1,200 ...

(b) Self-Employment Development Opportunities: Recipients who want to get off welfare by starting their own business will be referred to agencies that specialize in developing business opportunities. These business development agencies could be any organization in the private or non-profit sector that helps people develop self-employment opportunities.

These self-employment development agencies that help set people up in their own businesses are paid the same way as job placement agencies; on the basis of the social assistance savings they generate by helping recipients establish themselves in their own businesses.

The fee schedule for self-employment placements is designed to ensure that recipients developing business enterprises have support throughout the critical first year of operation. A refundable advance or a flat rate of up to $200 will be paid to the agency when a participant registers with the self-employment development program.

Option 3. Employment Support (Job Search)

Employment Support will support and encourage recipients to find paid jobs. Recipients will be supported with tools to help them get a job such as computers to generate resumes, fax machines, and computer job banks. Communities and public and non-profit, and private sector organizations can be involved in delivering Employment Support locally.

Participants will be required to complete approximately four months of an active job search, either independently or in a structured job-search program, prior to offers of community placement or referral to a job-placement or self-employment development agency. Where participants are not in need of basic education, the intent is to support early testing of a participant's employability through an active job search before placement matching occurs under Ontario Works.

Administrative Challenges: Making Workfare Work

The Ontario government faced a number of challenges to the introduction of workfare, not least of which was a bureaucracy that was not sympathetic to the cause. Generally, things took quite a while to get organized. According to a speech given by Ian Morrison, co-chair of the activist group Workfare Watch, at a 27 June 1998 conference entitled 'Communities Respond to Ontario Works,' the provincial government's attempt to introduce workfare could accurately be described as 'chaos.' Gerard Kennedy, former executive director of Toronto's Daily Bread Food Bank and current MPP for the opposition Liberal Party, claims that the government had no idea what it was doing when it set about designing workfare. Margaret Philip, writing in the *Globe and Mail* (4 June 1996) in the article 'Workfare Begins with a Whimper,' quotes Kennedy: 'From the beginning, workfare was and continues to be a cruel joke perpetrated on voters and low-income individuals alike. The reality is, the Conservative Party had no idea how workfare could be done. They milked it as an issue to be elected on, but didn't have a passing idea how to implement it.'

Another problem was the design of a 'community placement' plan that links welfare benefits to the completion of seventeen hours of work per week. This complicated design required steep costs in administration and policing. Moreover, the idea of working in exchange for one's benefits met with swift and strong resistance from anti-poverty groups and trade unions alike, which argued that the welfare recipient would in fact be performing 'free' labour. Ontario's workfare program was plagued by a series of delays, and program designers always seemed to be in catch-up mode. The official implementation date of Ontario Works was moved up from 1 January 1998 to 1 May 1998. Part of the delay stemmed from the attempt to consolidate three hundred sites into fifty. Regulations and guidelines appeared only days before the new law came into effect, and community agencies were not alerted to the changes. There was also very little training of caseworkers. In addition, there were serious problems of computer co-ordination associated with a change of this magnitude – despite a $190 million Business Transformation contract awarded to Andersen Consulting to modernize caseworker computer technology.

The delays in introducing Ontario Works did not appear to ruffle then Minister of Community and Social Services Janet Ecker, who herself announced that the government was phasing in the Ontario Works program very slowly. Although twenty communities were to have introduced workfare in September 1996, many of these were actually still negotiating the terms of their plans, including the *mix* of workfare activities (e.g., community service, job placement, or employment support). According to a James Rusk article 'Minister Unsure of Workfare Start' (*Globe and Mail*, 1 October 1996), Ecker told reporters: 'We want to do this right. We don't necessarily care if we do it fast.' A methodical approach became the convenient rationale for delays and internal bureaucratic squabbling.

One of the main challenges faced by the Progressive Conservative government was the resistance of administrators. Some municipalities (the front-line delivery point of welfare) were waging a rearguard battle against Ontario Works. Mike Harris and his workfare team ran afoul of the administrative culture of those charged with administering the welfare system. Thanks to the culture of social service agencies and its resistance to the idea of work placements, very few work placements were ever found, or monitored; as of 2001, recipients are still overwhelmingly enrolled in job-search activities or expensive training programs (the bread and butter of the old system). In fact, records show that those welfare recipients engaged in community service make up only a tiny handful in each municipality.

Premier Mike Harris was well aware that he was being blocked by administrators and bureaucrats, and he indicated that this resistance should be raised as a municipal election issue. At a press conference, the premier blamed 'the municipalities and unions' for the government's failure to achieve its workfare objectives:

> 'There's no secret that some municipalities and municipal leaders, and some unions, are fighting us on workfare ... I think it would be a good municipal election issue if there are municipalities that have not been as supportive in helping us implement workfare programs ... I'm disappointed that there has been opposition from some parties to workfare.

Some municipalities, some unions have slowed us down, there's no question about that.' He stressed, however, that this opposition has not weakened his faith in workfare. 'I am a firm believer in the principles of workfare. I'm a firm believer that individuals themselves will get far quicker entry back into the force if they begin to feel better about themselves, get skills, which is part of workfare, get training, begin to contribute.' (editorial, *Globe and Mail*, 21 August 1997)

In other words, Ontario's political leadership, unlike that of Mayor Rudolph Giuliani in New York, could not command the support of the municipalities and key social service agencies. The Ontario municipalities acted like powerful baronies to block, modify, or slow down the process. Janet Ecker, then minister of Community and Social Services, also recognized the difficulty in changing the administrative culture of welfare from an emphasis on training to an emphasis on hands-on work placements. Indeed, she appears to have factored this resistance into the government's time frames for implementation. Margaret Philip (*Globe and Mail*, 23 October 1997) quotes the minister as follows: 'We were quite aware that a reform of this magnitude, a cultural shift of this fundamental significance in how welfare has worked before, was going to take time ... In particular, a threat by some trade unions to pull their funding from United Way agencies participating in Ontario Works has denied opportunities for some people on welfare who wanted and could have benefited from a community placement.'

Even a leader as powerful and charismatic as Mike Harris could not remake society as he chose. His efforts to make workfare a success have been continually undermined. These forces of destabilization have begun to erode the very idea of workfare. In an effort to salvage his campaign promise that every able-bodied welfare recipient in Ontario would have to either work or train for his or her benefits, Harris decided to include the previously excluded private sector on the roster of possible work placement provides. This decision is, to a large extent, an admission that workfare has been hindered by the public and non-profit sectors.

Ontario Works has also been attacked for not protecting its workers. At the June 1998 Workfare Watch conference, activists complained that workfare participants would be exempt from the legislation that covers minimum wages, overtime payments, and hours of work. The government has been forced to admit that workfare recipients are in a legal grey area. While workfare recipients often perform work for municipalities, they are not paid employees. The government wants the municipalities to set up workfare programs that observe existing employment-standards practices in their placements, but critics want more guaranteed protection.

To date, union and advocacy groups have fought successfully against workfare, and workforce job placements have successfully been blocked. Not only have the public service unions discouraged the government's attempts to train welfare recipients within voluntary organizations, but they have also resisted, as far as possible, the training of welfare recipients within the government's own departments (this type of training proved to be very successful with single mothers in Alberta). After three years of recategorizing welfare recipients (for example, removing the disabled from the welfare category and moving them to a disability support plan), designing new legislation (merging the old General Welfare Act and Family Benefits Act into the new Ontario Works Act, effective 1 May 1998), monitoring the first twenty Ontario Works sites, and watching the gradual adoption of workfare throughout the province, it would appear that the community service part of the authentic workfare plan has not materialized.

Did Welfare Recipients Participate?

Despite its high-profile introduction and the great anxiety it created amongst welfare recipients (evidenced in Workfare Watch newsletters, protests, and marches), workfare has done little to change Ontario's welfare system. Ontario Works has tightened up eligibility criteria and established new rules, but, for the most part, recipients have not been mandated to perform community (or any other kind of) service to any great extent or in any appreciable numbers. Workfare in Ontario has come to mean the same old job-search/employment-training requirements that existed under previous governments; and filling in job-search forms or attending classroom training sessions are the only dimensions of workfare that caseworkers are familiar with and unions are willing to endorse. In other words, Ontario has a workfare program that doesn't make any new demands on most welfare recipients. The special interest groups know this. The politicians know this. For administrators and welfare recipients, it's business as usual.

For those few participants who have participated in workfare, the results are disappointing. Very little research has been done to follow up this group, but one study has been conducted. Entitled *Plain Speak-*

ing: Hope and Reality – Participants' Experience of Ontario Works, it was prepared by the Project Team for Monitoring Ontario Works (April 1999). This study looked at seventy-five welfare recipients over a one-year period (a six-month follow-up was possible with forty of these same recipients) in the Ottawa-Carlton region. Researchers set out to 'find out and document the experience of participants in the Ontario Works Program.' The following summary of findings illustrates how little the program affected this particular sample of welfare recipients:

> Many people hoped that the Ontario Works Program would help. Provincial government and media coverage of workfare as the fastest route to a job appeared to contribute to a high level of expectation among individuals. At the same time, participants expressed a certain skepticism about the government program:
> 'The government has their own agenda.'
> 'I am very angry with the government, they degrade the poor.'
> ... It appeared that for a number of individuals, participation in Ontario Works *(particularly in community placements)* actually compromised their choices and further hindered their ability to move forward. For most participants there was little gained. While they appreciated the opportunity to be out in the community and around other people, they told us that they did not, for the most part, learn new skills, gain new contacts, or see themselves as being closer to work. (1999, 3; emphasis added)

Workfare does not seem to have been of much benefit to those welfare recipients studied by the Project Team for Monitoring Ontario Works. Part of the reason may be that caseworkers did not specifically address the particular work-entry barrier faced by the welfare recipient. For example, the same survey found that there were quite specific barriers preventing Ottawa-Carleton welfare recipients from entering the workforce: 'Participants, at the outset and throughout the study, identified a great variety of barriers they experienced in gaining employment and independence. Many of these barriers were not or could not be addressed within the design of the Ontario Works Program' (Project Team 1999, 3). In that particular region, the barriers to work that were mentioned most often were 'need to speak both English and French; skills that were out of date or not relevant for the current job market; and the labour market reality of too many candidates for the jobs that were available ... age, gender, and the cost and availability of child care' (Project Team 1999, 25). In other words, the welfare recipients examined in that particular study did not feel that the design of Ontario Works met their specific needs. While the media often provides examples of work-placement success stories, the reality is that traditional training programs are still more often used by caseworkers to move welfare recipients into the job market.

The Official Record: What Do the Evaluators Say?

The actual workfare-participation rate is difficult to determine because workfare in Ontario can include almost anything. During the 1995 election campaign, workfare was clearly defined as mandatory community service in exchange for welfare support, but, as it turned out, the government merely added the community-placement option to already existing requirements. When Ontario Works was unveiled, there was some public concern that it was not quite the mandatory community service legislation for which citizens had voted; indeed, the only mandatory requirements were that participants either search or train for a job, be placed into a job by a placement agency, or participate in a community service job placement.

The premier requested that all municipalities enrol 15 per cent of welfare recipients in job placements. While the provincial government is responsible for 80 per cent of the welfare payments and 50 per cent of the administrative costs, it is the municipalities (who pay 20 per cent of the welfare cheque) that have to screen the applicants and develop the right mix between the three workfare components of community service, job placement, and training. Even though Mike Harris has announced that funding to municipalities will be increasingly tied to quotas for participation in Ontario Works, there is continued government concern that the municipalities, most of which are opposed to workfare, will take the easy way out by pushing everyone into résumé-writing courses and *calling* it workfare (Ian Urquart, in 'Tories' Workfare Program Neither Success Nor Failure,' *Toronto Star*, 23 April 1998).

In August 1999, the government admitted that only fourteen thousand of the three hundred thousand eligible for workfare had actually been compelled to take job placements; and few municipalities could show a community-placement rate higher than a paltry 2 per cent (Richard Mackie, in 'Premier Stands Behind Tests for Drugs, Literacy,' *Globe and Mail*, 26 August 1999). A specific example was provided by Ian Urquart, whose field research uncovered that of the eighty-five thousand people on the welfare rolls in Toronto, fewer than a hundred were engaged in community placement – far short of the ministry's expectation of twenty-five hundred. Toronto officials apparently claim that these numbers are low 'because volunteer agencies have been intimidated by anti-poverty groups and public sector unions into boy-cotting the program' (Urquart, *Toronto Star*, 23 April 1998).

Research conducted by Rick Salutin for his article 'Workfare, Boot Camps and Dr. Laura' (*Globe and Mail*, 7 January 2000) has forced him to conclude that, by 1999, only 5 per cent of municipalities had reached their target of 15 per cent and, to make matters worse, 'the Harris government has upped its target to 30 per cent. Clearly it isn't serious about these goals.' While there is certainly slow disclosure about the numbers associated with workfare, Mike Harris continues to be serious about these goals. In 2000, in response to a KPMG consultant's report that claimed that workfare would only achieve real results if Ontario spent substantial amounts of money (most especially on child care), Premier Harris announced the incentive of an extra thousand dollars per person for municipalities that reached their work placement objectives. The money might then be used to help with child-care costs tied to workfare. This offer did not sit well with the Association of Municipalities of Ontario, which complained that it had not been consulted, nor with the Canadian Union of Public Employees, representing almost all municipal workers in Ontario, which declared that it 'will fight any attempt to place workfare recipients in municipal positions' (James Rusk and Jennifer Lewington, 'Municipal Issues for the Millennium,' *Globe and Mail*, 1 January 2000).

Workfare has not turned out quite the way the Tories had hoped. As then Minister Janet Ecker told the legislature, 'I'm disappointed that there has been opposition from some parties to workfare. Some municipalities, some unions have slowed us down' (editorial, *Globe and Mail*, 21 August 1997). The unions are well aware that the government has not been successful in convincing the municipalities to focus on community placements. As Sid Ryan, president of the Canadian Union of Public Employees, has observed, few real workfare positions have been found (Gombu, in *Toronto Star*, 20 November 1996). Even Andy Mitchell, leader of Workfare Watch, the most powerful lobby group in Ontario opposed to workfare, admits that his organization's fears were never realized: 'Only a few hundred people are doing work for welfare at any one time. It never had a chance of being any different from that. Most people are simply doing variations of the things they always did' (John Ibbitson, 'Whatever Happened to Workfare?' *Ottawa Citizen*, 10 August 1998).

Did the Public Play a Role?

What went wrong in Ontario has much to do with the relentless efforts of unions and special interest groups to throw a wrench in the machinery of government. During his first term as premier of Ontario, Mike Harris eventually came to lock horns with teachers over education reform and later with health-care workers over hospital amalgamations, closures, and cutbacks, but his first real public enemies were the unions and anti-poverty groups that successfully fought, and keep on fighting, his welfare reforms. Michael MacIsaac, director of the Canadian Labour Congress's Ontario region, has attacked workfare because it does not create jobs. Workfare programs 'punish the unemployed and create more poverty by displacing public-sector workers' (MacIsaac, *Globe and Mail*, 28 November 1996). Anti-poverty groups have called workfare 'mean-spirited.' On 27 May 1995, Alan Borovoy, the Canadian Civil Liberties Union's general counsel, published an open letter to the minister of Community and Social Services in the *Globe and Mail* claiming that the forcing of hundreds of thousands of Ontario welfare recipients into compulsory work programs has prompted 'deep misgivings' within the organization and that work-for-welfare programs pose the serious civil-liberties concern of 'conscripting labour in a free society.' Opposition to workfare also came from the native community. Eight native communities asked a judge to strike down Ontario's workfare law because it violated treaties and brought hardship to a region where four out of five people were on welfare. Mike Harris said that 'Indians receiving social assistance will have workfare imposed on them whether they agree or not. They are subject to the same rules (as everyone else on social assistance)' (Richard Brennan, 'Workfare Applies to All: Harris,' *Toronto Star*, 2 March 2000). However, the Ontario government soon learned from the Ontario Court of Appeal that it could not force First Nations to implement workfare in their communities without their consent.

Union threats to cut off donations to volunteer and charitable organizations that participated in workfare proved to be a critical tactic. A report by the Ontario Social Safety Network and the Social Planning Council of Metropolitan Toronto (1996) claims that community agencies risk losing both their volunteers and workfare placements because confusion between workfare and volunteerism would devalue volunteer activity and create a negative image of volunteerism in the mind of the public and of other volunteers. Advocacy groups also claim that workfare conflicts with the mission of agencies to provide assistance to people in need while, at the same time, forcing agency workers to police a welfare recipient's continued welfare eligibility.

Labour councils also threatened the United Way with 'financial ruin' if it provided temporary work placements to welfare recipients in any of its member organizations. The United Way, the popular umbrella organization of almost all community and charitable organizations in the province, relies on donations for its survival. Some of these donations come from unions. The Canadian Union of Public Employees voted to boycott any United Way organization that would not openly oppose workfare. With charitable and community organizations unable or unwilling to train participants or allow community service, the government lost access to many potential hands-on work and training opportunities for welfare recipients.

The clash between the left and the right in Ontario continues. Unions and special interest groups have been successful in keeping the work experience and community service dimensions of workfare out of the formula – leaving the system with expensive training programs that have the usual dismal drop-out and failure rates (*The Economist* 1996). The lobby groups know that nothing new has happened in the area of workfare but continue to have conferences and rallies 'just in case,' or to 'strategize for when we do get workfare.' The last thing activist groups like Workfare Watch want is to draw public attention to the fact that workfare is not actually being implemented, in the event that, for the mere purpose of saving face, politicians become inflamed, heads start to roll, and workfare is actually made to happen. The reality of workfare is kept alive at conventions by various groups that make heated speeches, spout accusations of 'slavery,' and chant 'shame.'

What seems to be taking place in Ontario is a form of silent collusion between anti-workfare advocacy groups and the government. The politicians and administrators need to keep up the illusion that workfare is succeeding, while advocacy groups need to perpetuate the same illusion – so that they can continue to foster support for future attacks on welfare reform. For advocacy groups, workfare is still seen as unpaid labour, and allegations continue to be made that workfare participants have no health and safety protection and that they are exempt from legislation that guarantees a minimum wage, overtime payments, and hours of work (these claims are by and large true thanks to poor policy design, but they are being tackled by the government).

One of the most realistic assessments of Ontario's workfare program comes from journalist John Ibbitson, whose research has led him to conclude that workfare in Ontario is a 'phantom program.' Furthermore, across the province, municipalities themselves (which are charged with administering workfare) admit that only about 3 per cent of eligible welfare recipients are in government work programs, 7 per cent are in training programs, and the rest are cashing their welfare cheques and looking for employment 'much as they did before the Conservatives came to power and Ontario Works was born' (Ibbitson, *Ottawa Citizen*, 10 August 1998). Since neither the bureaucrats nor the lobby groups wish for it to come out that workfare is 'nothing,' this fact is not usually communicated to the public.

Writing in the *Toronto Star* of 18 August 1999, Ian Urquart also drew attention to the fact that 'workfare remains more a slogan than a program':

> Workfare is the Tories' dirty little secret. The truth is that the much ballyhooed program is mostly a fraud.
>
> That became evident on Monday as John Baird, the rookie minister of community and social services, held an ill-advised press conference to trumpet the latest drop in the welfare caseload.
>
> 'Another 15,638 people left welfare in July,' Baird boasted. "That brings the total since our government was first elected in 1995 to more than 412,000.'
>
> The press conference would have been a non-event if Baird had stopped there. But he went on to attribute the government's success largely to its mandatory 'work for welfare' program and that opened that the door to questions from reporters.
>
> Just how many welfare recipients are actually working for their cheques? Baird couldn't or wouldn't respond.
>
> When the questions kept coming, an aide abruptly ended the press conference and a red-faced Baird scurried out of the room.

The media were later telephoned and told that 'less than five percent of the province's welfare caseload' was doing chores for their cheque. Urquart concludes that 'the Tories have opted to do workfare on the cheap and hope no one notices.'

What Happened to the Good Idea?

Politics is to a great extent about impression management. Thanks to advertisements, press statements, and glossy brochures, the general public believes that large numbers of people are participating in workfare. Few people in Ontario have ever seen a workfare crew or a workfare project in action, yet they still seem to love the notion of workfare. The reality, however, is that the work placement dimension of workfare, as we have seen above, is very weak. The old welfare system continues to chug along, involving a lengthy job search followed by a training program (or a series of training programs).

What went wrong with Ontario's workfare? A number of factors seem to have been critical in the derailing of Ontario's program. First, it appears that the Harris government was simply content to make non-workfare changes to the system (e.g., reducing the amount of welfare payments, tightening welfare eligibility, and introducing new sanctions). The requirement for municipalities to have 15 per cent of eligible welfare recipients engaged in job placements fell far short of its goal. Why, therefore, did the government make such elaborate announcements of upping the required workfare participation targets to 30 per cent? Does this announcement not suggest to the public that the municipalities had already met their original 15 per cent target (even though 5 per cent was the *best* available result)? In other words, the illusion of success can sometimes be achieved in spite of actual failure.

Second, the institutional legacy of the old system was too great to break down – social workers and administrators continued to think along the traditional lines of classroom training as opposed to securing and monitoring work experience placements. Third, the power to interpret and administer welfare is distributed across the province's municipalities, and they were never really sold on the idea of workfare in the first place. Fourth, advocacy groups were well organized and were able to block key initiatives in workfare.

To date, union and advocacy groups have fought successfully against workfare, and work placements have successfully been blocked. Not only did the public service union block the government's attempts to train welfare recipients within voluntary organizations, but they also resisted, as far as possible, the training of welfare recipients within the government's own departments (this type of training had proved to be very successful with single mothers in Alberta). The Ontario social services bureaucracy is a believer in big government. This mentality is obvious. After a visit to Toronto, Jean Rogers, Wisconsin's most senior Wisconsin Works administrator, had the following to say:

> What you're seeing in Toronto is the same kind of thing that was true here in the 1960s ... They are still of the mode 'let's build bigger and better social

programs to help these poor families' rather than 'how do we help these families build an attachment to the workforce?'

You had a bunch of people who don't believe in people enough to think they can pull themselves up by their bootstraps and get on with their lives.' (Jeff Harder, 'Ontario Called Welfare Wimp,' *Toronto Sun*, 19 May 1996)

The government began to realize that it was being blocked in the area of community placements, but this realization only dawned after three years of recategorizing welfare recipients (removing the disabled from the welfare category and moving them to a guaranteed income support plan), designing new legislation (merging the old General Welfare Act and Family Benefits Act into the new Ontario Works Act), monitoring the first twenty Ontario Works sites, and watching the supposed formal adoption of workfare throughout the province. In 1998, refusing to give up, Mike Harris expanded workfare into the private sector, giving private employers financial incentives to cover the cost of training a welfare recipient for six months – the idea being that the welfare recipient would be kept on at the end of the placement. On 8 July 1998, Janet Ecker, then minister of Community and Social Services, announced that workfare would be extended to the for-profit sector. Accusations of 'corporate welfare' immediately began popping up in the press. According to Tom Blackwell, in the article 'Firms Can Use Workfare Free' (*Globe and Mail*, 9 July 1998), 'Ontario's labour umbrella group immediately condemned the move, calling it a gift to the Progressive Conservatives' corporate friends.' The swift union reaction is reported as follows:

Allowing the private sector to take on welfare recipients as workers will lead to exploitation and drive down wages over all, the province's top labour leader said yesterday. 'This is a huge issue,' Wayne Samuelson, president of the Ontario Federation of Labour, said in an interview. 'It's nothing short of disgusting ... Many employers will do anything it takes to get cheap labour and labour they can exploit.'

The government introduced legislation in the spring making it illegal to unionize workfare recipients. Critics say the province had no choice but to expand the program to the private sector because it couldn't find enough placements in the public and non-profit sectors.

The government also began preparations for expanding workfare to farms. By 1999, welfare rolls were continuing to drop, hitting their lowest level in ten years, although not necessarily as a result of ushering people from work placements into permanent jobs. Mike Harris called an election and ran a successful campaign in which he 'promises workfare will grow if the Tories are re-elected – and calls welfare reform one of his proudest achievements' (Caroline Mallan, 'Harris Promises Workfare Will Grow if Tories Re-elected,' *Toronto Star*, 27 April 1999). Again, Mike Harris swept to victory. In 2000 welfare rolls continued to fall, for the first time in years reaching less than half a million (487,424); the new minister of Social Services announced to the media that this was partly due to '57,000 jail inmates who were cut off welfare, as well as 42,000 people who refused to take part in workfare and were tossed off the list' (Canadian Press, 'Welfare Rolls Slashed to Decade-low Level,' *Globe and Mail*, 8 August 2000).

As of 2001, the attempt to expand the definition of 'community placement' to include subsidized employment in the private sector is showing few results. This is no surprise, given that the history of Ontario workfare is a story of institutional rigidity and constant grassroots resistance. How could the cornerstone of an election platform, and six years of political will, money, and resources, amount to so little? The answer is that union and advocacy groups and those who control the front-line social service machinery in the province were successful in avoiding the community participation dimension of workfare – an essential operational component of Ontario Works. Premier Mike Harris's recent decision to engage the help of the private sector to secure work placements and to link each municipality's financial allotment directly to their number of workfare participants proves that his administration has not given up on workfare. Inner government circles believe that Ernie Eves, the new leader of the Progressive Conservative Party (since Mike Harris stepped down in 2002), will also push for welfare recipients' increased participation in community service.

10.

Why Good Ideas Go Bad: A Six-Hazard Model

This chapter presents a summary sketch of what we have learned in previous chapters and assesses the implications that these lessons have for policy-makers. (Any conclusions about events in the 'real world' have their inadequecies, and those offered here are no exception.) Based on a study of six welfare-to-work stories, I have developed a six-hazard model that can be used to trace how a 'good idea' turns 'bad.' The model shows the problems associated with the implementation and evaluation of major policy initiatives. It is intended to offer the reader a comprehensive overview of otherwise confusing terrain, although, as with any model, it necessarily simplifies complex factors. Here, I have tried to develop a model that incorporates a fluid definition of workfare and takes into account the key players associated with any policy 'good idea': the politicians, the policy-makers, the administrators, the target group, the evaluators and the public (including lobby groups, the media, and the general public). This model recognizes the reality of charismatic leaders who rely on emotion to drive their promises, policy-makers who fail to clearly define procedures/rules/regulations, administrators who are reluctant to implement changes, target groups that engage in forms of disobedience and non-compliance, evaluators who report false results, and a public that has a constant need for the next good idea. The model recognizes that a form of collusion between the players may take place to keep a good idea alive long beyond its usefulness. It identifies six forces, any one of which can destabilize a good idea: the politician hazard, the policy-maker hazard, the administrator hazard, the target-group hazard, the evaluator hazard, and the public hazard. For a good idea to go bad, there does not necessarily have to be a rational-technical failure. An idea that is bad may simply be one that is no longer good.

The different forces, taken separately or together, all influence the good idea. In each of the six case stories, one or two hazards flashed more brightly than others; sometimes the pilot took heed of the warning, but generally not. In California, the evaluator hazard was the hazard light that flashed the brightest. By claiming that failure was success, the evaluators extended the life of a worthless workfare program. The GAIN program that Ronald Reagan raved about when he got to the White House became better and better, according to evaluators, even though welfare rolls did nothing but rise during GAIN's 1985–8 lifetime and less than 20 per cent of California's welfare recipients ever participated.

In New York the administrator hazard derailed workfare, with welfare workers going through the motions of administering a program that they saw to be contrary to their self-interest. Many recipients dropped off welfare before or during their actual placement. While caseload numbers did go down in New York City, it is hard to gauge the extent to which this was due to workfare or to other factors such as a tightening-up of eligibility requirements. In New York, the evaluator hazard also flashed warnings as politicians and bureaucrats claimed that the drop in welfare rolls was due to the workfare program, despite a lack of evidence to support this argument.

Any time the hazard light came on in Wisconsin, Governor Tommy Thompson heeded the warning. Wisconsin's ability to keep its 'good idea' good (in the rational-technical sense) owes much to Governor Thompson's persistence in pushing through his welfare reforms, but it is probably due more to the competence of the policy-makers who knew how to realize his political promises. Both the politicians and the policy-makers never took their eyes off the ball. With a governor who was truly committed to his cause and intelligent policy-makers who knew how to design a heavily interconnected, barrier-oriented program, the result was assured: reluctant administrators were not put in charge of moving people into the workforce, clients' needs were addressed on an individual basis, evaluators actually measured how many welfare recipients got a job (as opposed to the usual evaluation of the workfare participation rate), and the public was drawn into the program through business councils and direct requests from the governor to train and hire welfare recipients. Wisconsin removed welfare recipients' actual barriers to the workplace in a systematic and incremental way (e.g., investing heavily in child care, contracting out service delivery rather than using unwilling or inept county staff, linking welfare payments to the number of hours worked, not increasing benefits for each additional child born, providing short-term loans to get a car fixed to get to the workplace). Despite being armed with the political will and astute policy-making (which was constantly working towards improvement), Wisconsin's workfare program faced challenges from reluctant administrators, who constituted Wisconsin's biggest hazard. But Tommy Thompson out-smarted them. He divided the state into regions and contracted out the movement of welfare recipients into the workplace to profit and non-profit agencies (e.g., Goodwill Industries won the contract for Milwaukee's two most difficult inner-city regions).

Alberta was also one of the six jurisdictions that managed to keep its 'good idea' good, and that is largely because Progressive Conservative Premier Ralph Klein provided the political will to make the changes that had already been planned by the previous Progressive Conservative government. Ralph Klein made the decision to name Mike Cardinal, a Métis from a poor background who abhorred welfare, as minister of Alberta Family and Social Services. It was, in fact, Cardinal who gave the administrators the strong political support they needed to make the welfare reforms changes that had already been mapped out on paper, but which nobody would administer for fear of the political backlash.

Sometimes, a social policy can begin to unravel early, even during take-off. In New Brunswick, a closer look at the fantasy of the political promise in the very first instance might have revealed that there would be serious difficulties and enormous costs in the attempt to bring thousands of single welfare mothers, many of whom had only a primary school education, up to the college diploma level, in a scant three and a half years. New Brunswick's expensive 'learnfare' failure reveals a gap between attractive political imagery and the actual desires of the majority of single mothers, for whom the classroom had not been a great success earlier in their lives. Thanks to policy-makers who will admit no wrong, administrators who watched the failure and said nothing, recipients who dropped out of the program in droves, evaluators who gave rave reviews, and a public always ready for a new idea, the disaster went undetected. Yes, the idea had gone bad, but, thanks to the collusion of key players, the idea officially remained good, with people believing that this hugely expensive program (from which approximately 75 per cent of participants dropped out) was a good idea.

In Ontario, workfare is still seen as a good idea, even though it actually became derailed at a very early stage. There, the major hazard light flashing was the administrator hazard. Thanks to early days, and Premier Mike Harris's legacy, workfare may yet happen in Ontario. It is surprising, however, that the government assumed that administrators would co-operate with the government on an idea to which they were so loudly and vehemently opposed. The government's decision to allow existing municipal welfare workers (already known to be hostile to workfare) to remain as the front-line service providers of this new program practically guaranteed the demise of the good idea. Right-wing politicians' belief that left-wing ideologues would fall in line, follow the rules, and accept accountability for the results was naïve at best and costly at worst. Thanks to the rational assumptions that were made about the administrative culture of government, administrators were free to collude in the superficial success of workfare; and it is through this appearance of success that the very foundation of workfare is undermined. Anecdotes of work placements are fed to the politicians, who pepper political speeches with these good-news stories. At the same time, Mike Harris has recently engaged the private sector to provide work placements amidst roaring accusations of 'corporate welfare,' and he decided to turn up the heat on the bureaucrats by tying the money that each municipality receives to the number of work placements that they achieve. The workfare plane is going through a storm, but the pilot, Mike Harris's successor, Ernie Eves, is not likely to ignore the light that keeps flashing 'administrative hazard.'

In all six jurisdictions, the good idea was affected by the public hazard, whether it is lobby groups, the media, or the taxpayer. Even the whiff of a new idea that is contrary to the views of activists brings out the troops. Their boredom is often a hint that it is time for something new. The media survives by degrading the old and ushering in the new. And, thanks to human nature, we seem to welcome the new, even if it's merely the same policy in different wrapping. It is this aspect of ourselves that brought us the good idea in the first place. Figure 10.1 shows how the model works, starting with the political hazard and ending with the public hazard.

What the model points to is that good ideas go bad because the fantasy becomes exposed. As long as people pretend that the good idea is really taking place, then the good idea is alive. Once there is scrutiny and scandal, or even just plain boredom, the good idea is no longer good. Each one of the six hazards (alone or in conjunction with others) plays a role in determining the outcome of the good idea. So where does this model leave us? It leaves us with a useful analytical construct in deciding whether a good idea is actually workable, plausible, or even likely, or whether it is merely a political fantasy that serves a purpose at

Figure 10.1 Why Good Ideas Go Bad: A Six-Hazard Model

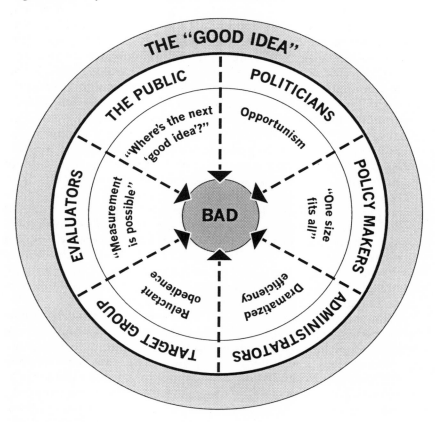

election time but is not really meant to go much further. The following section takes a look at each one of the six hazards, in turn, to show how powerful each force can be in derailing a good idea.

Politician Hazard: Opportunism

The lifeblood of politicians is the good idea. If politicians fail to offer new ideas, voters say 'nothing new' and move to the more compelling and innovative platform. In politics it is important to give the impression of bringing progress, innovation, improvement, and change into government. While politicians are always looking for the next good idea, the new solve-all must also conform to what is commonly accepted – what French philosopher Michel Foucault would call being 'in the truth' of its era – a type of policy chic. In the 1980s and 1990s politicians began to discover that the road to power could be paved with promises to get tough on welfare. Politicians took advantage of the new public mood to sell this particular good idea, providing effective economic and social rationales for forcing the poor to work for their benefits. Politicians, however, sometimes fail to examine their own assumptions or follow their own advice. They also fail to apply their well-honed critical capacities to an analysis of their own good ideas. The politician hazard addresses this incapacity to fully consider such initial assumptions and their consequences.

Workfare may be more about politics than poverty. In all six case stories, arguments of differing levels of sincerity were made for providing services of value in return for expenditures to increase welfare recipients' employability (directly through the acquisition of new skills and indirectly through the acquisition of new work habits). A work requirement would weed out those who had full-time jobs on the black market, for example, babysitting, house cleaning, or construction. Moreover, workfare would likely act as a disincentive to those currently employed who may be thinking of joining the welfare rolls. Despite certain fierce objections, the large majority of voters bought into the concept of workfare.

But how many politicians are truly committed to removing, in a direct and meaningful way, the major barriers to employment faced by welfare recipients? Workfare cannot work without adequate child care, but few politicians dug into their coffers to invest in such essential support. Only in the case of Governor Tommy Thompson of Wisconsin did we see serious commitment to making workfare work (in the sense of getting all welfare recipients to participate in work-related activities), and Thompson did not succeed overnight. This is a politician who thought long and hard about what would be needed to make workfare work. It took ten years and more than seventeen pieces of legislation for him to arrive at Wisconsin Works (W-2), a welfare program based on a 100 per cent work requirement. He undertook processes of creative destruction to adapt his vision of social programs to the realities of the workplace. To what extent did politicians in the other case stories address the major barriers that made it difficult or impossible for individuals to participate in training/community placements or even to obtain employment? How many politicians told their policy-makers to make sure that integrated essential supports such as accessible child care, transportation assistance, and accommodation for persons with disabilities were included in the design of the policy? How many politicians addressed the financial disincentives that resulted in people making less, rather than more, money by participating in workfare or leaving welfare for employment? How many politicians recognized the need to bridge supports such as health care to ease the difficult transition from welfare to self-sufficiency? Only in Wisconsin and, to a certain extent, Alberta, do we see a key politician going beyond the quick fix. As the case stories have shown, without significant attention to these barriers from the highest level, workfare is not a serious idea.

Most politicians promise that the good idea will bring about improvement, but in reality they have only a vague notion of the problem. All social policy necessarily has a political dimension, and, as Norris and Thompson point out, this is not necessarily a bad thing: 'To say that welfare reform is political, however, is not to condemn it. Rather it is to understand its essential character. Yet, it is not unfair to say that when the politics of an issue is mainly about politics (and not the issue), then both the politics and the issue are done a grave disservice' (1995, 236).

Another aspect of the politician hazard is the fact that good ideas are rarely, if ever, new; instead, they are often repackaged as new for political reasons. The good idea exists in effect as a recycled political platform. The brilliance of the good idea is to appear new without really having any such thing. Workfare is the perfect good idea for many reasons, one of which being that it always appears to be new. The United States has long had programs that required states to enrol welfare recipients in education and training programs. First there was the Work Incentive (WIN) program in 1967, followed by the Community Work Experience Program (CWEP) in 1971, the Family Support Act (FSA) in 1988, and the Personal Responsibility and Work Opportunity Reconciliation Act in 1996. All of these required states to enrol an ever-increasing proportion of the welfare population in so-called work activities (which could mean almost anything). Somehow each of these major U.S. social policy announcements managed to look new. The same applies to all of the case stories that we looked at in previous chapters. In the United States, California's Greater Avenues for Independence (GAIN) program was declared to be new, regardless of its similarity to the WIN program that preceded it. Because its training programs were now based on the principle of 'investment in human capital,' observers came from all over, including Washington, to have a look. California's GAIN program was held up as a model of a successful welfare-to-work program. No matter that there were few participants or that welfare rates went nowhere but up. GAIN appeared to be new and was a tremendous success at the political level.

In New York, the politician hazard helped ensure that workfare worked only at the surface level of reducing welfare numbers. The content and substance of workfare programs were relatively ineffectual but, because the mayor's political platform was intimately tied to solving the welfare problem, much energy was expended at managing impressions of success around the 'bottom line' (i.e., the reduction in absolute numbers of welfare recipients).

Tommy Thompson's promise to reform welfare was not an empty political promise, like that of so many other politicians. In 1986, Thompson presented his good idea for moving welfare recipients into jobs, and the people of Wisconsin voted him governor. Before his 1986 election, there had been serious federal programs to move people from welfare to work, but these had met with limited success. From 1987 to the present, Thompson has enjoyed the greatest success of any U.S. governor in moving people from welfare into self-sufficiency. He tackled each barrier to employment (e.g., child care, transportation, financial disincentives) piece by piece, and by 1999 he had reduced the welfare rolls by 91 per cent.

New Brunswick's new idea in welfare reform, called NB Works, drew the entire country's attention. Politically, NB Works was a tour-de-force, with its failure kept well under wraps. The idea of providing an intake of one thousand welfare single mothers a year (for three years) with the opportunity to complete high school and obtain specialized training at a community college, with full supports such as child care and transportation, provoked curiosity. The national press flocked to this small maritime province to witness the new experiment. Before receiving their three years of free schooling and supports, the mothers were given five months of work in order to qualify them for federal Unemployment Insurance (shifting them off provincial welfare rolls and onto the federal dole). The idea was interesting, the cost-sharing arrangement with the federal government was a brilliant financial coup for the province, but the fact is that people had always been able to get a quick job for a few months and then qualify for federal Unemployment Insurance to go back to school for three years. The only new elements were the program's formalized constitution and the expensive supports provided to the single mothers. Initial evaluations revealed that the vast majority of the first intake of one thousand dropped out of the program, and subsequent interim evaluations show no better results. As of 2000, the final program evaluation had not yet been released. The government managed to keep its 'good idea' good by hiding NB Works' failure and publicizing its next new idea, Jobs Plus (an extension of NB Works which is also now defunct).

In 1992, when Ralph Klein, the new leader of the long-governing Progressive Conservative Party, was campaigning on a platform of drastic reforms to education, health services, and welfare, he was not talking through his cowboy hat. The Conservatives won again, and he, as new leader, began welfare reforms in 1993 the likes of which Canadians had never seen. He cut welfare payments and, without ever using the word 'mandatory,' made sure that welfare recipients participated in either short work-related training programs or one his three hugely successful work experience programs: (1) paid training in the provincial government itself (mostly aimed at single mothers), (2) paid training in social service, community, or religious agencies (for those who needed more experience and supervision), and (3) paid training in the job corps (e.g., construction projects) for either the private or the public sector (for those with serious barriers to employment). He hired Mike Cardinal, who was known for his opposition to welfare, as his minister of Family and Social Services, and together they made sure that the work experience programs were designed in a motivating way. One example of innovation is that when welfare recipients went into one of these three work experience programs, they stopped being welfare recipients. They became 'employees' of the government. In other words, recipients went *off* welfare and received a pay cheque from their agency for hours worked (the government paid the agency). After an intensive paid work experience of three to six months, employment counsellors worked closely with the welfare recipients to help them find employment. According to Alberta Family and Social Services' records, more than 70 per cent were still employed one year after completing the program. Ralph Klein has kept his 'good idea' good. And although Klein has a reputation in Canada for having instituted welfare reforms that were unprecendently harsh and cruel, he was re-elected premier in 1998.

In 1995, Ontario's Mike Harris campaigned on a welfare-reform platform that focused on workfare, and his Progressive Conservative Party swept the province. His vision was that able-bodied welfare recipients (with children older than three years) would need to participate in active training or community-service programs for seventeen hours a week in exchange for their welfare cheque. The good idea still looks good in Ontario, thanks to excellent public relations. The lobby groups don't want the public to know that workfare isn't working in case the government starts making it work. The administrators pretend that it's working by signing up people for the same old job-search or training programs and calling it workfare. With the exception of a very few journalists (e.g., John Ibbitson, *Ottawa Sun*, 10 August 1998; Ian Urquart, *Toronto Star*, 23 April 1998; and Rick Salutin, *Globe and Mail*, 7 January 2000), the media still acts like workfare is actually happening. The puzzling thing about workfare in Ontario is that the previous New Democratic government said little about welfare reform, but actually tightened eligibility controls and introduced the highly successful JOBS program, which placed welfare applicants directly into the competitive labour market. The JOBS program was cancelled by Mike Harris in favour of his supposedly draconian workfare – and Harris's workfare is going nowhere fast because the front-line social workers won't add work placements to their routine of moving people through classroom-training programs. Still, because of the fuss that was made over workfare during the 1995 election campaign and the landslide victory of Mike Harris's party, the public naturally assumes that workfare has been implemented. Flyers dropped into the mail slots of thousands of households proclaimed the success of workfare. There were no details of how many welfare recipients were engaged in the same old job-hunting and training/education activities, compared with those engaged in actual work placements or community service: Mike Harris was elected again in 1999, promising more workfare. The important thing to remember about the political hazard is that opportunism, political expediency, and repackaging are among the elements that make up the good idea in the first place, and often they are all that is required. The Ontario government's announcement in January 2000 that it was going to re-quire 30 per cent of those on welfare to be engaged in job placements (up from the previous 15 per cent) overlooks the fact that a 5 per cent participation rate had never even been reached in the first place. As Henry Adams said in 1907, 'practical politics consists in ignoring facts.'

Policy-maker Hazard: One Size Fits All

What is the role of the policy-maker in determining the outcome of the

good idea? It is one thing for politicians to argue that traditional welfare policy doesn't work. It is quite another thing for policy-makers to
design a new program, especially one that is meant to alter the behaviour of a target group. Politicians usually have a major impact on how
policy-makers define a problem and solve it, since it is they who sold
the good idea in the first place. They tend to impose their assumptions
on the policy-makers, with the result that either the good idea goes bad
or the policy-makers gain influence and modify the idea into something realistic. The policy-makers are always affected by the politicians'
assumptions, and it is these assumptions which will have the biggest
impact on how the policy-makers actually approach the good idea.

It is often thought that policy-makers enjoy the guidance of clearly
defined, coherent goals. For the most part, thanks to the politicians, the
nature of any social problem is itself in question. Most policies have a
number of inconsistent features, relationships, and demands, workfare
being a perfect example. Even if policy-makers do know what results
they want, they are uncertain how to obtain them. The policy-maker
hazard refers to the lack of acceptance and appreciation of the nature of
a problem, in this case the employment barriers faced by individuals on
welfare.

In Canada, American examples of workfare and learnfare have been
studied and imitated by policy-makers, but to what extent has Canada
learned from the mistakes of the United States? Policy-makers' lack of
attention to, or disregard for, matching different aspects of workfare to
the different needs of welfare recipients is precisely the type of problem
that surfaces only after programs have been initiated. Despite the fact
that targeting a policy to the needs of different client groups may be the
single most important technical hazard in the success or failure of a
good idea, various U.S. government organizations have implemented a
blanket solution (e.g., workfare for entire welfare populations) without
looking at the specific needs of different sub-groups that face a wide
variety of work barriers. Ontario policy-makers followed the United
States in measuring workfare's success by the yardstick of enrolment,
content to require a 15 per cent participation in work placements (upped
to 30 per cent in January 2000) rather than movement into the workforce.
While Canada is in a position to benefit from the implementation
experiences of the United States, the influence of American programs
on Canadian policy design seems to begin and end with mere imitation.
There is little interest in learning from the United States's mistakes.
Canadian policy-makers seem unconcerned with how evaluation re-

sults might be fed back into workfare programs to modify or correct deficiencies. Most are already on to the next good idea. Although Canadians readily take advantage of American policy blueprints, Canadians have not actually learned much from the workfare experience south of the border.

The appropriate policy is rarely self-evident. Furthermore, it requires wisdom to realize that there are rarely blanket solutions, that a problem and its solution can be labelled 'something,' 'nothing,' or 'anything,' and that results cannot be planned on flip charts, but can develop only through trial and error. In almost all of the case stories, policy was undertaken from a politician's speech and rather than being based on a collection of data relating to welfare recipients' employment barriers. In some cases, policy-makers turned workfare into a whole new way of doing business (e.g., Wisconsin and Alberta), but other jurisdictions lacked either the will or the know-how to make workfare meaningful.

The case studies have shown that policy-makers rarely focused on a specific problem (e.g., getting welfare recipients into the workforce). In the United States, policy-makers were somewhat constrained by the federal JOBS program (1988–96). The creativity of each state was manifested in the waivers that it requested from Washington. While the JOBS program clearly stated that workfare was mandatory, each state could make of this what it wanted. California's GAIN program, introduced in 1985, was a forerunner to JOBS, and its long-term 'investment in human capital' theory fit well with liberal thinking of the times and enjoyed popular support. The 'education first' design was, according to California policy-makers, used as the model for the design of the federal JOBS program. GAIN continued to serve as a model for the nation for years, until Clinton's 1996 welfare reforms threatened to expose California's ever-mounting numbers on the welfare rolls and the lack of movement from welfare to work. In an effort to get serious and start producing the results that Clinton's 1996 welfare reforms (which included time-limited welfare and financial sanctions) sought, policy-makers amended GAIN and renamed it CalWORKS, a new welfare- to-work program that became effective 1 January 1998. The principles are similar, but there is more intensity in CalWORKS and a greater emphasis on work over education.

Policy-makers in Wisconsin directly addressed the problem and set about designing policies that would move welfare recipients into the workplace. Wisconsin insisted that its JOBS program achieve real results – at no time did Governor Tommy Thompson fall into the trap of emphasizing participant enrolment in welfare-to-work programs. His objective was to get people off welfare and into jobs, not just to focus on meeting a 20 per cent participation rate in the welfare-to-work program. Tommy Thompson's policy-makers understood his objectives, along with their attendant moral values and normative arguments. They also appreciated his seriousness: Thompson's proposed reforms were based on principles of social justice, and he was willing to mobilize the state's financial resources to make his vision a reality. The policy-makers sought out what was wrong with the system and worked closely with legislators to introduce necessary changes to fix it. Along the way, not all of the reforms were successful (e.g., the learnfare program for children of welfare recipients), but others surpassed expectations (e.g., tracking down non-custodial parents for child support). For more than ten years, policy-makers interpreted political promises and cleared away the debris that was blocking the road to employment and self-sufficiency for welfare recipients. The policy-makers correctly interpreted the politicians' new policies and implemented them successfully, in addition to the challenge of constantly adjusting and adapting complicated inter-agency operations and new technology, as well as training the front lines in the new changes.

In New York, policy-makers soon realized that it was the numbers game that was key, and as a result they focused their attention on the control, eligibility, and sanctions sides of welfare. As pressure increased to report good news, less attention was paid to the quality and efficacy of the work experience programs themselves. While the welfare rolls did decline, these changes had little to do with workfare.

Sometimes, the political agenda requires a policy to be produced immediately, regardless of workability, as in the case of New Brunswick's NB Works program. In the rush to get this high-profile national demonstration 'learnfare' project off the ground, policy-makers struggled so much with the design and the wording that the policy manual was not produced until the program's third year of operation. New Brunswick's good idea, an expensive three-and-a-half-year educational reform aimed at single mothers, was unrealistic in every sense of the word. Not only was the good idea out of touch with the lifestyle of welfare mothers, but the patchwork policies that provided the infrastructure for the program did little to capture the interest of participants, the vast majority of whom dropped out and returned to welfare. However, there was little that policy-makers could do with a good idea that was so bad in the first place.

Alberta had done a good job of overhauling its policy manual, aligning recipient categories with work demands, but the words of the policies did not come into practice until Ralph Klein swept to power. In Ontario, policy-makers chose to imitate the U.S. pattern (workfare as 'anything and everything') in that its design focus was the enrolment of welfare participants in the workfare program, either in job hunting, education/training, or work placement/community service. This loose design allowed municipalities – those resistant front-line service-delivery providers that were against work placement and community service – to continue their existing practices of rotating clients through endless training courses, ignoring the requirement that 15 per cent of welfare recipients be in work placements. The idea of work placements and community service had been abhorrent to municipalities in the first place, and the design of workfare policy was broad enough to allow them to carry out business as usual. The loose design worked well, since the program could still be called workfare while allowing the social-worker culture to run the show as it saw fit. Politicians could still report to the public that workfare was on track; and the fact that this broad definition of workfare was not quite what the politicians or the public had in mind during election campaigns was not important to the immediate survival of the good idea.

The policy-maker hazard relates to the fantasy that (1) policy is focused on a specific problem, (2) the good idea is actually 'something,' and (3) planning actually works. Normally, policy-makers are far removed from the reality of the poor. For many, poverty is the unpleasant experience of others. The gap between the concept of poverty and its reality might be filled with a little bit of truth, a lot of half-truth, and a dollop of myth. All these beliefs show up in the designs, procedures, and actions that policy-makers suggest. If the policies don't measure up to the theoretical specifications of the designers, it is easily concluded that the target group (in this case welfare recipients) is at fault.

Administrator Hazard: Dramatized Efficiency

How does the administrator affect the good idea? Struggles within the social services community itself cannot but influence the outcome of the good idea. The administrative culture of an organization is intangible, yet it is a dominant force. It can be a catalyst to the good idea, or an impediment.

There is a natural reluctance to embrace change. Change disrupts routines. It destroys accepted ways of doing things and often changes one's relationships with subordinates, superiors, co-workers, and clients. Acceptance or resistance to change depends on many factors, but in the case of workfare we are not talking merely about the introduction of a new accounting system, we are talking about a social policy that has ethical underpinnings. From what we know of the attitudes of the social service culture, it is obvious that most of its adherents are not supportive of workfare, mostly because of its mandatory work requirements. This culture has long favoured training over the labour market as the way to employability for welfare recipients. Workfare programs, however, usually emphasize employment over all other activities. When work is the clear object of reform, social workers are fundamentally reluctant to fulfil the new role that many governments have allocated to them; the shift from welfare worker to career counsellor is unlikely to occur. As a result, these case workers have a deep impact on how a policy is actually carried out.

Lipsky (1980) conducted a study of 'street level bureaucrats' (those who act as the interface between the organization and the clients) and concluded that the front line participated as much in the making of policy as those at the top. How a program is implemented reflects the administrators' interpretation of the policy. If the interpretation is off-track, one might expect the designers to adjust the program on a continuous basis in order to ensure that goals are being met. However, it is far more likely that the policy-makers have already often moved on to the next good idea. As Corbett remarks: '"People-changing" programs are expensive, hard to administer and labor-intensive' (1995, 45).

The administrative hazard relates to government bureaucrats appearing to implement a desired strategy when, in fact, they are doing no such thing – a form of dramatized efficiency. In other words, if a major attitude shift is required of caseworkers (as is the case with the introduction of workfare) and they don't want the change to occur, they will fake it. Meyer and Rowan (1977) have described the dramatized efficiency syndrome as an appearance of deliberation that is fostered for public consumption while a different set of procedures is used to get work done; in other words, while there is a visible plan in place, internal functioning often ignores it. This is a practical and realistic view of the situation. Why should people believe that, just because a new social policy is announced and administrators are trained, they should co-operate with the change and deliver the desired message to clients? Why should a new social policy, especially a right-wing policy in the hands of a left-wing administrative culture, change administrators' basic philosophy of welfare and how it should be paid out?

The introduction of workfare may not all of a sudden mobilize caseworkers to undertake the difficult task of locating the hundreds of thousands of work-experience assignments and jobs that are needed. When New Zealand briefly introduced a form of workfare in 1990, Maurice McTigue, New Zealand's High Commissioner to Canada, explained that 'the biggest problem with workfare is finding jobs for people' (Eric Beauchesne, 'Workfare's Track Record Is Weak,' Southam News, 11 April 1996). Governments seem to fall easily into the administrative hazard, since they rarely build in controls to make sure that front-line workers are held accountable for results. In the case of workfare, the administrative culture's hazard lies in its long-held assumption that the solution to finding work lies in classroom training. Despite the fact that programs to provide educational upgrading, employment preparation, and technical training have already been around for years and failed, social workers seem to be unwilling to embrace experiential learning. In view of their beliefs, it is unlikely that they would go to the trouble of making job contacts and negotiating work placements.

The six case stories have shown that some jurisdictions consider workfare to be just another training program (e.g., California and Ontario). Training assumes that there is a demand for what is being produced and that issues such as employer attitudes to class, racism and sexism in the workplace are secondary to a welfare recipient's lack of skills. As long as training is considered to be the solution to welfare recipients' unemployment problems, workfare cannot function. But the social-worker culture clings firmly to the assumption that it is only more training that will solve the unemployment problem, and it is this implicit refusal to follow orders that can cause the demise of the good idea. In the case of Ontario, there was an ideological disagreement with workfare. In other cases, administrative disobedience to the good idea can happen for other reasons, not least of which is simple resistance to change.

Regardless of political rhetoric, welfare workers maintained their position that welfare recipients would find work more readily only with improved qualifications. While this is a rationale to which adherents to the social service culture cling like a dog to a bone, training is a useful banner for a number of different groups. Swift and Peerla (1996) refer to the emergence of a 'training gospel' in which politicians, business leaders, and the journalists who interview them tell us about the 'new' job requirements of the innovation-based economy of the 1990s. They point out that people continue to spread the word that to get the good jobs requires training, despite the fact that training actually doesn't work: 'But despite all the talk of training, the reality has fallen short. Nowadays we're constantly hearing about people who have training, or university degrees, and still can't get jobs. There's a missing connection there, somewhere. As the chairman of the Business Council on National Issues told his audience of management enthusiasts, "Government labour-market programs have failed to equip the unemployed with marketable skills"' (Swift and Peerla 1996, 31). In spite of its terrible record, social-service workers still hold out training as the answer to insecurity and job loss. And if initial training fails, then train again. According to Swift and Peerla, 'some call it lifelong learning. For others it is learning a living' (1996, 31).

What about welfare recipients who are highly educated and possess solid work experience and impressive credentials? One press report referred to 1,308 welfare recipients in Toronto with a Master's degree or a PhD (Crawford, cited in Torjman 1996, 6). Naturally, there is a correlation between higher education and higher earnings, but that doesn't mean that higher education is for everybody. Both ability and motivation play a role in academic performance, and for many welfare clients the classroom was already a place of frustration and failure. A welfare-to-work study by the Social Research and Demonstration Corporation, a non-profit registered charity, claims that 'Experiential training is more effective than classroom-based adult education in producing positive labour outcomes' (SDRC 1998, 2). Administrators are not alone in their belief in the value of long-term investment in human capital; policymakers too have embraced training as a solution to complex social problems: 'Training has emerged of politicians and policy analysts alike. Once a relative backwater in the study of what used to be called "manpower" policy, it is now widely held to be the key to achieving economic competitiveness and to reconstructing the welfare state. But those exaggerated claims made on behalf of training, I believe, are highly suspect. Whatever concrete uses training may have – and there are certainly some – it is either foolish or dishonest to portray "more and more training" as a solution to the range of disturbing economic and social maladies that seem so constant in the 1990's' (Dunk et al. 1996, 1).

The culture of social work emphasizes self-improvement and long-term schooling. The case stories contained in this volume have revealed that this mentality does not appear to hold the key to the unemployment problem facing welfare recipients. Only in Wisconsin did administrators (often contracted agencies) place direct employment ahead of classroom-based education and training, under work-related activities. In the other jurisdictions, operating with a broad definition of workfare, administrators relied more on their personal or professional values in placing recipients. Different jurisdictions had different balances between the numbers of clients required to engage in the three main workfare activities (e.g., numbers enrolled in job hunting compared to those required to take courses, compared to those required to do a work placement or perform community service). California, which in 1985 originated the liberal-minded GAIN program, had a rich philosophy of 'education first,' despite the tough, employment-related talk in the GAIN brochures and literature. The unique Californian attachment (both administrative and political) to the theory of long-term investment in human capital is all the more remarkable in view of its dismal results. Were it not for the introduction of Clinton's time-limited welfare and the financial sanctions that Washington could apply to those states that were not meeting targets, it is not likely that California would have ever given up its philosophy. Even now, California is struggling under CalWORKS, GAIN's successor, to try to catch up to other states that did not have such a heavy emphasis on 'education first.' The high numbers of welfare recipients in California (the highest rate of any state) make this job especially challenging, as administrators dash about the state acquainting prospective employers with the CalWORKS program and trying to convince employers to hire CalWORKS clients.

It was really only Wisconsin that dodged the administrator hazard. Civil servants who did not like what Wisconsin was doing did not have to provide the service. Contracting out necessary government objectives was not new with W-2, since the earlier JOBS program had often been contracted out in order to get results. In some cases, progress was slower because of misunderstandings between state employees and contracted agencies regarding new goals and outcomes. Still, Wisconsin maintained the practice of subcontracting front-line service delivery of the welfare-to-work program to people who were willing and able to move clients into jobs, not just hand out cheques. Wisconsin contracts out its entire W-2 program at the local delivery level, using a competitive Request for Proposal bidding process. Agencies are responsible for the entire caseload within their boundary, including intake, eligibility, and W-2 placements. Moreover, while other jurisdictions might have restricted access to free education as part of their welfare reform, Wisconsin terminated welfare recipients' pursuit of free university and college degrees in favour of practical, job-focused training programs that could not extend beyond a twelve-week period.

In New York, administrators colluded in a good-news story that made the good idea look successful by avoiding any evaluation of inputs and process and concentrating instead on measuring outputs – in this case, the drop in welfare rolls. Evaluation biases always tend towards aspects of a program that are successful. If inputs look successful, then measure inputs, while if outputs appear more successful, then measure outputs.

New Brunswick administrators, like those in California, were officially firm believers in 'education first.' Administrators did not resist the will of the politicians because they were aligned along the same philosophical ground. New Brunswick's voluntary program was particularly generous, providing three and a half years of education to single mothers for free, allowing them to complete high school followed by community college training in an area of their choice. As it happens, the vast majority of participants dropped out, despite an expensive array of available supports such as child care and transportation. Neither the politicians nor the administrators wish to discuss the obvious failure.

Alberta's Ralph Klein, like Wisconsin's Tommy Thompson, knew that administrators could derail any planned change to the welfare system, and made very sure that he had the people in place who were going to see his vision through to the end. Ralph Klein's first brilliant step lay in the appointment of Mike Cardinal, who was adamantly against welfare, as his minister of Family and Social Services. Department employees responsible for important changes were screened for their support for the government's plans, and any necessary staff changes were made. While the work-experience programs in Alberta were referred to as voluntary, they actually operated as mandatory programs, and this was largely due to the front-line staff's assimilation of Mike Cardinal's philosophy that 'any job is a good job.' The deep level of commitment of those in charge to the success of the work-experience programs (two of which were introduced by Cardinal) was particularly evident in Alberta. The well-being of the welfare recipient was a major issue for staff, and they went to great lengths to boost the work habits, experience, and self-esteem of their clients (e.g., the Wall of Fame bulletin board that celebrated successfully employed workfare participants).

Ontario ran an election on the obligation of welfare recipients to perform community service or engage in active training for seventeen hours a week in exchange for their welfare cheques. Any such plans were sabotaged by Ontario bureaucrats who read the new rules regarding work placements and ignored them. The good idea ran full steam into the administrative hazard. The program was clearly labelled mandatory, but given the way in which choices were designed into the policy and caseworkers operated the program, it changed back to 'voluntary.' Despite the good-news reporting on the success of workfare in Ontario, municipalities report an unimpressive work-placement rate of between 2 and 5 per cent of those eligible for workfare.

The administrative hazard arises from an inability to recognize the bureaucrats' deeply rooted resistance to change and their fundamental disagreement with the social policy being introduced. When different values clash and the issue becomes politically and emotionally charged (workfare being a perfect example), the system is exposed to resistance and sabotage. As Schein observes, 'Once a group has a set of assumptions, it will tend to cling to those assumptions. Hence culture is very difficult to change unless one changes the people in the group' (1991: 14) While workfare might be intended as a work experience program, it may remain a training program for as long as the social service culture chooses.

Target-Group Hazard: Reluctant Obedience

What is the role of the target group in determining the outcome of the good idea? As Ernie Lightman remarked at a public talk, drawing an analogy between soldiers in Vietnam and welfare workers, 'unwilling soldiers do not fight good wars.' In other words, although welfare recipients are trained and provided with information that is meant to change their norms and values, the experience might leave them unmarked. The fourth hazard that can turn a good idea bad is the target-group hazard, the target group in this case being welfare recipients. This hazard relates to the recipient's enactment of empty ritual while firmly believing that participation in the program is counter to his or her self-interest. Trainers try to convince welfare recipients that it is only through participating in workfare that they may develop their true identity. But welfare recipients might remain sceptical of the new rules they are taught and the new ways of doing things – dressing, talking, working – advised in their workfare-orientation courses. And why shouldn't they? Conducted in an age of fragmentation and malaise, the assessment made by welfare recipients is likely to be negative and pessimistic. It appears to be in the best interest of recipients to find out how they can continue to receive benefits. Given their grim world, how could recipients not adopt the cynical attitudes of 'seen it all before' and 'nothing new is really possible'?

Recipients confronted with workfare have three choices: (1) embrace the changes and strive for self-sufficiency from the welfare system, (2) reluctantly enact the required rituals, or (3) disappear or drop out of the welfare system. There are also those would-be welfare applicants who are put off from applying in the first place. In fact, most of the six jurisdictions described in this volume tried to deter people from signing up for welfare in the first place by tightening up eligibility requirements and publicizing the rigorous work requirements that would be contained in the proposed changes. As Piven and Cloward have argued: 'Forced work programs are significant, not because they are likely to be implemented on a large-scale, but because the introduction of a punitive and stigmatizing workfare program will deter people from applying for aid at all, much as the threat of the workhouse deterred people from being supplicants' (1987, 38).

Most of the jurisdictions studied here also reduced welfare rates in an effort to bring them in line with the wages of the working poor. From the perspective of the welfare recipient, all these changes represent interrupted expectations. Such jolts can stimulate recipients to break free of routines, but, with the exception of the Workfairness activist organization in New York, welfare participants rarely participated in positive political action in the form of struggle and resistance.

Employers who have hired welfare recipients generally report mixed results. Deborah C. Washam, president and chief executive of a community home health care agency in Kansas City (a licensed agency that dispatches homemakers to assist elderly and disabled residents with light housework and shopping), claims that, of more than eighty women she hired as part of a generous welfare-to-work program, fewer than twenty-five remained on the job; many of the others apparently quit over perceived slights to their dignity: 'I don't think they've had much exposure to structure in their lives ... As single mothers, they are on their own and see themselves as authority figures. They won't take routine supervision at work' (Ian Nordheimer, 'Success Difficult to Achieve in Welfare-to-Work Plans,' *New York Times*, 1 September 1996). Apparently many among those hired, although the best qualified of those screened, had problems including absenteeism, lack of discipline about work hours, poor reading and communicative skills, and open resentment when given direction; and, as Nordheimer (*New York Times*, 1 September 1997) points out, a lot of the current workfare programs have not yet reached people on welfare who have even more serious problems, such as substance abuse or intellectual impairments.

In California, social workers so favoured long-term investment in human capital through lengthy training and education programs that the recipients might not have felt the effects of workfare until time-limited welfare was introduced. In Wisconsin, welfare recipients were boxed into a tight corner and had no way out. In New York, endless numbers filed through the required orientation sessions and went through all the motions with little hope of a permanent job. Many welfare recipients in New York were disillusioned with the system to the point that it reduced their resistance to fight Mayor Giuliani's aggressive social intervention.

Canadian welfare recipients did not appear to show much enthusiasm for workfare or learnfare. In New Brunswick, more than three thousand single welfare mothers signed up voluntarily for a learnfare program that would allow them to continue to receive benefits while completing high school and obtaining specialized training at a community college while receiving full supports in the form of subsidized child care and transportation. While the good idea was good for Premier Frank McKenna, who achieved a national reputation for innovation and forward thinking in social policy, what had originally seemed like a good idea to the learnfare participants soon became bad. The large majority dropped out of the program and returned to welfare, most quitting before they obtained their high school equivalency.

Another reluctant target group, at least at the beginning, was Alberta's welfare recipients. Across Canada, a huge amount of publicity was devoted to the claim that Alberta's recipients, faced with Ralph Klein's monstrous and inhuman social policy changes, were moving to the neighbouring province of British Columbia, where welfare rates were higher and recipients left in peace. Angry at the new arrivals, British Columbia accused Alberta of giving welfare recipients 'free bus tickets' to cross the provincial border, in order to reduce its caseload. (Alberta responded that British Columbia also had a policy of giving out free bus tickets, and it wasn't Alberta's fault if nobody used them.) To protect itself from a further inundation of welfare recipients, British Columbia subsequently tried to declare a three-month residency requirement for welfare eligibility, but this was struck down by Ottawa as unconstitutional. However, while some welfare recipients did leave the province, the overwhelming majority stayed. Welfare rolls have declined drastically in Alberta, and, according to the Canada West Foundation (1997), the majority of Albertans who left welfare did so because they found employment. While Ralph Klein's government did not use the word 'mandatory,' welfare recipients were correct in assuming that they would be forced to work, one way or the other.

Ontario's welfare recipients did experience considerable change under welfare reform, but these changes lay in such areas as a 22 per cent benefit reduction and tighter eligibility criteria. While there was much talk about welfare recipients having to work in order to earn their welfare cheques, little actually ever took place in the area of work placements. Supports such as child care were not introduced, so the government's decision to have Ontario Works apply to mothers of children over the age of three (under the previous law, single parents could collect welfare until the youngest child turned nineteen) could not really be applied. According to recipients, there is still little financial incentive to go off welfare. As one recipient said to me in an interview, 'What's to be gained by losing my "freedom" in exchange for minimum wage and no medication plan.'

Studies by Scott (1990) and Jordon (1993) reveal that welfare recipients do resist workfare in their own way, both individually and collectively, and they argue that the poor manipulate the welfare system to their own ends. However, most recipients shy away from affirming any ethic. Recipients' reactions are really a mix of hope and cynicism. According to William Morris (1896), work can be either a blessing and a lightening of life, or a mere curse and a burden to life. What is the difference between them? 'One has hope in it, the other has not.' Admittedly, when getting into symbolic value and emotional involvement, any researcher is dealing with a certain vagueness of attitude.

Workfare is a program that depends, to a large extent, on the welfare recipient's willingness to change. The recipient's capacity to change depends on his or her mind-set, which is heavily influenced by previous learning experiences and stored biases. Most people have an internalized set of beliefs and act on them without much thought. We do things the way we were taught, without probing too much into why. In an article entitled 'Poverty: How Little We Know,' Lawrence Mead (1994), one of the foremost experts on welfare in the United States, begs us to set aside the conventional belief that the psychology of the very poor resembles that of the middle class. Mead laments that, for reasons of political correctness, explicit appeals to culture as an explanation for poverty have faded out of research. According to Mead, this line of enquiry stopped partly because it showed a 'judgmental' perspective (i.e., the better off judging the poor) and partly because economists came to dominate poverty research, applying their maximizing psychology to all economic actors. According to Mead,

> We must return to the notion entertained by the poverty researchers of the 1960s that there is a distinctive 'culture of poverty.' 'Culture' here means a set of attitudes and beliefs that could cause people to persist in poverty or on welfare, especially by failing to work, in circumstances where someone with a more mainstream psychology would see an opportunity to escape. The need is to grasp how female-headedness or nonwork might appear inevitable to the deprived, even if the behaviour does not appear sensible to the better off.
>
> Many poverty researchers still affirm the essence of the culture of poverty, which is that the poor have orthodox values but cannot achieve them. Poor adults want to fulfil the work ethic and other mainstream norms but feel unable to do so because of the constraints they perceive around them. (1994, 336)

Welfare recipients faced with the prospect of mandatory workfare have the same concerns and fears that anyone would have, such as 'the appropriateness of the work and whether it will involve commuting. In Canada, cynicism still reigns, but in the United States, because of the introduction of the five-year lifetime limit on welfare (and not necessarily because of workfare), a sense of urgency has been added to the picture and welfare recipients have lost the luxury of cynicism. In Wisconsin, where most former workfare participants are in the workforce, the state is able to move onto the next challenge: that is, to *keep* former welfare recipients employed and *increase* their wages.

Evaluator Hazard: 'Measurement Is Possible'

How do the evaluators play a role in the life and death of the good idea? By shaping the results that are usually used to keep the good idea alive.

To what extent do evaluators base their evaluation on realistic assumptions about the nature of the problem, the organization, the policy, and the implementation? How can they evaluate a program in which the goals are haphazard and people can lay claim to any goal they want? Workfare is a social program that is poorly understood. The fifth hazard that may turn a good idea bad is the illusion that there is truth, as opposed to merely an opinion of the truth.

Evaluators' tendencies have introduced inaccuracy into most analyses of workfare. Their dependence on the rational portrays organizations as more cohesive than they are, operating in a more homogeneous environment than they do, and more capable of maintaining a clear strategy than they can. Underlying any evaluation of workfare (and there have been thousands) is the notion that clear goals and objectives have been established, information is available, and some measurement of before and after is actually possible. Unfortunately, as we have seen in the case stories, clear objectives are rarely set, data are either overwhelming, incomplete, or dubious, and no control group exists that might allow for a comparison between a workfare and a non-workfare situation.

In traditional public administration theory, the inability to measure would be corrected by following rational management principles such as an analysis of the objectives, a collection of available data, and a comparison between the old and the new. However, in the case of a 'good idea' such as workfare, where the definition of the question is in doubt (see Chapter 3: workfare can be 'something,' 'nothing,' or 'anything and everything'), administrators did not collect and categorize information in any relevant way for evaluation purposes. Rarely are there performance measures in place that relate to the stated objectives. But this does not stop the evaluations, or even summaries of evaluations. They continue to be produced, repeating their usual warnings about the accuracy of the data. In an Urban Institute study entitled 'Where Are They Now? What States' Studies of People Who Left Welfare Tell Us,' the authors point to the substantial decrease in welfare caseloads across the U.S. (a decrease of 43 per cent from March 1994 to September 1998) but then explain how incomplete a picture they can present due to the patchy nature of the data:

> All the studies discussed deal with leavers' well-being, but there are many differences among them that need to be considered when examining results. These studies are for different geographic areas, representing vary-

ing labor market conditions, urban and rural conditions, and state and local policies ... Except for Texas, neither the largest states in the United States nor the states with the highest population of welfare recipients are represented in this review ... Coverage by work requirements and sanction policies also differs across states ... Other differences in the studies are more subtle: differences in methods used can make comparisons tricky. These include differences in how the leaver population studied is defined (including the reason the person left welfare, whether he or she has remained off welfare, and the length of time since leaving welfare) and how specific outcomes, such as employment, are measured.' (Brauner and Loprest 1999, 1, 2)

Extreme variations in measures used make the Urban Institute survey of little value. The Institute for Women's Policy Research bemoans the fact that Clinton's 1996 welfare reforms did not include a requirement for rigorous measurement: 'Instead of tying evaluation efforts to grant receipt, the [Personal Responsibility and Work Opportunity Reconciliation Act] directs the Secretary of the U.S. Department of Health and Human Services (DHHS) to encourage states to continue evaluation of their waivers through random sampling, control groups, and other accepted experimental methods. It also authorizes $15 million annually for research activities (from fiscal year 1997 through fiscal year 2002), half of which DHSS is to allocate for federally initiated research and half for state-level evaluations' (*Welfare Reform Network News* 1997, 1).

In other words, Clinton's new law did not insist on any standardization of data collection, and the quality, scope, and very existence of evaluation on workfare are still left to the discretion of individual states and interested researchers and advocates.

The inability to measure the effects of welfare-to-work programs remains a constant challenge for researchers. In not one of the jurisdictions studied for this volume was measurement a priority at the time a work experience program was implemented. Data collection and management information systems first had to be developed to enable the monitoring of welfare recipients. The development of appropriate indicators and measurement standardization became an issue for Wisconsin and Alberta only later in the process, after they were aggressively challenged to reveal what had happened to all the welfare recipients who had dropped off the rolls. Wisconsin is now in the throes of refining its 'leavers' studies,' but in the early days recording was haphazard. Alberta claims that it is not the government's business to ask people why they left welfare, nor to keep records of their reasons, although graduates of the three hands-on work experience programs are tracked. Ontario cannot provide any evidence of the numbers who joined the workforce as a result of workfare. As of 2001, New Brunswick was still waiting for the 'final' evaluation of NB Works. New York's measurement focuses on how many people left the welfare rolls. California is currently struggling to turn around a massive system that never measured the value of its workfare program.

Failure to expose the good idea to rigorous testing incurs a heavy price: the impossibility of knowing its consequences. The very nature of the good idea, its organizational setting and its implementation, precludes rational evaluation. Billions of dollars in social spending may have gone into programs that were applied to only a small portion of the welfare rolls, and with only mixed results. In short, we are making policy decisions on the basis of perceptions. Public debates over workfare have been largely uninformed by data. Evaluators are hard-pressed to come up with anything more than the most limited assessments. As to whether workfare offers good value for taxpayer dollars, we actually have no idea.

A jurisdiction's inability to report accurate results is hardly desirable. However, if results are unobtainable, the acknowledgment of that reality is a more useful starting point than the false assumption that outcomes are measurable. But what is it exactly we wish to measure? And what are the evaluation priorities? It is hard to say what ought to take precedence among areas as varied as a drop in the welfare caseload, administrative efficiency/process, behavioural change, educational attainment, cost reduction, reduction in child poverty, numbers 'enrolled' in work activities, numbers who found jobs, numbers who increased their earnings, numbers who are still working after twelve months of leaving welfare, the effects of workfare on the use and quality of child care, teenage childbearing, homelessness, family violence, etc. Measures of well-being, however, are hard to define and unlikely to be recorded on an ongoing basis for the purposes of evaluation.

Evaluation is further complicated by the fact that whenever workfare programs are discussed, employment is the obvious goal, propelled by the assumption that the provision of employment will automatically remove poverty. However, obtaining a job does not necessarily ensure the elimination of poverty. In fact, the way out of poverty may often be through a continuous process of support. Determining the variables to be measured requires a number of trade-offs to be made (e.g., individual effects versus community effects) in the interest of efficiency.

Another issue confronting the evaluator is the choice of an appropriate comparison to the program being studied, if there is one. The evaluation dilemma, moreover, is made worse by the fact that the statistics provided to the evaluator may be exaggerated because the administrative bureaucrats, who record the information, convey what they know their superiors expect them to convey. Also, an evaluator's attempt to extract information about the efficiency and effectiveness of a program can be extremely threatening to service providers who want to hide their problems. In Canada, part of the reason for inconsistent welfare data across the country is that each province has jurisdiction over its own welfare program. Each province defines program eligibility, sets welfare rates, and designs its own system, with its own terminology. The only cross-province comparisons that can really be made relate to the actual number of welfare cases on file at any one time.

The United States is similarly fragmented in terms of language and standards of eligibility. Between 1988 and 1996, guidelines in the United States came from the federal JOBS program, but each state, through the waiver system, could opt to design its own version of JOBS. JOBS provided federal funding to the states for mandatory workfare, job-search, education, and job-training programs for welfare recipients. But each state collects its data differently, making it problematic when evaluators attempt to compare jurisdictions or when questions arise concerning national caseload trends. Complicated administrative issues also arise in evaluation, such as the evaluator's ability to distinguish between those who are unable to take part in a workfare program and those who refuse (one wonders if welfare statistics include seniors and the disabled as they did in Ontario prior to the introduction of workfare). Enforcement procedures also vary widely from one jurisdiction to another and sanctions, although written in policy, are rarely applied (although this is changing with time-limited welfare). Research on welfare dynamics is still relatively new in the United States, but many of the methods have some relevance to the Canadian context.

Evaluations on workfare have typically been associated with impact studies, which attempt to measure the effect of the intervention on selected variables. But an understanding of workfare rests not only with access to relevant data; it also rests with knowing which questions to ask in relation to what is being measured. As Lightman points out, 'the definition of success in a workfare program is highly problematic. "Success" can range from completed training and/or permanent employment through to short-term cost savings resulting from reduced caseload (viewing workfare as a screening mechanism, a form of tightened eligibility)' (1997, 98). Not only is certain information sure to be of questionable reliability, but if the right questions are not asked how can anyone know whether the program is worth pursuing? In the case of workfare, not one study has demonstrated that it provides value of any statistical significance. Most of the studies to date relate more to program compliance rather than program performance. There is limited value in a primary focus on how the service is delivered if what you really want to know is whether people are finding jobs and becoming self-sufficient. What does it matter if we know how many welfare recipients enrolled in work-related activity but have no idea how many are finding work and moving off welfare? Impact studies that have attempted to assess the degree to which a desired outcome is attributable to workfare have shown no significant results. In an article entitled 'Workfare in the U.S. – Empirically Tested Programs or Ideological Quagmire?' Donna Hardina (1997) concludes that right-wing ideology alone has guided the more radical efforts at welfare reform. Workfare is here defined as a program in which welfare recipients are required to work for government or private employers in exchange for welfare benefits it also includes mandatory work and job training schemes for welfare recipients. Hardina points out the lack of connection between workfare and permanent work: 'There is no sound empirical research that confirms that mandatory work and job training programs are effective in helping people leave the welfare system. On the contrary, most evaluations of state welfare reform projects have not produced statistically significant differences in job acquisitions, earnings, or decreases in welfare benefits' (1997, 131).

Most of what we know about the effectiveness of workfare in the United States comes from the hundreds of evaluations of state-operated JOBS programs. (JOBS was replaced in 1996 by the Temporary Assistance to Needy Families program.) The purpose of JOBS legislation was to transform welfare into a transitional program aimed at helping an increasing portion of Aid to Families with Dependent Children (AFDC) clients get jobs and avoid long-term dependence on welfare. Of all these evaluations (none of which show any statistically significant results, as Hardina has pointed out above), I found the 1993 evaluation of the JOBS program by the United States General Accounting Office

(GAO) to be the clearest and the closest to identifying the real problem with workfare in the United States:

> The current JOBS program has not served a large portion of the AFDC caseload and is not well focused on employment as the goal. Of the more than 4 million parents receiving AFDC cheques each month, JOBS served only about 11 percent in an average month from fiscal years 1991 to 1993. Furthermore, program administrators report that they lack the capacity to provide current JOBS participants with the services and assistance that they need ...
>
> Fiscal year 1993 spending (federal and state) for JOBS totalled $1.1 billion, yet *programs are generally not well focused on recipients' employment as the ultimate goal.* Our recent nationwide survey of local program administrators revealed that JOBS programs have generally not forged the strong links with employers that may be important to helping AFDC recipients gain work experience and find jobs. Many factors hamper the development of these ties to the workplace, including the JOBS performance measurement system. *This system holds states accountable for the number and type of AFDC recipients participating in JOBS activities but not for the number who get jobs or earn their way off AFDC. Thus, programs may focus more on preparing participants for employment than on getting them jobs. In fact, the number of JOBS participants who get jobs or leave AFDC annually is unknown.* (U.S. GAO/HEHS-95-28, 2; emphasis added)

The GAO's findings go a long way toward explaining the complexity of evaluation, especially when the goals are ambiguous (e.g., enrolment in JOBS versus finding a permanent job). Unfortunately, the GAO shows the typical belief in a rational fantasy zone that is removed from the real objectives of the program. Absurdly, the same evaluation body that pointed out all of the flaws above can still believe that things will get better with a bit of fixing, such as adding more resources: 'Proposals to reform the program will be challenged to balance increased participation with the need for additional resources and the need to develop additional capacity over time' (U.S. GAO/HEHS-95-28, 5).

And that is exactly what Clinton's 1996 welfare reform legislation looks like – a requirement to increase the numbers enrolled in work activities and the money allocated to make it happen. If it were not for the addition of 'time limited welfare,' the welfare reform legislation would have been just another version of the same old workfare 'good idea' trotted out three times before. Instead, the time limits have sent the states into a panic, scrambling to move people off welfare. But why did workfare live on for so long when it was such a costly, useless program? Rarely, if ever, did government-commissioned evaluations discuss the realities of workfare. The evaluators placed themselves in the same fantasy land as the administrators in explaining away less-than-perfect results in terms of a lack of resources, a poor economy, and the like.

In California, the Manpower and Development Research Corporation (MDRC)'s (Riccio et al. 1994) evaluation of GAIN over several years used the results from Riverside County (which went against GAIN's 'long-term investment in human capital' theory and matched welfare clients directly to the labour market) to show that GAIN had some hope. Nothing of much value could be gleaned from the other five counties in the study, which put classroom training and education before employment. Again, the MDRC recommended that more money and more resources would make GAIN a better program. GAIN basked in glory for many years as the model of a human approach to welfare. While the rest of the nation's welfare caseload declined, California's rose steadily. Clinton's time-limited welfare has put and end to California's motto of 'education first,' as counties risk having their funding cut off if they don't hurry up and get welfare recipients into work-related activities.

The formal evaluators of New York's workfare scheme used an output-based system, restricting evaluation to the numbers dropping off the welfare rolls. Whether or not welfare recipients were actually getting jobs as a result of their six months of job experience was not important, or at least not important for the government. Indeed, one internal study that attempted to track what happened to welfare recipients has been kept confidential (awaiting a lawsuit to move the results into the public domain).

Wisconsin had years of repeated experimentation in welfare reform. All of its major reforms were evaluated, and these evaluations seem to have been carried out in a fairly critical way. When something didn't work, the government wanted to know. The learnfare program, designed to keep the children of welfare recipients in school longer, was a failure. But the attempt to find non-custodial parents and obtain child support for their child or children was very effective in meeting its objectives. Wisconsin was an early laboratory of success in reducing its welfare load and helping people ease the transition from welfare to work (e.g., one year of free health care after a mother has entered employment, continued assistance with child care). Wisconsin is currently concerned with improving its welfare 'leavers' data, to find out more about the large numbers (91 per cent) of those who have left the caseload.

In New Brunswick, evaluations of the learnfare program consisted of process issues such as how often the staff held their meetings and how well the different levels of government (e.g., federal and provincial) interacted. One early report somehow revealed the disastrous results of the first one thousand single mothers (two-thirds of whom dropped out in the first year), but after that little could be obtained beyond behavioural information such as how well the learnfare participants 'liked their teachers.' The major report summarizing the real effects of NB Works was scheduled to appear sometime in 2000, but the government has long moved on from that program, and any such report is likely to have a low profile. Moreover, the premier responsible for the program resigned in 1998, the year that the final Intake 3 (the last one thousand single mothers) completed its three and a half years of schooling. In 1999 the Liberals lost the provincial election to the Progressive Conservatives and are no longer in power. As of 2000, a number of vague and obfuscating interim evaluations had appeared, but still no final report, even though, according to the ministry, as of June 2000, Baseline Norpack was still under contract to provide this evaluation.

Alberta's welfare reforms led to a drastic drop in the welfare rolls. The government does not itself track why welfare recipients leave, but it did commission the Canada West Foundation to conduct a survey and report back on what had happened to former recipients. The evaluators found that most had found jobs (and not gone to British Columbia as many suspected). The flaw of the survey was that it was a telephone and mail survey, and not likely to reach those who may possibly have become homeless.

Ontario's workfare program is relatively new, but because it measures participation in workfare as opposed to the number of those who go from workfare to employment, no formal evaluation is likely to reveal much failure. No large-scale survey has been undertaken in the three years since workfare was officially introduced. And although no municipality has been able to show that more than 5 per cent of welfare recipients were engaged in 'work placement,' the government's officially required 15 per cent participation rate was raised to 30 per cent in early 2000. Anti-workfare activists know that mandatory workfare (forced training or community service for seventeen hours a week in exchange for welfare) has not occurred, but they don't want this to get out, lest the government be pressured into making it happen.

Finally, the assessment of a program's effectiveness in terms of goal achievement is a tricky process, not least because the stated goals of a project are just artefacts of those drawing up the list – only the *people* involved with the program have goals, and the program may or may not be the means for achieving these goals (Legge 1984, 44). The introduction of a new government program is inevitably political. It is likely, therefore, that any such evaluation that takes place will scarcely remain untouched by political considerations. Paul Light, director of the public policy program at the Pew Charitable Trusts in Philadelphia, which has funded research at Brookings, the American Enterprise Institute, and the Heritage Foundation, claims the following: 'Twenty, 30 years ago, policy research was directed towards a generalized search for truth. Now it's just plot your curves and get your data. The left and right both have their scholars on call. It's post-Enlightenment or maybe anti-Enlightenment – the notion that there is no truth, only opinion about truth' (quoted in Paul Starobin, 'The War of the New Combat Intellectuals,' *Globe and Mail*, 13 September 1997). It is possible that evaluations are being created by goverment's political allies. After all, why produce results that your intended audience is unwilling to digest? Starobin laments the old days of unbiased and unpredictable analysis, claiming: 'Washington no longer sees scholarship as a tool to think with. Both Democratic and Republican party ranks are riven with factions, and each has its platoons of scholars whose job it is to provide the ammunition for ideological battle' (*Globe and Mail*, 13 September 1997). Whether evaluation was ever unbiased is another question. However, since workfare is such a heated and controversial issue, it is worth noting that evaluations are usually requested and paid for by someone who has an interest in the outcome. Had each workfare program clearly defined its intended objectives and measured whether these were being achieved, most jurisdictions would have known that they faced a massive and expensive failure. But actual results are not necessarily required of a good idea, as the California, New York, New Brunswick, and Ontario case stories have revealed.

Public Hazard: 'We're Bored. What's the Next Good Idea?'

How might the public play a role in bringing down the good idea, in making the good idea turn bad? Just as the public cries out for the first good idea, so does it cry out for the next. The media keeps the good idea alive to the public. Taxpayers are happy with the good idea until they learn, from the media, that there has been abuse. This tells the politicians (if they have not already had a role in degrading the good idea) that it is time for a new good idea.

Interest groups and activists typically adopt positions on moral and political issues that are in opposition to the larger political community. Workfare is one such moral issue, and it probably attracts more critical attention than a lot of other good ideas. In all six jurisdictions covered in this volume, activists attempted to derail workfare. Protests by activists were often ineffective, but they were important for their claim to represent the voice of welfare recipients. The rich imagery conjured up by the activists (e.g., workhouse, slavery, chain gangs) keeps the good idea alive even when it is having little success. Most anti-workfare criticisms are aimed at the quality of work placements, claiming that they lack intrinsic value and require few skills. Other criticisms are that workfare displaces existing workers and causes lower wages (this argument was especially prevalent in New York). Richards points out that an important aspect of interest-group lobbying is exploitation of 'rational ignorance': 'Citizens will quite rationally remain ignorant of any political issue as long as the cost of learning about it exceeds the per capita benefit of a government's adopting an alternative policy multiplied by the subjective probability that citizen intervention will affect the policy choice' (1997, 172).

In the United States, where workfare is firmly entrenched as a standard feature of the welfare landscape, protests are now little more than empty rituals. In Canada, where workfare is still a relatively new concept, protests are impassioned, even powerful: people don striped prison garb, tie bowling balls to their ankles with heavy bicycle chains, and lumber onto anti-workfare buses carrying 'Don't punish the poor!' placards. In Ontario, Andy Mitchell, head of the Workfare Watch anti-workfare group, admitted at a Workfare Watch conference (on 27 June 1998) that hardly anything had actually taken place in the dreaded 'work experience' area, but that activists had to keep up the momentum 'just in case.' Even though activists try to play a role in the demise of the good idea, their marches and demonstrations often make the public think that the program is working better than it actually does.

The media also plays an important role in keeping the good idea alive in the eyes of the public – but the media is also in a powerful position to decide when the time has come for a new good idea. Thanks to a strange form of collusion between politicians, policy-makers, administrators, welfare recipients, and lobby groups, none of these groups is likely to admit that the good idea was a mess. That is why it is the media, looking for the next good idea, that alerts the public to the rat. The fever begins in the shape of a breaking story about a 'wrong,' be it some form of abuse or neglect on the part of the government. Investigations are called for, task forces are struck, more anecdotes are reported in the media. There are endless examples of wasted money, and things reach a crisis. The media has given the kiss of death to the good idea, and the quest is on for the next innovation. Depending on the political cycle, that is usually the point at which a new good idea is required, whether it be from the existing government or the opposition. An Anglo-Quebec journalist based in Montreal, William Johnson (2000) wrote the following after a particularly boring federal election campaign in which the Canadian Liberal leader had just won power for the third consecutive time: 'You must grasp that we journalists have a professional bias, a marked predisposition, in favour of news. We're for the new, the trendy, the different, the exciting. Good government is not enough. We want change. For us, day by day, it's always time for a change. Otherwise, what would we talk about?' ('We Were the Losers in this Election,' *Globe and Mail*, 29 November 2000).

In the United States, each resurrection of workfare (there have been two since WIN) was treated as a new good idea, even though the idea was, at best, only more of the same (e.g., higher participation rates required in work-related activities in JOBS [1988] and the Personal Responsibility and Work Opportunity Reconciliation Act, [1996]. In California the GAIN program was touted as a great success for more than ten years, then abruptly regarded as a waste of time and replaced by the more rigorous CalWORKS. Stories abounded in the news that people on welfare would no longer be able to opt for a so-called life of ease and that they would have to work in exchange for their benefits, even though the earlier program had also used the very same language about change. In New York, the press carried endless articles of protest against the damage that would be caused by 'displacement' thanks to the Work Experience Programs. Wisconsin's reaction to Tommy Thompson's welfare reforms was mostly negative for the first few years (viewing the reforms as cruel and drastic), but public opinion has swung around to supporting W-2 in light of the 91 per cent drop in the welfare rolls.

In Canada, the media welcomed New Brunswick's 1992 learnfare program with great excitement. Premier Frank McKenna played host to reporters from all over Canada who flew into the maritime province to learn more about this interesting social experiment. Early evaluations showed a 75 per cent drop-out rate, but as of 2000, the final evaluation was still unavailable and the government had long moved on from NB Works to Jobs Plus and similar programs. The media seemed unwilling to underline NB Works' failure, especially in view of such an exciting start. In Alberta, the press went wild with the claims that welfare recipients were fleeing to nearby British Columbia to get away from Premier Ralph Klein's draconian welfare reforms. In Ontario, jubilant voters, promised that welfare recipients would be put to work for their benefits, swept Mike Harris to victory in 1995 and again in 1999 (with the promise of 'more workfare'). The media made it clear that voters liked what they heard on the campaign trail. Some cracks are showing in Ontario, but Premier Harris has paved these over by raising the required percentage of people on welfare who would be required to participate in work placements. The media enacted the success fantasy of the good idea by reporting that the required workfare participation rate was being upped from 15 to 30 per cent, enraging interest groups and selling more newspapers.

The general public also plays a role in turning the good idea bad. When Clinton said that he would change 'welfare as we know it,' the American people were more than ready. Welfare was out of control, numbers higher than ever, and people feeling over-taxed. In the case of workfare in the United States, a natural human phenomenon asserted itself – the herd instinct – the tendency of people to follow an idea, a slogan, a concept. Sure, they had heard the word 'workfare' before, in fact since the 1970s, but that did not seem to matter. They were hooked on the idea of changing the welfare system, and they gave Clinton the power to do just that. The 1988 JOBS program (the last 'good idea' of which Clinton himself was a key architect) was discredited and the groundwork laid for a new good idea. Clinton's 1996 welfare reforms seemed harsh to some (including a number of his own staff), but he proceeded to insist on higher participation rates in work-related activities and introduced time-limited welfare (a lifetime limit of five years). Clinton's subsequent re-election is further evidence that he had his finger on the pulse of America. Clinton's 1996 good idea, the PRWORA, is still good, made even better by the introduction of time-limited welfare, which provides bureaucrats with a dimension of urgency. California and New York are scrambling to move people into the

workplace, while Wisconsin is looking for ways to keep people working and raise their wages. Workfare in the United States is successful
because people believe in it.

Canadians are generally less interested in making demands on welfare recipients than their counterparts in the United States. In 1992,
New Brunswick was the first Canadian province to break away from
the norm of cheque dispensation by designing its ambitious learnfare
program for single mothers. Premier McKenna followed the advice of
his American image consultant and persuaded the province that investment in human capital was the way to go. It seemed like a good idea,
and since the formal evaluation had still not appeared by 2001, it will
probably remain a good idea in the minds of many. Alberta in 1993
became the first province in Canada to take a tough stance on welfare.
Albertans thought it was about time. They supported Ralph Klein's
welfare cuts and his supposedly voluntary work-experience programs,
and they later re-elected him to another term as premier. Albertans
have no reason to demand a new good idea from Ralph Klein, for his
idea is still regarded as good. The Ontario public bought into major
welfare reform in 1995, as part of Mike Harris's Common Sense Revolution. The voters loved the idea of workfare, and they believed that it
had been implemented as promised (although a couple of journalists
dissented). Workfare is still a good idea, in Ontario, although Mike
Harris's successor, Ernie Eves, will have to feverishly battle the bureaucrats to actually make it happen. Other provinces seem to be content
with the status quo.

Conclusion: Reality Is Not What It Used to Be

In this book, I have attempted to explain what happens to a good idea
in social policy, using workfare as the example. In the six-hazard model,
all six players collude to some extent in producing the illusion that
the good idea is good for their own individual goals – that is, until it's
time for the next good idea. The field of policy studies has always
been in quest of good ideas. Workfare, with its connotations of self-
improvement and promises of a new and better life, has a seductive
ring. But the attractiveness of the good idea is never completely illu-
sory. Underpinning the good idea there has always been an assumption
of rationality: choice will be deliberate and actions taken in an orderly
sequence. Decisions, after all, are made in a rational way. When something doesn't work, it's because one of the rational comprehensive

planning steps was not undertaken properly. What gets lost in this scenario is that, even though rationality is important, people rarely exercise it. We need to acknowledge that our capacity for rationality is limited, and that this leads to our concealment of negative outcomes and grand collusion in false assumptions. At the same time, we continue to read rational books, make rational plans, and conduct our lives on a rational basis. This is not surprising since this ideology has permeated every corner of our existence since the 1950s. As Legge points out, 'Much of the literature about social and organizational change assumes without question that change is an objective phenomenon, that occurs outside the mind, that it is a "fact" of life that can be planned, initiated and managed, or if unplanned, can be "reacted to" or "contained" and so forth ... most people involved in the design and management of programmes of planned change do not question its objective nature, and, until very recently, the same could be said of most evaluation researchers' (1984, 16).

The three American case stories (California, Wisconsin, and New York) and the three Canadian case stories (New Brunswick, Alberta, and Ontario) have all demonstrated that social policy is more about plausibility, acceptance, and reasonableness than about accuracy. The case studies make the point that program results are desirable (if you can produce them), but not really necessary. The reason we persist with the good idea is that it fits in with the fantasy that we have about how organizations work. Perhaps the time has come to bring a sense of reality to our ongoing series of social policy experiments. A feasible idea is not necessarily inferior to a good idea.

At the beginning of this book I claimed that the six-hazard model was also applicable to other social policies. In the years to come, the implementation of good ideas will be more challenging than ever. Governments all over the world are facing new pressures in the areas of health care, education, child care, unemployment insurance, pensions, and so on, and they are coming to realize that they cannot live up to their earlier promises – promises to which the public has grown accustomed and feels entitled. Social policy innovations in any of these areas may be derailed by the hazards that have been identified in the six-hazard model. Without an understanding of these hazards, a 'good idea' will likely not be sufficient for the transformation of established practice.

References

Abramson, Eric. 1996. 'Management Fashion.' *Academy of Management Review* 21 (1): 254–85.

Alberta Family and Social Services (AFSS). 1993–4, 1994–5, 1996–7, 1997–8. *Annual Report.*

Baseline/Norpack Evaluation Consortium. 1995. *NB Works Process Evaluation Year-End Report.* Prepared for NB Works Evaluation Committee, 23 June.

Berger, Peter, and Thomas Luckmann. 1967. *The Social Construction of Reality.* New York: Doubleday Anchor.

Blum, A., and P. McHugh. 1971. 'The Social Ascription of Motives.' *American Sociological Review* 36 (December): 98–109.

Boessenkool, Kenneth J. 1997. 'Back to Work: Learning from the Alberta Welfare Experiment.' C.D. Howe Institute *Commentary* 17 April: 10–17.

Boychuk, Gerald. 1998. 'Canada West Foundation, "Where Are They Now?" A Critical Assessment.' Unpublished paper, 5 October.

Brauner, Sarah, and Pamela Loprest. 1999. 'Where Are They Now? What States' Studies of People Who Left Welfare Tell Us.' No. A-32 in series New Federalism: Issues and Options for States. Urban Institute.

Brown, David. 1995. 'Welfare Caseloads: Trends in Canada.' In John Richards and William Watson, series co-eds., Social Policy Challenge no. 5. *Helping the Poor: A Qualified Case for Workfare.* Toronto: C.D. Howe Institute.

Byrne, John A. 1990. 'Business Fads: What's In – and Out.' In *Managerial Reality*, eds. P. Frost, V. Mitchell, and W. Nord, 10–18. New York: Harper Collins.

California Department of Social Services (CDSS). 1997. "Welfare-to-Work. Fact Sheet." Internal report.

California State Senate Report. 1996. 'From Welfare to Work – A Briefing Paper on Welfare-to-Work Aspects of the New Federal Welfare Reform Law.'

Prepared for Senate President Bill Lockyer by staff of the California Senate, 4 December.

Canada. 1994a. 'Reforming the Canada Assistance Plan: A Supplementary Paper.' Ottawa: Department of Human Resources.

– 1994b. 'Improving Social Security in Canada: A Discussion Paper.' Ottawa: Department of Human Resources.

Canada West Foundation. 1997. *Where Are They Now? Assessing the Impact of Welfare Reform on Former Recipients, 1993–1996.* Calgary, June.

Carney, James. 1997. 'Clinton's Dealmakers.' In 'Getting Welfare.' *George* (January).

City Journal. 1997. Editorial, 'Welfare Reform Discoveries' (winter): 24–30.

Collins, James. 1996. 'Workfare Means Daycare.' *Time* 148 (28), 23 December: 38–40. *Common Sense Revolution.* 1995. Ontario Progressive Conservative Party publication.

Corbett, Thomas, J. 1995. 'Welfare Reform in Wisconsin – the Rhetoric and the Reality.' In D.F. Norris and L. Thompson, eds., 19–53. *The Politics of Welfare Reform.* Thousand Oaks, CA: Sage Publications.

Creating New Options – Public Consultation Report. 1994. Human Resources Development New Brunswick. Government of New Brunswick. Fredericton, NB.

DeParle, Jason. 1997. 'Getting Opal Caples to Work.' *New York Times Magazine.* 24 August, 32–47, 59–61.

Dialogue – The Staff Newsletter of the Ministry of Community and Social Services. 1996. 'Ontario Works Begins in September.' Summer, 19 (3): 1.

Dunk, T., S. McBride, and R. Nelson, eds. 1996. *The Training Trap: Ideology, Training and the Labour Market.* Socialist Studies II. Winnipeg, Society for Socialist Studies/Halifax: Fernwood Publishing.

Edmonton Social Planning Council/Edmonton Gleaners Association. 1996. *Two Paycheques Away: Social Policy and Hunger in Edmonton.* An Edmonton Social Planning Council/Edmonton Gleaners' Association Publication, December.

Evans, Patricia. 1993. 'From Workfare to the Social Contract: Implications for Canada of Recent U.S. Welfare Reforms.' *Canadian Public Policy* (March) 19 (1) 57.

– 1995. 'Linking Welfare to Jobs: Canadian Style.' In Adil Sayeed, ed., 75–104. *Workfare: Does It Work? Is It Fair?* Montreal: Institute for Research on Public Policy.

GAIN Guidebook. 1988. California Department of Social Services. Sacramento, CA.

Goldman, Barbara, et al., 1985. *California: Findings from the San Diego Demonstration.* New York: Manpower Demonstration Research Corporation, March.

Green, Mark. 1997. From Welfare to Work: Getting Lost Along the Way.

Gueron, J., and E. Pauly. 1991. *From Welfare to Work.* New York: Russell Sage Foundation.

Hardina, Donna. 1997. 'Workfare in the U.S. – Empirically Tested Programs or Ideological Quagmire?.' In Eric Shragge, ed., 131–48. *Workfare – Ideology for a New Under-Class.* Toronto: Garamond Press.

Haywood, Steven. 1998. 'The Shocking Success of Welfare Reform.' *Policy Review* (January-February): 6–10.

Hess, Melanie. 1987. 'Traditional Workfare: Pros and Cons.' Research and Policy Workplan Report Sheet. Toronto: Social Assistance Review.

Hogan, Lyn. 1995. 'Jobs, not JOBS – What It Takes to Put Welfare Recipients to Work.' Policy briefing. Washington, DC: Progressive Policy Institute.

Holmes, Larry, and Shelley Ettinger. 1997. *Workfare Workers Organize: We Won't Be Slaves.* New York: Workfairness, International Action Center.

Human Resources Administration (HRA) Offices of Program Operations and Data Analysis and Research. 1997. HRA Facts. April.

Institute for Survey and Policy Research at the University of Wisconsin. 1998. Survey of Support for Welfare Reform. In *Madison Capital Times*, 24 November.

Jacobs, Lesley A. 1995. 'What Are the Normative Foundations of Workfare?' In Adil Sayeed, ed., 14–37. *Workfare: Does It Work? Is It Fair?* Montreal: Institute for Research on Public Policy.

Jordon, B. 1993. 'Framing Claims and the Weapons of the Weak.' In G. Drover and P. Kerans, eds., 53–80. *New Approaches to Welfare Theory.* Aldershot, U.K., and Brookfield, U.S.A.: Edward Elgar.

Kirp, D.M. 1986. 'The California Work/Welfare Scheme.' *Public Interest* 43 (spring): 292–6.

Klein, Ross. A. 1996. 'Training for What? A Critical Analysis of Provincial Initiatives to Foster Labour Force Attachment among Recipients of Social Assistance.' In T. Dunk, S. McBride, and R. Nelson, eds., 125–43. *The Training Trap: Ideology, Training and the Labour Market.* Socialist Studies II. Winnipeg: Society for Socialist Studies. Halifax: Fernwood Publishing.

Krashinsky, Michael. 1995. 'Putting the Poor to Work: Why Workfare Is an Idea Whose Time Has Come.' In John Richards and William Watson, series co-eds., Social Policy Challenge no. 5, *Helping the Poor: A Qualified Case for Workfare.* Toronto: C.D. Howe Institute.

Laframboise, Patti and P.Kirkham. 1994. 'Workfare Explored in the Companion Guide IV to Obstacles and Opportunities for London's GWA Clients. London: Department of Social Services, Policy and Planning Division, July.

Legge, Karen. 1984. *Evaluating Planned Organizational Change.* London: Academic Press.

Lightman, Ernie. 1991. 'Work Incentives Across Canada.' *Journal of Canadian Studies* 20 (1): 120–37.

– 1997. 'It's Not a Walk in the Park.' In Eric Shragge, ed., 85–107. *Workfare: Ideology for a New Under-Class.* 1998. Toronto: Garamond Press.

Lipsky, M. 1980. *Street Level Bureaucracy.* New York: Russell Sage Foundation.

Los Angeles County, Department of Public and Social Services (LADPSS). 1997. 'Draft Calworks Implementation Plan.' Internal document, 3 December.

Liu, John C. 1997. 'The Overlooked Fact About Welfare in California.' Briefing May 1997. San Francisco: Pacific Research Institute for Public Policy.

Mascarenhas, R.C. 1993. 'Building an Enterprise Culture in the Public Sector: Reform of the Public Sector in Australia, Britain, and New Zealand. *Public Administration Review* 53 (4): 319–26.

Maximus. 1995. 'Evaluation of the Wisconsin AFDC Benefit Cap Waiver Demonstration.' Prepared for State of Wisconsin Department of Health and Social Services, Washington, December.

Mayor's Management Report. Preliminary Fiscal 1998. Rudolph Giulani, RAndy Mastu, William Carnecle. Vol 1. Agency Narratives, City of New York.

McFarland, Joan, and Robert Mullaly. 1996. 'NB Works: Image versus Reality.' In J. Pulkingham and G. Ternowetsky, eds. 202–19 *Remaking Canadian Social Policy: Staking Claims Forging Change.* Halifax: Fernwood Publishing.

MCSS (Ontario Ministry of Community and Social Services). 1996. 'Research Paper on Welfare Reform.' Internal document, September.

MDRC (Manpower Demonstration Research Corporation). 1994. 'GAIN: Benefits, Costs, and Three-Year Impacts of a Welfare-to-Work Program – Executive Summary. September.

– 2000. 'Evaluation of CalWORKS in Los Angeles County.' August.

Mead, Lawrence. M. 1994. 'Poverty: How Little We Know.' *Social Service Review* 68 (3) Sepember: 322–51.

– 1995. *The New Paternalism: Welfare Reform in Wisconsin – Wisconsin Policy Research Institute Report* 8 (1) January.

– 1996. *The Decline of Welfare in Wisconsin – Wisconsin Policy Research Institute Report* 9 (3), March.

Meyer, J.W., and B. Rowan. 1977. 'Institutional Organizations: Formal Structure as Myth and Ceremony. *American Journal of Sociology* 83: 340–63.

Mills, C. Wright. 1940. 'Situated Actions and Vocabularies of Motive.' *American Sociological Review* 5 (February): 904–13.

Milne, William J. 1996. *The McKenna Miracle: Myth or Reality?* Monograph Series on Public Policy and Public Administration. Toronto: University of Toronto Faculty of Management, Centre for Public Management.

Milwaukee Women and Poverty Public Education Initiative. 1998. 'W-2 Community Impact Study.' Prepared for the Milwaukee County Board of Supervisors, November.

Ministère de la Sécurité du Revenu. 1994. *Rapport statistique mensuel.* Programmes de la Sécurité du Revenu du Québec, mai.

Mintzberg, Henry, Bruce Ahlstrand, and Joe Lampel. 1998. *Strategy Safari: A Guided Tour Through the Wilds of Strategic Management.* New York: Free Press.

Morris, William. 1896. 'Useful Work versus Useless Toil.' London: Freedom Press.

Mullaly, Robert. 1997. 'The Politics of Workfare: NB Works.' In Eric Shragge, ed., 35–57. *Workfare: Ideology for a New Under-Class.* Toronto: Garamond Press.

Mullaly, Robert, and Joan Weinman. 1994. 'A Response to the New Brunswick Government's "Creating New Options."' Discussion paper. 8 February.

Murphy, Jonathan. 1997. 'Alberta and the Workfare Myth.' In Eric Shragge, ed., 109–29. *Workfare: Ideology for a New Under-Class.* Toronto: Garamond Press.

Nathan, Richard. 1993. *Turning Promises into Performance: The Management Challenge of Implementing Workfare.* New York: Columbia University Press.

National Council of Welfare. 1992. 'Welfare Reform.' Ministry of Supply and Services Canada. Summer.

NB Works. Undated. N.B. provincial government publication.

NB Works. 1995–96. *Annual Report.* Human Resources Development New Brunswick. Fredericton, NB.

Nightingale, Demetra, and Robert Haveman, eds. 1994. *The Work Alternative – Welfare Reform and the Realities of the Market.* Washington, DC: Urban Institute Press.

Norris, Donald F., and Lyke Thompson. 1995. 'Findings and Lessons from the Politics of Welfare Reform.' In Norris and Thompson, eds., 1–18. *The Politics of Welfare Reform.* Thousand Oaks, CA: Sage Publications.

Ontario. 1996. *A Summary of the Ontario Works Program.* August.

Pal, Leslie. 1987. 'Tools for the Job: Canada's Evolution from Public Works to Mandated Employment.' In Jacqueline S. Ismael, ed., 33–62. *The Canadian Welfare State: Evolution and Transition.* Edmonton: University of Alberta Press.

Palumbo, Dennis J. 1985 'Foreword: Future Directions for Research in Policy Studies.' In Yvonna Lincoln, ed., 7–20. *Organizational Theory and Inquiry – The Paradigm Revolution*. Newbury Park, CA: Sage Publications.

Personal Responsibility and Work Opportunity Reconciliation Act (PRA). 1996. HR. 3734, Title IV. Subtitle B. Section 405.

Piven, F., and R. Cloward. 1987. 'The Historical Sources of the Contemporary Relief Debate.' In F. Block, R. Cloward, B. Ehrenreich, and F. Piven, eds., 3–44. *The Mean Season: The Attack on the Welfare State*. New York: Pantheon.

Powell, W., and P.J. DiMaggio, eds. 1991. *The New Institutionalism in Organizational Analysis*. Chicago: University of Chicago Press.

Project Team for Monitoring Ontario Works. 1999. *Plain Speaking: Hope and Reality – Participants' Experience of Ontario Works*. Ottawa: Social Planning Council of Ottawa-Carlton.

Rawlinson, Graham, and L.B. Mussio. 1995. 'Workfare: We've Been There Before.' *Toronto Star*, 4 July.

Riccio, James, Daniel Friedlander, and Stephen Freedman. 1994. 'GAIN: Benefits, Costs, and Three Year Impacts of a Welfare-to Work Program – Executive Summary. Manpower Demonstration Research Corporation, September.

Richards, John. 1997. *Retooling the Welfare State: What's Right, What's Wrong, What's to Be Done*. Policy Study 31. Toronto: C.D. Howe Institute.

Richards, John, and Aidan Vining. 1995. 'Welfare Reform: What Can We Learn from the Americans?' In J. Richards and W. Watson, series co-eds., 1–36. Social Policy Challenge no. 5. *Helping the Poor: A Qualified Case for Workfare*. Toronto: C.D. Howe Institute.

Rose, Nancy. 1995. *Workfare or Fair Work – Women, Welfare and Government Work Programs*. New Brunswick, NJ: Rutgers University Press.

Rusk, James. 1996. 'Minister Unsure of Workfare Start.' *Globe and Mail*, 1 October.

Sabatini, E., with Sandra Nightingale. 1996. *Welfare – No Fair: A Critical Analysis of Ontario's Welfare System (1985–1994)*. Vancouver, BC.: Fraser Institute.

Sayers, Sean. 1987. 'The Need to Work: A Perspective from Philosophy.' *Radical Philosophy* 46 (summer 1987): 17–26.

Schein, E. 1991. 'The Role of the Founder in the Creation of Organizational Culture.' In P. Frost, L. Moore, M. Reis Louis, C. Lundberg, and J. Martin eds., 14–25. *Reframing Organizational Culture*. Newbury Park, CA: Sage Publishing.

Scott, J. 1990. *Domination and the Arts of Resistance: Hidden Transcripts*. New Haven and London: Yale University Press.

Sen, Amartya, 1980. 'Description as Choice.' *Oxford Economic Papers* 3: 353–69.

Shillington, Richard. 1998. *Social Assistance and Paid Employment in Alberta*. A report prepared for the Population Research Laboratory, Department of Sociology, University of Alberta. Manotick: Tristat Resources.

Shragge, Eric., ed. 1997. *Workfare: Ideology for a New Under-Class*. Toronto: Garamond Press.

Simpson, Jeffrey. 1998. 'Everywhere, Welfare Systems Are Getting a Dose of Tough Love.' *Globe and Mail*, 21 January.

Smith, Ralph. 1987. 'Work-related Programs for Welfare Recipients. Washington, DC: Congressional Budget Office, Government Printing Office, April.

Social Research and Demonstration Corporation. 1998. *What Works? Lessons from Welfare-to-Work Programs*. Vancouver, BC: Social Research and Demonstration Corp.

Struthers, James. 1994. *The Limits of Affluence: Welfare in Ontario 1920–1970*. Toronto: University of Toronto Press.

– 1996. 'Can Workfare Work? Reflections from History.' Ottawa: Caledon Institute of Social Policy publication.

Swift, J. 1995. *Wheel of Fortune: Work and Life in the Age of Falling Expectations*. Toronto: Between the Lines.

Swift, J., and D. Peerla. 1996. 'Attitude Adjustment: The Brave New World of Work and the Revolution of Falling Expectations.' In T. Dunk, S. McBride and R. Nelson, eds., 29–51. *The Training Trap: Ideology, Training and the Labour Market*. Socialist Studies II. Winnipeg: Society for Socialist Studies/Halifax: Fernwood Publishing.

Torjman, Sherri. 1996. *Workfare: A Poor Law*.' Caledon Institute of Social Policy, February.

'Training and Jobs – What Works.' 1996. *Economist* 339 (7960): 19–21.

Trutko, John, Demetra Nightingale, and Burt Barnow. 1999. 'Post-Employment Education and Training Models in the Welfare-To-Work Grants Program.' Washington, DC: Urban Institute.

United States General Accounting Office. 1987. 'Work and Welfare: Current AFDC Programs and Implications for Federal Policy.' Washington D.C.: GAO/HRD-87-34, January.

– 1995a. 'Welfare to Work – State Programs Have Tested Some of the Reforms.' Program Evaluation and Methodology Division. U.S. GAO/PEMD-95-26, July.

– 1995b. 'Welfare to Work: Current AFDC Program not Sufficiently Focussed on Employment.' Report to the Chairman, Committee on Finance, U.S. Senate. GAO/HEHS-95-28, December.

– 1997a. 'Welfare Reform – States' Early Experiences with Benefit Termina-

240 References

tion.' Washington, DC. U.S. GAO/HEHS-97-74, May.
– 1997b. 'Welfare Reform: Three States' Approaches Show Promise of Increasing Work Participation.' Washington, DC. U.S. GAO/HEHS-97-80.
– 1999. 'Welfare Reform – States' Implementation Progress and Information on Former Recipients.' Testimony before the Subcommittee on Human Resources, Committee on Ways and Means, House of Representatives. U.S. GAO/T-HEHS-99-116, 27 May.
Wallace, J., and D. Long. 1987. 'GAIN: Planning and Early Implementation.' New York: Manpower Demonstration Research Corporation (MDRC).
Waste, R.J. 1989. 'Déjà vu and Disaster: Federal-Urban Policy in the 1990s. *Urban Resources* (Spring): 21–4, 33.
– 1995. 'From Workfare for the Poor to Warfare on the Poor in California.' In Donald Norris and Lyke Thompson, eds., 55–78. *The Politics of Welfare Reform*. Thousand Oaks, CA: Sage Publications.
Weick, Karl. 1995. *Sensemaking in Organizations*. Foundations for Organizational Science. Thousand Oaks, CA: Sage Publications.
Welfare Reform Network News. 1997. 'Multi-State Welfare Monitoring Projects.' 3, 20 February.
'Wisconsin Welfare Reform – a History in Progress, a Plan for the Future.' 1996. Government document prepared by Governor Tommy Thompson's office, April.
Wiseman, M. 1985. 'Workfare.' *California Journal*, 16 (July): 292–5.
Work Experience Program: Policy and Procedures Manual. 1997. City of New York, Human Resources Administration, Office of Employment Services.
Zucker, L.G. 1987. 'Institutional Theories of Organizations.' In W.R. Scott and J.F. Short, Jr., eds., 443–64, *Annual Review of Sociology 13*. Palo Alto, CA: Annual Reviews.

Index